SOME

OF THE

WORDS

ARE

THEIRS

a memoir of an alcoholic family

GEORGE H. JENSEN, JR.

FOREWORD BY WILLIAM L. WHITE

Springfield, Missouri
2009

For inquiries contact:
Moon City Press
Department of English
Missouri State University
901 S. National Avenue
Springfield, MO 65897
Website: http://English.MissouriState.edu/moon_city_press.htm

Front cover: George H. Jensen and George H. Jensen, Jr. on the parade
   field of Fort Slocum, New York, circa 1953. Photograph courtesy of the
   author.
In-text photographs courtesy of the author.

Text editor: Craig A. Meyer
Text design: Ben Pfeiffer and Angelia Northrip-Rivera
Cover design: Ben Pfeiffer and Rebecca Sloane

Library of Congress Cataloging-in-Publication Data

Jensen, George H.
 Some of the words are theirs : a memoir of an alcoholic family / George H.
Jensen, Jr. ; foreword by William L. White.
     p. cm.
 Includes bibliographical references.
 ISBN 978-0-913785-09-6
 1. Jensen, George H. 2. Alcoholics—United States—Biography. 3.
Alcoholics—Family relationships—United States—Biography. 4. College
teachers—United States—Biography. I. Title.
 HV5293.J46A3 2009
 362.292092—dc22
 [B]   2009048214

To my families

past, present, and future,

to Donna Barkan Jensen (1962-2008),

and to the crew of the USS *Dewey*

CONTENTS

FOREWORD
BY WILLIAM L. WHITE

"Your father is a good man. He just has a disease."

George Jensen's Some of the Words Are Theirs will find many appreciative audiences. It is far more than the grown tale of an abandoned seven year-old boy whose alcoholic father went on to drink himself to death. For those whose lives have been touched by alcoholism, you will explore the subtle ways parental alcoholism shapes personal development and find clues on how to give up life-shaping family myths. You will discover how one man forged his own healing narrative. Members of Alcoholics Anonymous will be particularly moved by this book. In his search for missing parts of his life story, George Jensen found answers from men who offered what his father could not. Men and women in Alcoholics Anonymous may in turn find a surrogate son in these pages whose growing understanding of alcoholism followed a path to acceptance and love.

Readers of biography and memoir will find in *Some of the Words Are Theirs* an engaging narrative of self-discovery cast in the shadow of local culture and global events. The section on the Japanese bombing of Pearl Harbor is a particularly fascinating example of how a rich personal story can be constructed from only fragments of available detail. Readers who are interested in the role of story and storytelling in personal identity are going to be particularly pleased with this book.

This work can also be read within a rich American history of alcoholic and alcoholic family memoirs dating from the dramatic increase in alcohol consumption following the Revolutionary War and the birth of the American Temperance Movement. Temperance literature, works such as *The Drunkard, One Cup More,* and *The Doom of the Drunkard,* portrayed the way in which alcoholism ravaged the family through violence, economic hardship, abandonment, and death. These morality tales were stories with an agenda: the prohibition of the sale of alcohol. As such, they focused more on the evils of alcohol than on an intimate portrayal of family experience. When inebriate homes and inebriate asylums dotted the American landscape in the late nineteenth century, the professional inebriety literature referred to spouses and families only peripherally, or portrayed the family as a potential cause of alcoholism or a source of sabotage to recovery.

It wasn't until the late twentieth century that the focus shifted from the "disease of alcoholism" and the alcoholic to the impact of alcoholism on the family. The resulting body of literature tended to portray family members as being as "sick" as the alcoholic and in need of sustained therapy. This pathologization of the alcoholic family crested in the late 1980s via such concepts as "para-alcoholism" and "co-dependency." Memoirs of alcoholic families in this era were heavily influenced by popular depictions of highly predictable role adaptations that unfolded within families through the progressive insults of alcoholism. Children and adult children of alcoholics were portrayed as uniformly suffering and in need of treatment in their own right. To the family's rescue came a plague of pop psychologists and pseudo-therapists whose proclamations triggered their own backlash movement in publications like *The Codependence Conspiracy, I'm Dysfunctional, You're Dysfunctional* and *The Diseasing of America.*

The memoirs of adult children of alcoholics in the late twentieth century contained stories of alcoholism-shaped family life, but complexities and layers of meaning were often missing from these portrayals. Fueled by anger, sadness, and loss, such tales conveyed the impression that the protagonist's life would have been idyllic but for the insults of alcoholism on his or her family. Missing were tales of greater depth and nuance and stories, not of psychopathology and psychotherapy, but of natural resilience, maturation, and wisdom.

GEORGE H. JENSEN, JR.

That tide may be turning with the publication of *Some of the Words Are Theirs.*

Jensen's memoir is a lesson in how lives are shaped more by attitudes than by events. In this richly layered and evolving story, Jensen finds a way to shed his own personal myth (all the problems in my life resulted from my father's alcoholism) and the sorrow and loss that permeated it. The life story at the end is very different than the opening life story. On a journey through anger, resentment, and grief, he achieves a state of maturity and wisdom—the recognition that removal of alcoholism and abandonment from his story would not have produced a perfect life, but a life with other issues that would have similarly challenged his development as a person.

There is a sense of liberation at the end of this book that most readers will find very comforting and personally empowering. I think some readers turning the last page of this book will be open to new possibilities and will have found their own life story becoming less about events and more about meanings.

—William L. White
Author, *Slaying the Dragon*

PREFACE

THE STORY BEHIND THE STORY OF THIS MEMOIR BEGINS WITH AN ACADEMIC book—*Storytelling in Alcoholics Anonymous: A Rhetorical Analysis* (Southern Illinois University Press, 2000). This book is a study of how alcoholics tell their stories and how these stories move them through recovery. When I wrote the preface for *Storytelling*, I felt readers would want to know what drew me to write a book on that topic. Even in academic circles, most readers assume that all scholars studying alcoholism are themselves alcoholics.

While I certainly wouldn't mind being known as a recovering alcoholic, that's not the truth. And I preferred to begin a book that consumed a large segment of my professional life (about six or seven years) with the truth. So, for the first time in my career, I provided a personal back story in the preface of a scholarly book:

> Long after I was an adult, my mother told me that my father had
> gone to Alcoholics Anonymous for six months. One day, he came
> home from a meeting and said, "I don't think I'm an alcoholic."
> I suspect that it was less than a year later—I was six—when my
> mother reached her breaking point and asked my father to leave.
> He eventually drifted to New Orleans, where he slowly drank
> himself to death. I have little doubt that my family was better off
> once my father left, even though my mother struggled to support
> us on a teacher's salary, but we were still an alcoholic family.

So, even though *Storytelling in Alcoholics Anonymous* was scholarship, it was also very personal, even spiritual. It was an opportunity to work through some of the issues of growing up in a family that had been transformed by alcohol.

Now, let me take another move backwards, to a back story behind the back story. In the early stages of writing *Storytelling in Alcoholics Anonymous*, friends and colleagues who read drafts and found themselves sloshing through rhetorical theory, told me I should do a version of the book for "regular" readers. I tried to write something like that, but I found myself drifting away from the topic of Alcoholics Anonymous to memories of my father's drinking and how it affected my family. I found myself wanting to write about how attending open meetings of Alcoholics Anonymous had helped me to understand my father. Slowly, I turned from a short paragraph in a preface of a scholarly book to a full-blown memoir; the back story became *the* story.

A memoir about an alcoholic family? Even I wondered why I was bothering. One afternoon, while I was still in the research phase of *Storytelling in Alcoholics Anonymous*, I walked up and down the autobiography/memoir section of a local bookstore, pulling books off the shelf, reading the blurbs on the back cover. From this quick and sloppy survey, I concluded that about two-thirds of the memoirs published each year are more or less gruesome tales about alcoholism. The others document the true lives of actors, politicians, authors, and dogs, roughly in that order. I said the "true" lives, but that may inaccurate. We all know that the autobiographies of politicians may contain lies, but I am more inclined to believe the self-reported yarns of politicians than I am memoirs about dogs. I've have come across some smart dogs in my life, I even owned a few, but not one is worthy of an entire book. Back to alcoholics. If so many memoirs are more or less about alcoholism, why bother to add to the heap? More to the point, why would anyone, other than a relative who owes me money (a lot), want to read it?

I'm not so sure I could have answered that question when I began to write about my family, partly because I wasn't even focused on readers or publication. Once I began to work through family documents, dredge up memories, talk to family and old friends, I was sucked in. I had always enjoyed trying to solve the mysteries of a research project. Now, in a similar way, I became intrigued by what I thought happened in my family and how that differed from what really seemed to happen and how no one seemed to agree on what really did happen. I was so intrigued that it felt like I was researching someone else's life. And, in a way, I was. The more I researched, the more I wrote, the more I became a different person. As the project developed, I created more and more distance between the memories I had carried, almost as a burden, and the person I was becoming. Oddly, I was experiencing the kind of change that I witnessed and analyzed as I studied how members of AA told their stories.

I soon discovered that a memoir is not about writing down memories; it is about testing the limits of memories, questioning memories, even shaping new memories. I began to understand a simple equation: reworking memories is reworking family history is reworking my past is reworking my future.

When I wrote that brief paragraph about my life for the Preface of *Storytelling in Alcoholics Anonymous*, every word was true. It was true to my memories. About six months later, after the book was published, beyond revision, after I had begun to research and write a memoir, the paragraph was riddled with lies. Not a word had changed, but now it was no longer true.

By that time, I knew more. The story I had always told myself about my family had changed. I had changed. I soon realized that I wasn't writing a memoir. At least, not a memoir in the sense of "let me share my memories." I wasn't even writing a memoir about the ravages of alcoholism. I was writing a healing narrative.

After some point in the writing, I realized I didn't want to tell a story of abuse. I probably couldn't have, even if I wanted to. (One editor who decided to turn down the manuscript of this book said it was not sufficiently "melodramatic." I wanted to write him back and say, "Thank you very much." The editor must have wanted a tale of martyrdom, a popular genre since about the first century of the Common Era. Excuse me, but I decided I didn't want to suffer for my readers.) My childhood had its difficulties, but the hardships were, for the most part, in the greater scheme of things, not much more dramatic than anything found in the typical first-year college essay, which is sometimes called the "essay of personal disaster." (As a college writing teacher, I know this genre well. I have read thousands of these tales.) I didn't want to suppress the bad times, but I found myself more interested in moving on, exploring possibilities, finding alternative ways of thinking about my family, as many ways as I could imagine.

This is how members of AA tell their stories. When new members of AA first stand up at a meeting to speak, knees shaking, they focus on the drunkolog (a truly great bit of lingo), the portion of the story that deals with their drinking days. They talk about the string of dark events that led up to hitting bottom, and they often have to stop, cry a while or take a few breaths, then muddle on. As members move deeper into their recovery, they focus on how the program has helped them change. They tell jokes, and they laugh. Some of the best entertainment I've had in my life was listening to oldtimers tell their stories. I hope I have followed this model and that something of my journey through draft after draft is visible to the reader. So, this memoir may not entirely line up with what readers expect to find.

As readers, we expect a linear story. We want to begin at the beginning and move toward the end—preferably, to an end with no loose threads—in chronological order, without too many side trips. But the plot of a healing narrative is about how we come to know our stories and how these stories can change. The plot is more about how attitudes—not events—are the stuff of our lives and how we need to trade them in from time to time. Let me give a brief example. I grew up feeling like my father had abandoned me. He left our family when I was pretty young, and I never saw him again. The following passage is only one of the points where I loop through that event, trying to tell it in a new way. Just before this paragraph, I had written about how my mother asked my father to leave and how my father had sent my mother a dark letter shortly after he took off for the West Coast:

I marvel at how my mother found the conviction to raise the issue of separation. She must have feared that her husband would erupt, that the barely controlled tension in the household would surface, that he would argue with her, try to manipulate her, that she might not be able to remain strong, navigate the course from "We can't go on like this" to separation to divorce. After her husband left, I wonder how she remained firm. When she read his letter, when he wrote that he thought of suicide, that she was the only woman in the world for him, I wonder how she kept from writing back, "I can't raise these kids alone. I'm too frightened. I'm too lonely. Come home. We'll work things out." Yet, she held fast. Although I only thought of this recently, my father needs to be given some credit for leaving without a fight. Many practicing alcoholics refuse to leave or try to manipulate their wives into letting them stay. Many stalk their wives for years. For so long, I wondered how he could stay away, how he could abandon his kids. Now, I think that it took considerable strength on his part to leave us alone and let us get on with our lives.

Not much happens in this paragraph. Or, maybe a lot happens. The plot of this paragraph is series of shifts in attitudes and beliefs that came to be over decades. As I hope is clear in this passage, writing a healing narrative is a historical process of reframing stories within stories. The writer allows geological layers of attitudes and beliefs to build, like sediment, epoch after epoch. In geology, a quarter inch of sediment could represent hundreds of years, thousands of past lives. In a healing memoir, a paragraph can represent half a lifetime of beliefs.

The reader of a healing narrative is like a geologist who finds meaning in the layers of sediment. If you don't know how to look for the layers of sediment, it doesn't even seem to be a story. It just looks like a scar cut into a hillside or bunch of rocks in an old cardboard box.

I began writing about my family by focusing on the trauma of my childhood. At this point, as ridiculous as it seems, I was sharing my memories with myself. Then, at some point, I began writing for others.

I started to share drafts with friends and family. However, before I sent the manuscript to anyone who was a character in the story, I would revise the manuscript one more time—reading through it chapter by chapter, trying to see it from the perspective of the real person who would soon read about my view of his or her life. I was amazed by how much I revised as I shifted my reading to the perspective of others. Of course, I never anticipated all of their reactions. They were sometimes hard on me—deservedly so—and their comments forced me to revise again and again. One friend told me that I was acting like a "victim" through a long chapter, some eighty pages. (At some point in healing narratives, the speaker needs to move from being a victim to an agent, and I wasn't quite there yet.) I realized she was right, so I trashed the eighty pages and started over. I don't know how many times I revised this memoir, each draft trying to get the story right, but I am sure I went through it more than a hundred times, maybe two or three hundred. The reader, as geologist, will see some of these layers. I hope the reader can also see how writing and revising is more than shifting around words on a page.

The sequence of revisions is also a story, but certainly not the kind of story most readers expect. The plot of this book—if it could be called plot—is a movement from a simple story to a complex story, from blame to acceptance, from not caring to caring, from failing to understand to learning how to love completely without complete understanding. These movements come to the reader more in a sequence of emotional development or a string of imaginings than in a constructed chronology of memories. So, this book is about creating a story as much as it is about remembering or discovering one. That does not mean, I hope, that it is fiction or dishonest. Foremost, a healing narrative needs honesty, as much honesty as a horribly flawed human (that would be me) can deliver.

That honesty comes as much in what is said (truth as a finished story, a product) as it does in letting the reader know the source (truth as finding a story, a process). Let me explain with an example of what you will read. Toward the end of the memoir, I write a letter to my sons about my father (whose nickname, when in the navy, was Jens) to share some of his experiences in World War II. I never heard my father talk about the war, so the story in the letter is entirely a construction from multiple sources—my father's military records, histories of the war, and letters from my father's shipmates. As I pieced fragments together, I sometimes felt a need to fill in the gaps with my imagination. Some readers might think that, the moment I drew upon my imagination, I passed over into fiction, but I didn't. The following passage comes after the factual version of a story about a torpedo that went under the USS *Dewey* while my father manned the phone on the bridge, his battle station. The facts are, I am sure, as true as Truth. A Japanese plane launched a torpedo. It swam deep in a direct line toward the *Dewey*, went under it, leveled off, then hit another destroyer. It's a good story in itself, but I wanted to know what my father did as a torpedo moved toward his ship. Here's what I imagined for my sons:

I want you to try to understand what your grandfather and his shipmates did in the minutes between the second the Japanese plane released its torpedo to the second they knew the torpedo had cleared the ship. If Jens didn't see the plane launch the torpedo, he would have heard someone at one of the 50 caliber machine guns send the message that a torpedo was heading straight toward the ship. He would have relayed this message to the captain, and the captain would have ordered hard rudder right. Jens would have relayed this message to the engine room and then waited. He wouldn't have moved. He might have wanted to run to the starboard side to see if the torpedo was going to hit his ship and then run to the port side to see it level off, and know that his ship was safe, as some of the crew had when a torpedo ran under the *Dewey* during the attack on Pearl Harbor. But he didn't move for thirty or forty seconds. He and his shipmates were now seasoned in battle. I am sure he stayed at his post and did his job. And I am sure that the entire crew of the *Dewey* stayed at their battle stations. They were all doing their jobs, even though they might only have seconds to live.

SOME OF THE WORDS ARE THEIRS

I say with some conviction that my father stood there at his post for thirty or forty seconds, knowing that he might be wounded or die in the next moment, and that he continued to do his job. He didn't run to one side of the ship to see if the torpedo would hit and then run to the other side to see it reappear. He stood there, doing his job.

I made all of that up. It came from my imagination, but I am pretty sure that I am right, and I am certain that this section of the memoir is as true as anything else I wrote. It is made up and true and, for any careful reader, it is completely honest because I let the reader know it is made up, my best effort to allow imagination to bridge a gap in the narrative. It was not, by any means, an insignificant gap. I really needed to know this event that I made up. If my father had sobered up, if he had stayed with our family, he would have told me this story. So, I had found (created) one of the pieces of my father's life that I needed to reclaim *so that I could get better* because I needed to know my father as a man apart from his drinking.

Good things can definitely come from writing and reading healing narratives; we can only hope that they will produce no harm, either to the living or the dead. Part of the journey is through dark places, and we cannot write our own stories without writing the stories of others. We might begin writing healing narratives for our own benefit, to explore and express all the feelings we have suppressed or forgotten, collected and prized, all the resentments that, at some point, grow into burdens. We end writing about and for others, to try to see our lives from their perspectives, to release it all.

To move through the process of healing or recovery, I had to write about my father's drinking. Even though all the members of my family have passed on, I often revised by trying to imagine how they might be affected by my words. Sometimes, I read my manuscript by trying to imagine how they would read it if they were still alive. At other times, I read trying to imagine how they might read it now, as people who have passed on, who are not so concerned about what the neighbors might think, who could understand my failings as a writer and person within the context of my desire to change. I also sent drafts of the manuscript to family and friends, as many as I could locate, and allowed them to question my memories. If they wished me to change their names, I did so. I didn't, however, always accept their suggestions for revision. One neighbor from my childhood days asked me to revise out the parts about my father's drinking and write more about neighborhood cookouts and trips to the beach. Her memories and my memories didn't match up. While her comments did help me to reframe some parts of the story, I was not interested in writing a story about cookouts and beach parties.

In the end, we can never resolve all of the differences between our memories and the memories of others. In the end, after all the ways others had changed my story, I had to write my version of the events. I needed to write about the bad times for my own personal growth, but I also wanted to respect the pain of my father, mother, and brother. If I glossed over their pain, I could not respect it. Surprisingly, most of my relatives and friends were very supportive of the project. I even felt that sharing drafts of the memoir brought us closer together.

I began writing this book around 1993; it did not begin to feel complete until about ten years later. As I began to look for a publisher, I continued to revise the story that felt complete without continuing to update it. Since 2003, many significant events have happened to me and my family, including the death of my wife on June 2, 2008. At some point, you have to say, "This is all I can deal with in this story." So, readers need to image that the telling of this story happened about 2003 and that some of the characters continue on.

I am indebted to many people who served as readers of drafts early and late. Donna, my wife, and my two sons, Jay and Jeffrey. Too many students to mention, but especially Heidi Skurat Harris, who read more than one draft carefully and honestly. A number of close colleagues: James Baumlin, Nancy Walker, Patrick O'Reilly, W.D. Blackmon, Mike Burns, Sally Crisp, Huey Crisp, Michael Kleine, Chuck Anderson, Karen "Flash" Palmer, and Angelia Northrip-Rivera. Vicki Jensen Bushnell, my west coast cousin, provided enormous support. She was, in many ways, my co-researcher. Special thanks to

Craig A. Meyer who edited the book as a student project. I presented an early chapter at a works-in-progress conference sponsored by Brown University; there, I received much encouragement from Ernie Kurtz, William White, John Crowley, Bruce Donovan, David Lewis, Jared Lobdell, Trysh Travis, Maria Swora, Joli Jensen (no relation), Linda Kurtz, Etta Madden, James Swan-Tuitt, Wally Pansing, Matthew J. Raphael, and Jay Williams. Most importantly, I need to thank my father's shipmates, who were kind enough to write me. My heartfelt thanks to Jack Aldis (who tracked down my office phone number and called me twice), Merlin E. Cone, Arthur L. Critchett (who wrote me a two-page letter in script even thought he suffers from Muscular Dystrophy), Marie Dawson (who wrote for Joseph H. Dawson, her deceased husband, and sent me a videotape of her husband being interviewed about the Pearl Harbor attack), Marvin Funk, Edward L. Gilbert, Lloyd Gwinner, Dorwin D. Hill, Robert Reece, and Stephen P. Yorden. I cannot overstate what they did for me: *They gave me back my father.* This was a magnificent gift from strangers.

xxiv

This book includes the words of all these people. With each draft, I moved further from myself. With each draft, I moved toward others.

If parts of the story are disturbing, I hope that readers will understand that the book ends with a chapter entitled "A Brief Sermon on Love." Equally important, the book ends with a question mark.

GEORGE H. JENSEN, JR.

STORYTELLING

ALMOST AS IF REMEMBERING SOMEONE ELSE'S LIFE, I HAVE TO REMIND myself that my older brother and I were separated by only three years. He had only three more years with our father before the man disappeared, only three more years to watch, listen, grow, learn, and yet it feels like we came from different families, like we had to find a way to make ourselves into brothers. Separated by three years. Separated by half a lifetime of memories. Two brothers from different families, different eras.

John Charles—the family called him J.C.—could even remember the day that television entered our family, appeared unannounced, almost as if a third child. He sat, my brother once told me, quietly, patiently, on our well-worn couch—its age hidden beneath a slip cover—in the living room of our apartment in navy housing. He watched the man, his father, I mean *our* father, and a neighbor carry in a huge cardboard box, cut away the box with a kitchen knife, insert the plug into a socket that was almost two feet above the floor, twist a knob, and stand back, far back, to watch something, anything, materialize. He saw the man—our father—fiddle with the antenna and curse for a long time before a snowy channel appeared, and even then the picture faded in and out, could not be brought back, started to roll, could hardly be set right with any knob or slap, word or kick. He heard the man curse, stand back, then sigh with relief as the picture righted itself.

J.C. watched the set, hardly blinking, hardly noticing the man—our father—was now gone.

Alone, my brother spent the rest of the day lying on the oval cord rug that covered a linoleum floor, his hands behind his head as a pillow, watching show after show, mesmerized by a new world of images—black,

3

white, and shades of gray, so like the muted colors of navy housing, our 1950s clothes, our 1940s furniture. When the picture faded or began to roll, he called to our mother. She stopped cleaning or cooking long enough to bring back the picture. She never cursed. She never hit it with her fist.

At that time, the networks didn't have enough programs to fill the airways. Even in the middle of the day, unpredictably, a test pattern might appear for half an hour, sometimes for several hours. As I imagine it, J.C. spent some long stretches of the day staring at the test pattern, waiting for another program, any program. Only after the final show of the evening, after the waving flag and "The Star Spangled Banner," the test pattern and the high pitched whine, did he drag himself to bed. The next morning, he woke up early, turned on the set and sat with legs crossed, eating a bowl of corn flakes and sugar, lots of sugar, watching the test pattern, listening to the high pitched whine, waiting patiently for the first children's show of the day, probably *Howdy Doody* or *Romper Room*, certainly a show with avuncular adults, part of a new extended family for a country on the move. He listened as they told him to obey his parents, which he would, as long as his parents did not ask him to turn off the television.

All this happened about 1954, in Norfolk, Virginia, when J.C. was seven years old and I was four. I have only one memory before this time, a memory I have some trouble sorting out, so television was always a part of my world.

In my early memories (at least, of consistent memories), I don't know if we were able to pick up all three networks, but I remember television being more satisfying than it seems to be for my children, who are surrounded by televisions. A few years ago, the cable man promised my sons they would soon have five hundred channels; less than a year ago, during a family trip to Chicago, we watched television as we rode up the elevator at the Hilton. In 1954, when televisions were almost as large as refrigerators (televisions were larger and refrigerators were smaller), who would have thought that one day we would watch television in an elevator? Even Walt Disney could not have imagined it.

GEORGE H. JENSEN, JR.

When I was a little older, even after we had moved to Virginia Beach, about the time the man disappeared, I watched cartoons as if the animated characters were my friends, real people who were like me and could understand what I couldn't even begin to put into words. *Heckle and Jeckle*, one of my mainstays, was about two proletariat black magpies. At the time, I thought they were Black Crows and I felt they acted out my anger—although this was something sensed, certainly not a conscious thought. Heckle spoke with a New York accent, and Jeckle was vaguely British. Together, they worked cons on the upper class, and they usually prevailed with witty banter. As the cartoon developed over several years, their wit and reason seemed to fail. They began to swing sledge hammers and throw sticks of dynamite. Throughout their history, they found some means to be in absolute control. A few years later, I gravitated toward *Rocky and His Friends*, especially the "Peabody's Improbable History" segment. Mr. Peabody, both dog and genius, and his pet Sherman, both boy and (intellectually speaking) a little behind the curve (even for the average farm animal), traveled through time to important historical events, like the Battle of Waterloo, where the dog, a true statesman, advised some historical figure, like Wellington, and kept the events of history on track. I wanted to be Mr. Peabody, but I knew I was more like Sherman. A few years later, even though I was still very young, I realized that *The Bugs Bunny Show* would become a classic. I was fond of the segment (I can't remember the title) in which a sneaky little trickster mouse badgered a large dim-witted cat. Like the cat, I was often back on my heels, spinning in circles, muttering, "Which way did he go? Which way did he go?"

As I moved toward my teen years, long after the man retired from the navy and then disappeared, some of our family rituals surrounded the television. Every Saturday night, my mother made two pizzas from Chef Boyardee's Complete Pizza Mix, which could only be considered "complete" by someone with a Third World concept of pizza. My mother–I mean *our* mother, also J.C.'s mother—always added extra cheese, real mozzarella, not the powdered parmesan that came in the box, and real sausage or real pepperoni. At 5:00 pm, the three of us who remained ate pizza off of shaky metal TV trays (furniture specially made for the new television age), drank Pepsi (it was the only night we could drink more than one soda), and watched *The Wide World of Sports* (one of the rare sports shows at the time). It always began with a ski jumper careening off the side of a ski ramp just as Jim McKay, the show's anchor, said "the agony of defeat." The ski jumper always got to me. Years later, when I heard an interview with that very ski jumper on National Public Radio, I learned that he wasn't even hurt in the fall, and I felt cheated out of a significant part of my childhood. I wanted him to be hurt, but not because I had a cruel streak. For ten or twelve years of pizza nights, I had felt sorry for the poor guy, who was, I imagined, a sports klutz like myself, and then I learned he walked away from the tumble that made America cringe every week. The ski jumper, in the same interview, even cataloged his many championships. I was more than a little pissed off.

While pizza night was a good family ritual, one of the simple but important ways my mother held the three of us together, I more often watched television by myself. One of my favorite shows was *Queen for a Day*. It aired in the afternoon, about two o'clock, Monday through Friday, so I could only watch it during summer vacation. Each episode followed the same pattern, but I didn't mind. Three women (all white and working class) were picked from the studio audience (or maybe off the street) to share their tales of woe. One by one, each woman took turns whimpering about how her family was in bad shape: Her husband had lost his job (the cause left to your imagination), they were behind in their bills (thousands and thousands of dollars), the kids had no shoes (so they couldn't go to school and would never be upwardly mobile, economically speaking), their car needed a new carburetor (so her husband couldn't get to a job, even if he had one), Sears had just repossessed their television (and so she couldn't watch *Queen for a Day*, which caused the studio audience to "oooooooh" with sympathy), she had to cook spaghetti with a meatless sauce (particularly sad in the late 1950s and early 1960s, before vegetarians, much less vegans, appeared in America), she had a heart condition (never specified), their cat had just died (a beautiful tabby kitten, just a few months old), on and on. I listened and cried along with housewives all across the land. At the end of the show, the studio audience voted by applause for the woman with the most pathetic story, and an applause-o-meter let us at home in TV Land see which woman had won. Then, the *denouement*. The host walked the winner to center stage, where he draped her pudgy body with a regal cape (red with a white fur border, little black spots on the fur), placed a crown over her stringy hair (this was, after all, before Oprah and the make-overs that transformed frumpy housewives into Super Models), and seated her on a throne (where life took a turn for the better). The fortunate woman wept as the host told her that she had won a new Kenmore washing machine, a set of Firestone tires, two cases of Rice-a-Roni ("the San Francisco treat"), a month's supply of Purina dog food, and two hundred dollars in cash, all in crisp twenties, fanned in the right hand of the host, looking like much more than a few hundred. The queen cried as the host sang her the *Queen for a Day* song (I can't remember the lyrics, so use your imagination here), and the credits rolled over the entire scene. We all, the housewives and me, believed her life would be better now. It got to me every time. And I never wasted a thought on the two women who lost and didn't get all the cool stuff.

During this time network television was replacing local community, yet the oral tradition of storytelling lived on in our home. Neighbors and friends often visited unannounced. We usually entertained in the kitchen, where my mother made pot after pot of coffee in an old aluminum percolator. I liked to listen to it gurgle and accelerate—blup . . . blup . . . blup, blup . . . blup, blup, blup—and think about the Maxwell House coffee ads. The adults sat in the chairs, sipping coffee from mugs and chain smoking. Soon a huge cloud of smoke mushroomed toward the ceiling and hung several feet deep. We kids sat on the floor. The Smiths—Ben, Linda, and their children, Karen, Rebecca, and Ben Jr., who lived just down the street in a house just like ours—were often there, as was Elsie Tereskerz, one of my mother's best friends. Sometimes Rita and Harry French, friends from my father's days in the navy, came all the way from Norfolk.

Ben Smith was a great storyteller. He was a big man, about 6' 2", with weathered skin, a flattop, and a booming voice that commanded an audience; his speech was peppered with "hot damn" and "crap" and an entire class of mild profanity (by today's standards) that jarred the room and sometimes caused the kids to giggle, then smile faintly, then hardly notice as the years passed.

Ben rarely repeated a story. When he did, the details changed and the chronology shifted. Listening to him weave a tale was like watching a good novelist revise his prose and mold the identity of his characters. I heard him tell stories about growing up in the mountains of Virginia, working in Panama, trying to break into professional baseball, arguing with his boss, and soldiering in World War II. During his time in the war, he was only seventeen, just barely out of high school. He drove a truck and was never in battle, but his stories were still riveting. When he spoke about driving an Army truck through mountain roads in Italy, headlights dimmed to avert aerial attacks, he made the experience sound more exciting than hand-to-hand combat. Years later, in an undergraduate film course at Old Dominion University, I thought about Ben's truck story as I watched *Wages of Fear*, the French film about men who transported nitroglycerin across potholed mountain roads.

Around the time of the Cuban Missile Crisis, when I was thirteen, Ben, Linda and my mother spent several months talking about building a bomb shelter in our back yard. Ben even drew out some plans on an envelope. They talked about air filters, beds, jugs of water, and dehydrated food. I listened and fantasized about being one of the few families in our area to survive a nuclear attack. We would stay down there a few weeks and then pop out to a deserted town. We could go to the new mall and get whatever we wanted. I didn't think about radiation. How could I know? No one understood nuclear war at the time. Our teachers taught us to protect ourselves in the advent of a nuclear attack by crawling under our desks and covering our heads with our skinny little arms. Once I hit high school and read John Hersey's *Hiroshima,* I understood it all better. Then I understood the absurdity of a bomb shelter. Our house was about five miles from the world's largest navy base, which would have been ground zero during a nuclear war. We were so close that the initial strike of World War III would have vaporized the bomb shelter and us in it. But, before I knew all this, I loved to listen to Ben talk about his plans.

I can't remember the details of any of Ben's stories well enough to retell them. Even if I could remember the sequence of events, I wouldn't want to tell them with my nasal twang. I wish I had taped his stories. My mother gave me a tape recorder for Christmas when I was about twenty-four, but I didn't think to tape Ben's stories. I guess I thought he would always be around.

Only once did Ben seem at a loss for words. It was a few days after Linda had given birth to their fourth child. Rebecca and I were walking home from the bus stop after an hour and twenty minute trip from a school on the other side of the county, and Ben was waiting at my house. He called to Rebecca, who immediately asked, "What's wrong, Daddy?" He didn't say anything until she was almost close enough to touch. Then, he said, "Our baby's dead." It was the last he spoke of that child. He didn't speak of troubles or the moment. His stories were always about another place and they had something like magic in them.

I wasn't, however, a fan of Rita's stories. When the Frenches visited the same kitchen, Harry rarely spoke. He sat as Rita told the same stories over and over. Never a detail altered. Her tales were faux epics about her victories over store clerks, car salesmen, butchers, even her husband and her children. With almost all her stories, she repeated the same basic phrase as she dragged loose ends into a conclusion: "... and then *I* told him ...," or "... and then *I* told her ..." She always delivered this phrase, her cachet, by lifting her chin and then dropping it, as if scribing an exclamation point in the air. Rita only broke from her standard style for one brief period, when I was probably fifteen or sixteen, to tell about her daughter, who had married a worthless man (probably an alcoholic), birthed two children, and then divorced. She was killed in a car accident late at night (probably by a drunk driver) as she was returning home from one of her jobs. After their daughter's death, Rita and Harry moved their grandchildren into their small house. They planned to adopt them. The boys were still only three and four; Rita and Harry were, by this time, in their sixties. In the months that followed, they found they didn't have the energy or space to handle young kids, so they allowed a couple who owned a farm in West Virginia to adopt them.

Rita's stories about her daughter and her grandchildren, told over the span of seven to eight months, touched me. These were about her love for her daughter and grandchildren, and I am sure that I identified with two brothers being raised by their mother. Maybe at some level I even wondered: What if my mother had been killed by a drunk driver when she was returning home from one of her jobs? As time passed, Rita spoke less often of her loss. She returned to stories about prevailing over small-minded bureaucrats and clerks. When Rita's language turned biblical again, I usually sat on the floor long enough to feign a polite interest and then excused myself to watch *Leave It to Beaver, The Andy Griffith Show, Father Knows Best,* or *My Three Sons.* By this time, I had already given up on my Southern Baptist upbringing. I preferred the folksy, fatherly morality of sit-coms.

Ben Smith and Rita French were rarely in our kitchen at the same time, but, on one particularly tense night, they were seated across from each other at our kitchen table. My mother sat between them, serving as a human buffer. Ben and Rita spent the evening trying to tell story after story–simultaneously. Ben started a story, then Rita interrupted and started a story, then Ben interrupted and picked up his story right where he left off, in mid-sentence, then Rita interrupted . . . for about three hours. I watched my mother's head turn to the right and then the left, as if she were watching a ping-pong match. I don't ever remember both Ben and Rita seated at our kitchen table on the same night again. From this point, I assume that Ben chose to stay away whenever the French's black Ford Fairlane was in our driveway.

Many other stories came to our kitchen. When I was about fourteen, for a long string of nights, I sat on the floor and listened to Elsie Tereskerz tell the story of how Karl, her oldest son, was killed. I never knew Karl well. He was about ten years older. When he commuted to Old Dominion College (before it became a university) around the early 1960s, he grew a beard. One day, he and Elsie came by in a VW Beetle to pick up my mother (I think they were all going to shop at the commissary on the navy base), and my mother called me out to the driveway so that I could see Karl's beard. I had seen men with flattops or crew cuts, a few men with well trimmed mustaches, but I had never seen a man with a beard. I remember that Karl chuckled to himself as I stared at his whiskers, eyes wide. He soon moved to San Francisco and became part of the hippie scene, living with a number of friends—men and women—in a commune of sorts. They supported themselves by selling homemade candles on street corners. Then, at some point, they started to sell marijuana. One Saturday night, Karl was selected to meet a buyer—a friend of a friend. The buyer turned out to be an undercover police officer, who drew his gun. Then, Karl drew his gun. After a brief blaze of pistol fire, both men were dead. Elsie and Terry, Karl's younger brother, went to San Francisco to bring back Karl's body. While they were there, they tried to piece together what happened by talking to Karl's friends and the police. None of what they heard made much sense. They couldn't reconcile the Karl of San Francisco with the Karl of their family or even the Karl with a beard who went to Old Dominion College.

One night, Elsie was telling it all to my mother, who had already heard the story more than once. Still, my mother sat and patiently listened to her best friend search for meaning in the last moments of her son's life. As Elsie spoke, she took off her wedding band and turned it over and over in her fingers, as if she were praying with rosary beads, but not praying, trying instead to find a way to understand her own words. As she was repeating what she had heard from the police, who were convinced that Karl "got what he deserved," she dropped her ring and it rolled across the floor. She was silent for a few moments, until I handed her the ring, and then she continued, fingering the ring, speaking of Karl. She said, "On the flight back, Terry kept saying, 'You know, Elsie, I'm sure Karl is up there watching us, and he's going to be mad that we're moping around.'" Then she gave a short laugh (she had a great laugh) and continued, speaking of Karl (not laughing any more), turning the wedding band in her fingers, recounting what the police said, what Karl's friends said, what the coroner said, trying to shape fragments, different world views, together into a single narrative.

SOME OF THE WORDS ARE THEIRS

As these stories found a forum around our table, my mother was a good audience, but she rarely spoke. When she did find her voice, her stories rarely grew beyond a few sentences, like her story about the ham in her family's pantry. I remember this story word for word, but first I need to set it up. The context is important. Every month or so, my mother spent the better part of her day cooking navy beans with a ham bone. This dish was apparently a delicacy in the mountains of Virginia, where she was born and raised, so she would always invite the Smiths, who were also mountain people, to share the meal. She served the beans up in bowls with chopped onions and canned tomatoes and a side of cornbread. (J.C. and I couldn't tolerate any of it. We were flatlanders.) On one Sunday night, as the Smiths and my mother were eating their beans, cooing about how much they missed the home cooking of their childhoods, my mother said: "Every winter, my father bought a smoked ham. He hung it in the pantry. Whenever we ate beans, he would go out to the pantry and cut a few slices for everyone." This tale, like all her stories, was short, yet even such brief tales seemed to push the limits of my mother's skill as a storyteller. Unlike Ben's stories, it had no excitement. Unlike Rita's stories, it hardly led to a moral triumph. Unlike Elsie's stories, it bore no crisis. Still, it was a story, and there was something important in it. The entire narrative, all thirty-two words, was about a feeling—being at home, surrounded by family, feeling secure.

All the families who brought their tales to our kitchen had their dramas and tragedies, yet my family seemed to muddle along without a story worth telling. If my father had not disappeared, I imagine he would have told stories about his father and his father's father, their emigration from Denmark, the Old Country, and their cowboy life in Colorado, or said something about his father's work as a logger in Washington. He might have talked about being at Pearl Harbor on December 7, 1941, or spoken of battles in the Pacific campaign. If my mother had felt more comfortable with the past, she might have said more about living through the Great Depression, working for the Red Cross during World War II, and traveling around the country as a navy wife. After my father was gone, she could have told stories about living with an alcoholic, but she never did.

The entire time I was growing up, the single story she told my brother and me about our father was, typical of her other stories, short: "Your father is a good man. He just has a disease." This story was what she repeated to us as if nothing else need be said. I don't know that she said even this much about her absent husband to others. On one occasion, probably not until I was in my early teens, she said to me, "Your father went to AA for six months. Then he came home one night and said that he didn't think he was an alcoholic." I was an adult before she spoke to me about a specific event related to my father's drinking. Even then, she spoke of his drinking only briefly, on two occasions.

A family without a man was so rare in the 1950s that it seems like she would have tried to explain my father's absence, even if she had to make up a story, not a long one, just a few facts to halt idle curiosity, just enough of a lie so that others, who had normal families, could say, "Oh, I see." But I never heard my mother offer anyone, old friend or new, neighbor or stranger, any kind of excuse for being alone with two kids.

Maybe she thought it was better to let others invent their own tales about our family. Maybe she knew that they would gravitate to a fairly conventional explanation—that my father was killed in a car accident or that he died of a heart attack.

Since my mother didn't speak much, my brother and I were left to develop our own stories, which we only told to ourselves for a long time, then, after years of silence, to others. We were adults before we shared our stories with each other. Even then, I heard most of my brother's story from his friends, after his death.

The versions of the story I invented were simple, without elaboration and, like the stories my mother told, more a string of statements than a narrative:

My parents are separated/divorced. By the time that I was sixteen, I told this to most of my friends, usually at that point

---

when kids start to develop intimacy by asking what your father did for a living. Sometimes, I said "separated," which was the more accurate statement. My mother never actually divorced my father so that we could continue to receive privileges as navy dependents, including medical care. Sometimes, I said "divorced" because, by the time I was sixteen, my parents had been separated for nine years and who stays "separated" for that long without getting "divorced"? This was usually enough to satisfy most people.

My father is/was an alcoholic. I didn't volunteer this part unless a new friend asked why my parents were separated/ divorced. Even the most inquisitive/intrusive people were satisfied by this statement.

My father went to AA meetings for six months. He came home from a meeting and told my mother he didn't think he was really an alcoholic. Then he drank himself to death. I only said this to my wife and sons, mostly to my sons so they would be scared to death about taking a drink.

When I was six, my mother asked my father to leave. I never saw him again. By the time I was in my twenties, this became my standard way of summing up my entire past. It had just enough of a hint of martyrdom that no one ever asked follow-up questions.

After he left, my father sent a few postcards to me, but none to J.C., my older brother. For two years, he sent me birthday presents, but none to my brother. I never said this to anyone but my wife. Maybe because my brother often said something like this, and it was really more his story than mine.

My father only sent money once, about five years after he left, and then only under duress. I might have said this to my wife, once or twice.

My father chose the bottle over his family. I only said this to myself from about nine years old to about twelve. By the time I was about twelve, I had stopped caring about my father, so repeating this part of the story was pointless.

My mother had spared J.C. and me from growing up in an alcoholic family. I knew this, and my brother knew this, and we both knew that we knew this, so we didn't have to say it to anyone, not even each other.

For a long time, my simple story (whatever version of it I was then telling) felt complete because it made my family seem less confusing. At least, to me. My story was, after all, about me, about dealing with my pain and my fears. The rest of my family, my father, mother, and brother, remained in the background, like flat characters in a bad novel, who have names and faces but speak the words of a narrator, who is really just the author. Within my simple story, I could know them and predict how they would act and I felt safe.

It wasn't until 1985, when I was thirty-five, that my simple story began to change. It was then that I started to understand how alcohol had affected my family even after my father left, long after he left. Then, in 1993, I read a letter that my father wrote to my mother shortly after he left but before he had totally disappeared, and I began to see him outside the role of husband or father or alcoholic. Later, as I worked my way through a chest of family documents, I found other words written by my father, mother and brother, and their words further changed my story. Even the facts of it. I had always believed that my father left when I was six years old, but a postcard he sent shortly after he left is postdated April 8, 1958, so I was seven when my father left, almost eight. For some reason, I erased an entire year with him. Maybe I thought he left soon after he retired from the navy in 1956 because

I have so few memories of him once we moved from naval housing to a small house in Aragona Village. Maybe I thought my story sounded better if I said that I never saw my father after I was six. I'm sure I wanted sympathy.

As I looked at family documents, the very facts of my story were shifting, but even the facts could not contain the story that began to emerge. I began to see beyond what happened, or what I thought happened, or what I wanted to believe happened. I became interested in possibilities, the persons that we might have become, the kind of family we might have been, if circumstances were different. Then, in 2002, I began to search for my father, some twenty-eight years after his death. I found a man who knew my father in New Orleans, and I wrote to my father's shipmates, the men who were with him when Pearl Harbor was attacked. In a way, I found what I had been looking for most of my life. I found my father, and I found a story to tell my sons.

MEMORIES, FIRST AND LAST

I AM NOT SURE HOW LONG IT TOOK ME TO FIGURE OUT THAT MY FIRST memory was tied to my mother's last memory. It seems like I would have immediately understood that I had stumbled across my beginning as I watched my mother act out her last memory in a nursing home, but I didn't. Yes, she acted it out. Alzheimer patients don't tell stories or have flashbacks; they relive memories. The future disappears, the present fades, and the past is all.

Maybe I didn't identify the past event that created my mother's panic because I was too worn down by my own present, trying to handle work, care for my kids, and visit my mother. So it took years to piece together the two events, make sense of my mother's ramblings. Now that I've made the connection, discovered this peculiar bond with my mother, it all seems like a prophecy. It contains the kernel of my life, as if I started to loop through it again at the moment my father disappeared on his binges, when he left us for good, and as I tried to deal with his departure.

But I need to move past memories to the event, which was simple enough, spanning no more than part of an afternoon.

It took place at Fort Slocum, an army base, on an island not too far from Manhattan, around 1954. My father, then a Chief in the navy, was stationed there. Apparently, many sailors and their families were living on this army base, but I am not sure why. My family had moved there from Charleston, the place of my birth, shortly before my second birthday, and the event probably happened a little more than a year later.

Not surprisingly, the memory has such a fuzzy feel that I occasionally think it is not really a memory at all. More than once, I have wondered if I made it up, fabricated it whole cloth from old photographs, imagining motion between the stills, adding a story to the motion, but I only know of one photograph from this time and place. It is a picture of my father and me. We are on the parade field of Fort Slocum. My father is in his khaki noncom uniform, with rows of stripes on the sleeve for his years of service. He is squatting down to make himself closer to the size of his son so both silhouettes will fit in the viewfinder of a Brownie box camera, and I am squatting also, a small boy, maybe only three years old—already imitating his father. If this is the one photograph that exists from this time and place, a photograph that has nothing to do with the memory, I don't know how I could have constructed it. And, when I think about it, the memory is not really like a series of photographs, even if I filled in the gaps. It has its own motion long before most families—certainly mine—had 8mm cameras. I see my movement across a field from the perspective of a toddler, as if my eyes were bouncing a few feet above the ground. The more I think it through, the more I have learned to trust that this must be my first memory, but I can't be certain that it happened exactly as it plays in my mind.

Behind our apartment, our quarters, I am in a playpen. I see other buildings, all together, one after another. I am going to say I was almost three, maybe a little older. We were at Fort Slocum from the time I was about two until I was about four. If I were still in a playpen, I couldn't have been very old, certainly not four. But, if I remember this, I couldn't have been too young. *I see my mother walk inside. A dog, which belongs to our neighbors, is leashed to a heavy wire clothesline. The dog runs back and forth, the entire length of the clothesline, barking. I smell dog crap. A great deal of dog crap. My brother is not there.* J.C. should have been there. But I am fairly sure he was not around because he was older and he would have stopped me. *I decide that I want to find my father, so I climb from the playpen and begin to walk. It seems like I know where I am going. I am moving across a parade field, which is in the center of the base, the parade field in the one existing photograph, bouncing as I walk. I am surrounded by brick buildings, big buildings.* Even at this young age, I knew to look for my father at the base bar, although, at the time, I couldn't have known it was a bar. Or even what a bar was. I must have figured that out later. *I see the bar in the basement of a building. Concrete steps lead down to a glass door. Writing is on the door.* How could I have remembered that there was writing on the door? Did I remember the visual image and later, after I was in school, maybe even after my father disappeared for good, begin to describe the image as writing? Or did I assume that there had to be writing on the door? Something like "CHIEF'S CLUB | Closed Sundays | Monday thru Thursday 11:30 am til 11:30 pm | Friday and Saturday 11:30 am til 3:00 am"? *A row of long windows runs close to the ground. I kneel down to look in. The bar is empty and all of the chairs are upside down on top of the tables.* It must have been early. *From there, I wander. I am lost but I don't know it or I don't care. I come to the sea wall. The wall is only a few inches high. I step onto it, spread my arms wide for balance, and follow its course. When I look down, beyond the wall, to the other side, which was hidden before I stepped on top, I see waves breaking on huge rocks. Far down.* That is where they must have found me, walking along the sea wall, balancing myself, because I had forgotten for the moment that I was searching for my father. They must have asked me to come to them, to step away from the sea wall, and when I did, they grabbed me and rushed me to my mother. I probably didn't understand why my mother was crying when she saw me, alive and safe.

Even though I have come to believe this memory as something close to what happened on that day, it still has the feel of a dream, like the most vivid dreams, the ones that we wake from confused, not sure where dream ends and reality begins. Such dreams are apart from time because they come to us night after night, like we're caught in the alchemical symbol for eternity, a snake eating its own tail. There must be some reason I keep coming back to it. There must be some reason my mother also came back to it.

A day much later, when I was in my early forties, after my mother's Alzheimer's had become advanced, I went to visit her at the nursing home. As I entered, she was pacing up and down the hallway, frantic. She came toward me and I realized that she recognized me without knowing I was her son, without even knowing where she was, and she said, "I've lost my baby. I've lost my baby."

She was somewhere in the past. For a few more weeks, each day the same panic and the same words, "I lost my baby. I lost my baby." Each day, I tried to console her, but I didn't know what to say. I said, "It's okay." I said, "You don't have a baby. Your babies are grown men." On one day I even said, "I found your baby. He is safe." Nothing I said consoled her.

For a long time, she had been moving further and further into distant memories, so I tried to place her panic in time. Maybe she was babysitting when she was a teenager and she had lost the child she was supposed to protect. Maybe this was all symbolic and she was afraid that she was losing her grasp on those she loved, or on her own sanity. I couldn't figure it out.

Years later, after her death, as I began to write about my first memory, the obvious finally hit me. I came to believe that she was on that island, reliving the day that I went searching for my father. She was hoping someone would find her son, that he would be safe. I was the baby she had lost, and she relived the events and emotions of my first memory when she still knew my forty-two year old face, knew I was a person who came to see her every day, knew I was someone who helped to care for her, but when she could no longer connect that familiar feeling with the person who was her son, when she knew, at some level, that she really was losing her baby.

Several years later, as I began to work through my mother's papers, I found a clipping from *The National Observer,* a newspaper published in New Rochelle, New York, near Fort Slocum. In the article, dated December 28, 1974, Douglas Looney reflects on the years he was stationed at Fort Slocum, from 1963 to 1965, long after my family had moved to Virginia. Looney writes of how he had returned to the deserted military base. He sadly recalls his lost friends and his good times drinking at the Officers' Club. In the midst of his recollections, he mentions that, while he was stationed on the island, a "little boy drowned when he toppled from the sea wall." Then, I believed my memory even more. There was a sea wall, and there was danger in it.

A FATHER ABANDONED

SHORT TIMERS

IN 1954, WE MOVED INTO NAVAL HOUSING IN NORFOLK, WHICH WOULD BE my father's last transfer before retiring from the service. We all became "short timers." This is a military term for someone who is close enough to retirement that he can get away with almost anything. If a superior officer asks a short timer to work on the duty roster before he finishes his morning coffee, he is well within his rights to say, "Don't bother me. I'm short." In Norfolk, when my family was "short," I began to have more memories, not just one single isolated memory like my first, but a string of memories, enough to convince myself that I can find a story to tell of those times.

While I haven't been able to locate the exact date of the move to Norfolk, I can recall most of what happened that day. After we drove up to the complex of naval housing, I jumped out of our family car, ran through our new quarters and then headed to the playground. It was spring, I would guess, because I wore short pants and a white T-shirt but the days were not yet arctic in length. While I played, my parents worked all day moving our scant bits of furniture into the small, two bedroom apartment on the ground floor. When I think back on this memory, I am amazed at how long my parents let me play by myself, unsupervised, in such a new place. I had probably not reached my fifth birthday, and they left me alone for hours. Of course, they might have walked down to the playground to glance at me on the swings or the monkey bars, a brief sighting, long enough to know I was okay, but I don't remember seeing them. Naval housing in the 1950s, especially housing so far from the Chesapeake Bay, far from a sea wall, must have been a different time and place—a safe, enclosed world.

When I started toward my new home, around dinner time, I discovered that the buildings in the complex, maybe twenty, thirty, or forty of them, all looked the same. I moved from one back door to the next, looking in, cupping my hands around my eyes so I could see through the screen door, calling out "Mom." All the families were eating. The mother at each household came to the screen door to tell me that she wasn't my mom, that she didn't know where I lived. I started to be scared and wondered how I would ever find my way home. Somehow, I ended up at the MP station. One of the MPs, if I remember this correctly, made an announcement over a loudspeaker that could be heard throughout the complex, "We have a little lost boy at the MP station. His name is George." Then they gave me an ice cream cone and kidded me about being lost. I was safe with these men, and happy. Both my parents came for me. My father smiled and joked with the MPs. After I finished my ice cream cone, my parents took me to our new home. I don't remember being lost again.

Because this memory of my first day in Norfolk is so detailed, I could lapse into believing that I saw and remembered everything from this period of my life, or at least the essence of it, but I didn't. Through the two years that we lived in Norfolk, I have only one memory of my father with a drink in his hand, which probably dates to around 1955, when I was about five. And, as memories go, this one is fairly puny, a quick visual glance. I remember looking up at my father as he sipped a dark liquid from a short glass, smiling broadly, laughing with his buddies, the neighbors who lived above us or beside us. The only other evidence I have of his drinking at the time is a pen and ink caricature, sketched, I assume, by a fellow sailor. The resemblance is quite striking. My father is sitting in a lounge chair, wearing a bathrobe and slippers, his eyes directed toward the drink in his hand, that I've-already-had-a-few smile on his face. He must have sat for the artist, as if to say, "Capture this pose. This is who I am, how I want others to see me." A man relaxing with his drink. Happy in this moment. I should hate this caricature. I should read into its negative space all of the pain his drinking caused himself and others, but I don't. I've always been very fond of it. I find it comforting to think, at one time, in the early going, he was at peace with his drinking.

And, I am sure, that drinking surrounded us. In the two-story, clapboard buildings, each with four apartments, families lived in close quarters, next to each other, on top of each other, almost like the unmarried sailors who lived in barracks on base, so parties must have erupted spontaneously and frequently. To my eyes, this was all part of the horizon, innocent fun, the kind of thing that all adults do in one apartment as the kids play in another. Everyone seemed to have a grand time.

The parties could even have the feel of fantasia. One morning, during this time in Norfolk, my mother interrupted my play. She had a surprise for me, she said. She told me to go next door, and then I walked into a strange and wonderful scene—an apartment full of pizzas. They were everywhere, on the table, sofa, chairs, beds. No people, just pizzas. This is all I remember. A moment. In a world where pizzerias were rare and pizza deliveries were decades off, I magically entered a place where childhood desires were fulfilled.

But there was no magic. I can, as an adult, imagine what led up to the scene, and it is only through imagination—not memory—that I can find a fuller story. My father and a friend, probably a sailor from New Jersey or New York, some place where pizzas were then more common, started to drink, first slowly, then with some momentum. After their drinking had some pace, they decided to cook for the entire world. The more they drank, the more pizzas they made. They must have made forty or fifty pies before they slowed enough for the booze to lay them low. It's odd that I don't even remember eating one slice. I just remember the sight of all those pies. This is a great memory, even when supplemented with a back story, but it hardly tells me anything about my father. I don't even remember seeing him that day. The times in naval housing, as far as I was concerned, were wonderful, and I suspect that all of my memories from then are focused and glossy, the numbers inflated. When I walked into that apartment, there couldn't have possibly been forty or fifty pizzas. How could my father and his friend even have found that many cookie sheets or pie pans? But I remember pizzas everywhere, so, in my memory, I saw an impossible bounty of pizzas.

It was a good time for me. A time when I even did pretty well with girls. At least, for a five year old. Certainly, much better than I did as a teenager. Once, I was locked in a bathroom with a girl. We were probably playing doctor; then, we couldn't figure out how to unlock the door. The girl's older brother had to remove the screen from the window and wiggle through a narrow band of sunlight to unlock the door. We didn't even get in trouble. The moms just laughed about it. I also remember standing outside of our building with a girl, I think a different girl. She said, "I'll show you mine if you show me yours." I agreed. She pulled down her pants briefly. I pulled down mine. Then she said, "I didn't see it." So I pulled mine down again. Immediately, I realized I had been tricked. She just wanted a second peek. This is the only bad memory I have of naval housing in Norfolk, and it's not really bad. It's more of a sweet story about a slight loss of innocence. As far as I was concerned, life was grand. Judging from a family portrait, it wasn't so happy for the rest of my family.

THE FAMILY PORTRAIT

OUR FAMILY PORTRAIT OF THE TIME WAS A CLEARLY STAGED, 1950S VERSION of the oh-aren't-we-a-happy-family photograph, or, in this case, a series of photographs. My father, I would guess, asked one of his navy friends, a photographer, to come over on a Sunday afternoon with a navy issue camera so we could pose for what would amount to a professional family portrait for free. The friend shot the photographs, developed them and gave my father several copies, which, I am sure, were never framed.

For the longest time, I thought I had five identical copies of one pose of a black and white portrait, but I eventually discovered I actually have three shots, three separate photographs that were taken on the same day, probably in a span of a few minutes. This line of discovery started when I found a smaller photograph, obviously taken on the same day, probably with a different camera. The discovery of the smaller photograph prompted me to look closer at the larger photographs. When I spread them across a table and compared details, I realized that what I thought was multiple copies of the same shot was actually multiple copies of two shots. So, with the smaller photo, I actually had three moments in time, three shots that can be placed in a sequence. It reminded me of how I used to draw stick figures in the margins of my textbooks, with the figures moving slightly on each page. When I thumbed the pages of the textbook slowly, the figures moved. When I looked at the three photographs in sequence, my family began to move and speak. It almost as if I had found a home movie.

The first photograph, which is smaller (3" by 4"), with a glossy finish, seems to have been taken with the Brownie Instamatic camera that my family owned at the time. The camera, which was probably handheld, captures a wider angle. My mother is wearing a nice dress, my father a suit, my brother and I white shirts, cuff links, and bow ties. I sport suspenders. We sit on an old couch. The broad floral design of the slip cover doesn't serve as a very good background, clashing with the needlework on my mother's collar, the twisted tropical vegetation on my father's tie, and the horizontal stripes on the boys' socks. When I look at the photograph, I can almost lose myself in the floral design, the same swirling pattern that was everywhere in the 1950s. Wallpaper with the same basic pattern would soon be hung in the kitchen and my parents' bedroom in our first house in Aragona Village, almost as if the vegetation spread from slip cover to my father's tie to kitchen to bedroom. When I pull back from the flora design, I notice that none of us looks into the camera, and I am the only one who smiles. This shot was taken first, I believe, because J.C. had not started to cry, but my mother and father already look tense. It is not hard to imagine a story to explain the tension that is already present in this shot. We were playing roles, acting out a myth, posing, creating an artifact that we would one day believe to be a memory. I think I know what actually happened. *Days before the photograph is taken, Mother probably begins to talk to Brother and me about how we are going to have a picture made of our family. A man will be coming to our house. A friend of Father. We will need to dress up, and we will need to be good. We will need to be on our best behavior and sit still. Then the day arrives. Brother doesn't want to dress up. We are all sitting on the couch, waiting. We are not even posed, but Brother is already restless. Father asks Friend to take a few shots with our Brownie Instamatic. Flash. Then Father realizes Brother is not going to sit for long. He tells Friend to go ahead and take the shots with the good camera.*

The second shot is larger (8" by 10"), more carefully framed, and printed with a matte finish. It was probably taken with a navy issue

30

camera sitting on a tripod. My mother manages a slight smile and looks directly into the camera. She almost seems serene. My father, clearly distressed, looks down toward the floor. J.C. is bawling, his eyes closed. My father's fingertips touch J.C.'s arm. I flash a huge smile and, like my mother, I look directly at the camera. *After the first shot with the Instamatic, Brother can't sit still. Friend has to set up the camera, maybe lights, too. Brother has already been sitting for about five or ten minutes. Father doesn't want Brother to embarrass him in front of Friend. Father starts yelling, maybe more like navy talk, maybe not quite yelling, but it feels like yelling to Brother, who starts to cry huge tears. Father feels bad and touches Brother's arm gently with his fingertips, a faint attempt to calm him down. Mother doesn't know what to do. She doesn't want to embarrass Father, but she wants to comfort Brother. She is torn. Father tells Friend to go ahead and take the shot, hoping Brother will stop crying. Flash.*

In the last shot, also taken with the navy issue camera, we all look into the lens, but it is still not the pose my parents had envisioned. My mother's eyes are wide, her face tight. She looks like a deer caught in the headlights of pickup truck. My father looks angry, maybe also embarrassed. He no longer touches J.C.'s arm with his fingertips. He seems to be leaning away from the rest of us. My brother is trying to stop crying. In the calm eye of the photograph, I flash another smile, oblivious to the tension of the moment. *Father and Mother both try to calm Brother, and Brother moves from tears to sniffles. Brother has almost stopped crying. We are almost in the pose my parents want. Friend feels awkward. He tells us to look at the camera and smile. We all look at him. Only I smile. Flash. Friend asks Father if he wants another shot. Brother is still sniffling. Father tells Friend, "Forget it, thanks, but no, go home." Mother takes Brother back to his bedroom. Friend packs up and leaves. Father leaves. Maybe even with Friend. Maybe for drinks. Mother is glad Father is gone. Now she can comfort Brother. I sit on the couch wondering, "What's for dinner?"*

Unless some additional photographs were lost, we went to all the trouble of dressing up for three shots. When a family poses like this, a professional photographer shoots at least one roll of film, maybe two or three, but we couldn't even hold things together for ten minutes, a dozen extra shots. Not one of the three existing shots was able to capture my family in a happy moment, no matter how transitory. A terrible afternoon, certainly, and I have no memory of any of it. This part of the story is entirely constructed.

It is intriguing that my mother saved these three photographs, some in multiple copies. Many people would have shredded all of the copies as they repeated, "This didn't really happen. My family is not like this." But my mother saved five prints of the three shots. I wonder if this wasn't her way of having some evidence of the difficult times. One of my students once wrote an essay about how she tape-recorded her parents' fights. Then she placed the tapes in plastic bags and buried them in a flower bed. She knew she would need the tapes later, to remind her about how bad her parents had fought. Maybe this is why my mother saved the photographs. She could look at them and tell herself, "Yes, it really was that bad. I really did need to ask him to leave." Judging from the photographs, J.C. must have been caught up in the tension of a marriage in its final stage. From the huge grin on my face, it is equally clear that I was clueless.

Conjectures

Even when I supplement memories and photographs with my imagination, all I can scrape together is scant evidence that provides little more than glimpses of my father, as if I am still a boy, ignorant of the world and its ways, watching a stranger pass on a crowded avenue, forced to fabricate a life to go with a face. And the memories are so few that I worry about whether or not I am making too much of them, imposing a pattern on a single event. It's almost like I have to preface every statement about my father with "I think that I know" and end it with "maybe even this is not true."

I think that I know my father was not funny. When I was about six years old, the entire family was driving someplace in my father's new 1955 Ford. He was proud of that car. It had a low-tech, early attempt at a sunroof, although it might not have been called that at the time. The front half of the roof was all glass. People often looked at the glass roof, astonished amidst their 1950s naive faith in technology, and showered him with questions. He seemed to enjoy spinning a yarn about his car, but I'm fairly sure he never admitted that the roof was an engineering failure. The sun poured in, always. The car was often uncomfortably hot or painfully bright. Engineers would not even attempt to redesign sun roofs until the late 1970s, and then sunroofs or moonroofs would be smaller, designed to pop open to let in air, the cars would be air conditioned, and every member of every family would be wearing cool sunglasses.

On this particular ride in the 1955 Ford with a glass top, I said, "I'm thirsty." My father replied, "I'm Friday, glad to meet you." Then he looked at my mother to see if she laughed. She didn't. I said louder, "I'm thirsty." My father replied, "I'm Friday, glad to meet you." Then he looked at my mother again, waiting for her to laugh. Their eyes met. Silence. Her face expressionless. Meanwhile, in the back seat, my frustration was growing. All I wanted was some water or someone to tell me that I could have water soon, not immediately, but sometime that day. So, again, I said, "I'm thirsty." My father said, "I'm Friday." My mother said, "We'll be home soon." And that silenced both of us, but something hung heavy in the air, unresolved.

Even at that age, I got the joke. I understood why it was supposed to be funny. It just wasn't funny. When my mother's eyes met my father's, I want to believe she was thinking, "You're not funny." But all this is my interpretation of my memory. Maybe even this is not true. Maybe my father was funny. Or maybe he was hilarious, when he drank. Or maybe his friends thought he was hilarious, when they drank with him. All I really know is that I didn't think he was funny on that day, at that moment, when our family was about to split apart.

My father retired from the navy in April, 1956. This I know from his military records. It seems like we would have had to move from naval housing immediately, yet I remember us moving after June 14th because my mother gave me a huge birthday party on the lawn in front of our building, inviting forty or fifty other navy brats. Maybe it was really only thirty. Maybe only twenty. But I remember forty or fifty. In the middle of the party, a scruffy kid who wasn't invited walked into the group, and I told him to go away. My mother scolded me. She turned to the boy, invited him to stay, and gave him cake and ice cream. This might be one slight sign of the effects of my father's drinking on me. I was already insecure. To feel like I belonged at my own party, I had to exclude this other kid. I repeated the same behavior for a long time, and I'm not proud of any of it.

About this time, we went to look over our new house, which was almost finished. I watched my father walk around the yard, which had recently been seeded. He carried a cardboard cylinder of clover seeds, spreading them without any apparent design as he walked. I think that he was inspecting his quarter acre of America, claiming it with his clover seeds. The soil was soft and his feet left impressions, an inch or so deep. Then it started to rain hard, a squall off the Atlantic, and we rushed inside. My parents walked around, opening closet doors, flushing the single toilet, and measuring windows. J.C. went off to explore the unfinished upstairs. I had brought my model car, a Thunderbird with headlamps that lit up, and I lay on my side in the middle of the empty living room, which seemed huge, rolling my model car over the hardwood floor, trying to imagine myself small enough to fit into the driver's seat. In the dark room, the headlights seemed to glare and I was lost in my own world, a place distant.

My father was proud of his new property, which was, I am sure, the first he had ever owned. It was also the first place I felt settled. When I recently saw Linda Smith, our neighbor from the days of Aragona Village, she said, "What I always remember about you is how you would tell people, 'Get off my property.'" I must have often said this to other kids in the neighborhood. My obsession with protecting the parameter of "my property" was probably related to living my entire life, to that point, in navy housing, where there are no property lines. Like my father, I wanted to claim this piece of land and the hope it promised. Months after we moved in, well into the summer, I noticed that the places where my father had walked when we visited on that rainy day sprouted grass and clover first. I could see the path he had taken as he crisscrossed the yard. I could follow his steps for a while, and then I was lost. It was like he vanished.

The Village

ARAGONA VILLAGE WAS ONE OF THE MANY POST WORLD WAR II developments that popped up across the country to promise a piece of the American dream. The houses were small (about 1,200 square feet) and inexpensive. We bought ours for $11,000 and change, with a 5½ percent loan, which meant my parents had a monthly payment of $66.27. All of the Aragona Village models—the Cape Cod, the Ranch, the Split-Level, the same three models offered in other fabricated communities in New York, California, Colorado, Wisconsin, and pretty much everywhere else—were quickly constructed, poorly insulated, and covered with asbestos shingles. Later, rumors circulated that John Aragona, the developer, was connected to the Mafia and that he imported cheap materials from Italy, like small metal windows that could hardly be cranked open and, even when fully open, allowed in too little of the Atlantic breeze to break summer heat. Yet, military families continued to pick out their favorite model, street after street of houses appeared, and more families moved in. Miraculously, as the families planted gardens, added shutters, erected fences, grew trees from seedlings, and converted carports to family rooms, the houses actually started to look different, each taking on a style of its own. Some of the families even added columns in front of the brick facade (none of the houses in Aragona Village were all brick) or plaster lawn jockeys with black faces. The lawn jockeys, about two feet high and dressed in riding garb, held a brass ring so visitors from a nearby plantation could tether their horses and walk in for a mint julep. After the Civil Rights movement of the 1960s, the African-American lawn jockeys were traded in for Mexican lawn jockeys. Eventually, thank God, the lawn jockeys disappeared all together, replaced by plaster deer and plastic flamingos.

Even during an era of post-war optimism, buying a house was an act of faith. My mother and father, despite the problems in their marriage, must have had some sense of hope. My father, who had been a public relations officer toward the end of his time in the navy, thought about attending the University of Missouri to study journalism. He had taken a few courses there in 1949, while still in the navy. When he retired, he wrote a letter to the Head of the Department of Journalism, but I don't think he ever actually applied. Something happened; the plan fell apart.

Despite the change of plans, my parents must have believed he would find a good job and begin to build a second career. However, the only job I remember my father having during this period was filming events for the telecasts of the local news with a handheld 8mm camera. It was a good job, one that could have led to a career. One Saturday, he took my mother and me along (I don't remember my brother being there) as he filmed a re-enactment of a meeting of the House of Burgesses in Williamsburg. One of the burgesses, dressed in a red cape with a white fur border, saw me, called me over, and handed me his scepter. The man laughed because I held it upside down. My father filmed the event, and he later woke me so I could see myself on the late news. In fact, I think I remember the entire scene from seeing it on television rather than being there, because I remember seeing the man and me and the scepter from a distance, from the perspective of the camera held by my father. So, this memory, which is vivid, is at least one degree of separation from my actual experience, maybe more.

About this time, though it might not be connected to the same day, I remember being with my father at the news station in Norfolk. We were all there, even my brother. My father had taken in some of his film, and I watched as a man, who had just finished processing the footage, criticized my father. The film had not turned out. My father was wearing a nervous, self-deprecating smile, trying to placate the man, explain what happened, hunching up his shoulders, as if to say, "I'm new at this. I'll get better. I can do it." The man's expression remained stern, critical. I didn't like the man. I didn't like how he was treating my father. But I could do nothing, except watch. I would guess that my father soon lost this job, not necessarily because of this incident, probably because he missed work for days at a stretch.

For about a year and a half, my father was with us but not in the navy, a time when he was probably out of work more than in work. He couldn't have been very busy, but I don't remember our spending much time involved in father-son activities—doing chores, playing catch, wrestling, burping, farting, that sort of thing. Bonding. Being men together. Pissing in the same pot. I can remember only two father-son activities. The first was a boxing lesson. Someone, maybe Santa Claus (i.e., my mother), gave me boxing gloves and a kiddie punching bag. It was more like a speed bag that was mounted on a metal rod, which was in turn attached to a small metal platform. The metal platform, in some inconspicuous place, was probably stamped with "Made in Japan." (At that time, almost everything that was inexpensive and mass produced bore the same stamp. In the 1970s, it was a real shock to every American when Japan started to make more reliable automobiles than Detroit.) I am not sure why my father decided to give me a few tips on boxing, maybe I whined at him long enough or maybe he realized that he was going to leave us soon and he felt a need to give me a life lesson. Anyway, he helped me lace up my gloves and showed me how to stand on the platform and whale away at the bag. He told me to jab twice ("one, two") with my left, then throw a right cross ("three"). Then he said, "Practice." And he was gone.

I practiced and I followed his advice. I was not the kind of kid who had to go looking for a fight. My brother also gave me boxing lessons. His were a little more experiential, so I had enough of boxing at home. Yet, on the few occasions when I was forced to fight outside the home, I always followed my father's advice. I jabbed twice with my left ("one, two"), then tried to throw a right cross ("three"). The fight always ended the same way. I was in the process of throwing the second jab ("two"), holding some dream of throwing the deciding right cross ("three") when the other guy's fist smashed into my face ("two and a half"). The other guy's dad must have taught him to lead with a right cross.

Besides the boxing tips, the only other life lesson I remember was a father-son talk, delivered shortly before my father left. We were driving down Virginia Beach Boulevard when, out of the blue (at least, I didn't expect it), he said something about how there are times when men and women are naked and it is bad and other times when it is okay. I can't recall his exact words or where he went from there, maybe because I was utterly confused, even though I was trying hard to understand. He might have felt that he needed to tell me the facts of life before he left, even though I was far from an age when I would need the information. Or I might have seen him and my mother together, so he felt the need to offer some kind of explanation. But I think I would have remembered an event that shocking, especially in 1958. So, he must have been trying to educate his son. I came to call this my father's "naked ladies" lecture, only I liked to pronounce "naked" as Billy Graham did in his sermon about the "neck-ed devil in the wilderness," which he delivered during one of his many televised crusades. Whatever the purpose behind the strange chat, I would guess my father was trying to be a good and caring father—maybe even one of those sit-com dads—and not really pulling it off.

It seems like my father would have taught me something about baseball, but he didn't. By the summer after first grade, Bobby and Tommy Southard moved into a house on Tyson Road, one street over. Bobby was one year older than I, and Tommy was a year younger. Their father was then a Commander in the navy, a mustang, which meant that he began as an enlisted man and advanced through superior merit into the officer corps. He was a flat-topped tough guy who believed in firm handshakes and discipline. After I knew him a while, I also realized he had a big heart. He was a devoted father, especially to Marty, Bobby and Tommy's younger brother, who was mentally retarded. Anyway, during that summer, Bobby, Tommy, and I were in their backyard feeling more than a little bored, so they suggested we play baseball.

"What's that?" I asked.

"You mean you don't know what baseball is?" they replied, in unison, as if they were twins.

This memory is surprising because, in the 1950s and 1960s, baseball was still our unchallenged national pastime. The NBA and NFL were struggling to find an audience and were rarely televised, but a baseball game was telecast every Saturday, usually the Yankees against some other team. So it's odd that I was seven years old and had never heard of baseball. This memory seems to suggest that my father was not around much before he left for good.

The Business Trip

In the winter of 1958, about a year and a half after we had moved to Virginia Beach, my father came home in a taxi late on a Sunday night. My brother and I ran to the door yelling, "Daddy, Daddy!" He had been gone for several weeks and returned with not a dime. I would guess he had stayed gone as long as his money lasted, until he could no longer find anyone to buy him a drink, until he had to sober up and return home, ashamed, like a little boy. My mother emptied her purse to pay the cab driver, who seemed as embarrassed as my father. I remember that the cab driver apologized again and again. Of course, none of this was the cabbie's fault, but he still felt bad about taking the woman's last dollar. When my mother put me to bed, she looked sad. I asked her, "Are we out of money?" She said, "No. We have some more money in the bank." But something was clearly wrong. I think that was the night—the moment— she made the decision.

41

A few weeks later, or a few months, my father called me in from play. It was a cold day, shortly before spring. I had that vague sense again that something was wrong. My father seemed serious, or angry, or worried. I had no idea what he was going to say, but I feared it would be important, and bad. I was a little confused, and I wondered if I had done something wrong. As we stood in the kitchen, the father kneeling to look his son in the eyes, he told me that he was going away on a business trip, that he would be gone for a while. I was relieved. Everything was okay, so I returned to play, without even asking what a "business trip" was or how long a "business trip" lasts. Then, without any fanfare, he was gone.

It is odd, the way he slipped away. I don't remember saying goodbye or seeing him off. I guess I really believed that he was going on a short trip, maybe for a few days. This is how much of my childhood felt, like I didn't really know what was going on and I didn't really feel anything, and I was under water, pulled by currents, looking at images distorted by the refracted light. Whatever clarity I have about my childhood was, I am sure, constructed later, after rethinking events, after I had more information and a little more perspective.

I know now, from reading a post card, that my father took a bus across the country to Bremerton, Washington, where he stayed with his mother, Grandma Musa, for a while. On a postcard, he wrote: "The bus ride was a killer, but I made it." Only later, much later, from relatives in Washington, I learned that he soon moved in with his brother Forrest, whom the family called Frosty. At Frosty's, he quickly wore out his welcome. One day, the two brothers where drinking, and they decided to make pizza and chicken cacciatore. By the time Della, Frosty's wife, came home, the brothers were falling-down drunk and the kitchen was a mess. Tomato sauce was on the walls and ceiling, and, soon, I would guess, my father was packing his bags. In a few months, he lost contact with everyone, even his mother.

Shortly after Grandmother Musa had a stroke in the early 1960s and moved into a nursing home, she wrote a letter to my mother. Her health was failing, and she said that she had to write standing at a dresser. It is clear from her script that her hand shook as she wrote. She used little punctuation. This woman, who was educated in a Normal School in Nebraska and taught school for a while, strained to scribble simple thoughts:

> Im writing this to ask a favor do you have a late address of George Im going to have Forrest write Know no one has let him know where I am no doubt he won't care either Dale does not care either but he does not know how however. I

42

have only seen Vicki twice she is so sweet Forrest brought she and Delias little girl up this afternoon for a short call. I thot Id find out the reaction of either Dale tried to come but couldnt have him in his condition most the time he is in seattle & has been all the time.

Grandma Musa had four sons. She didn't mention Russell, my uncle Rusty, because he was working as a logger in Alaska. While in Alaska, he drank with the other loggers, as loggers drink, but no more than the other loggers. He kept his job and remained married. He did, however, have problems with Sharon, his daughter, who drank a lot. I once heard him say, "I think she has a complex." Grandma Musa had already lost track of George, my father. Dale, she said couldn't visit in "his condition." (Dale eventually disappeared, and all Aunt Jean, Rusty's wife, would say about it was, "He did something very bad.") Grandma didn't feel that either of them cared about her. Frosty was taking care of her when she had her stroke. He had, my cousin Vicki later told me, broken down and sobbed when he found her on the floor of her house, when he realized she had been lying there for three days, paralyzed by a stroke. He moved her into a nursing home and brought Della and Vicki to visit. He cared, but Frosty's drinking would progress. He and Della would later divorce.

I didn't know about all this until much later. At the time, submerged in my watery haze, I only knew that my father was on a business trip. Each night I prayed for his return. Often, I asked my mother, "When's Daddy coming back?"

She always said, "I don't know."

After about three years, I finally asked, "Is Daddy ever coming back?"

She said, "No. I don't think so." I never had to ask about my father again, and I am sure my mother was relieved to be done with the silly lie about a business trip taken by a man who didn't even have a job.

After my father left in April, he sent me a birthday present in June of 1958, a toy rocket that, once hooked up to a hose, filled with water and pumped with air, blasted over a hundred feet straight up, over roof tops, even over tree tops, stage after stage, until the top stage, a little spaceship, came drifting down safely under a parachute. In the late 1950s, only eight months after the Soviets launched Sputnik, about three years before President Kennedy promised we would go to the moon by the end of the 1960s, it was an amazing feat of toy engineering. For a while, I was the most popular boy on the street. As August 4th approached, I am sure that J.C. expected an equally wonderful gift. Nothing came. When June 14th came next year, our father sent me another present, a badminton set. Our mother hid it until late in the summer, well past J.C.'s birthday on August 4th, and then she told J.C. and me that it was a present from her to both of us. She had feared our father would again fail to send J.C. a present. Of course, I only heard that the second present was from our father years later, and I'm sure our mother never told this to J.C. He often spoke of the one present that our father sent me and how he didn't receive anything. It seems like a simple act of omission, but I don't think J.C. ever got over it. From then on, he assumed I had been our father's favorite.

This business about me being the favorite, if it were true, is puzzling. I don't remember our father spending more time with me, but maybe he did. Certainly, the birthday presents suggest favoritism. If I were the favorite, the real question is why. I can only make guesses here. J.C., who was older, saw more of my father's drinking. He remembered more. Things I didn't even learn about until much later. He might have looked at our father with a knowledge beyond his years, a gaze that made the father feel uncomfortable, more like a son in his son's eyes. My mother later told me that J.C. overheard the conversation when she asked our father to leave. She said, "We can't go on like this." Then she saw J.C. and realized he had been listening. He turned and ran.

But maybe there was something else, something as simple as the temperaments of the men in my family. I sense that my father was needy, at least, by the time we moved to Virginia Beach. He probably felt worthless because he had trouble holding a job. He probably also felt bad about his drinking. He seemed to look to my mother for approval, affirmation. J.C. was an active child who also wanted attention. Maybe my father felt burdened by this. He may have felt that he couldn't satisfy this kid. He may have even resented the attention my mother gave to J.C. Two males in the same household who both need attention is not a good mix. I was a quiet kid who didn't ask for much. Give me a stick, a couple of marbles and the corner of an empty room and I was happy for hours. I might have been the favorite because I was low maintenance.

The second birthday present was the last time we heard from my father for a long time. We just went on with our lives, without really understanding how his leaving affected us. Years after he left, when I was maybe fourteen or so, I watched *The Days of Wine and Roses* on television while I was at home alone. The movie is a love story derailed by booze. Joe Clay, played by Jack Lemmon, works in public relations for a Madison Avenue advertising agency. He meets Kirsten Arensen, a secretary for the same firm, and they begin to date, and he introduces her to drinking. They marry and have a daughter, Debbie, and then their lives slowly spiral out of control. Kirsten passes out one night, and her cigarette sets the apartment on fire. Joe loses a series of jobs. He wakes up in the "violent ward." Eventually, Joe finds his way to AA and sobers up. Kirsten, however, moves through a string of "bums," who supply her with companionship and booze. I watched the movie without feeling much of anything. If we had more than three channels at the time, I probably wouldn't have watched it at all. As I drifted through the story, snacking on cheese and crackers and Kool Aid, I don't think I connected the movie family to my family. Then, in the last scene, Debbie asks her father, "When is Mommy coming home?" Joe answers, "Mommy is sick." This hit home. It was the first and last time I cried about the loss of my father. Even then, I only identified with Debbie, the daughter, and her question about the missing parent. I still didn't think about how the film was related to my father. *The Days of Wine and Roses* is a weepy melodrama. My family plodded along, seemingly without crisis.

As I grew older, I learned to talk about my father, but I never moved past the past. I also learned a little more about him, but not much. I knew he had a "disease." I knew he had been at Pearl Harbor when it was bombed. But, basically, I tried to forget him. I told myself, even at a young age, maybe by the time I was nine years old or so, "He had a choice between us and the bottle, and he chose the bottle." I don't think that I blamed him or consciously felt anger toward him, probably because I told myself I didn't care.

It was easy to push him from my life because I never had any sense that he thought about us. He only sent money once, a $500 money order, when I was about twelve. And this only because a friend of my mother (actually, a man who had served in the navy with my father) somehow arranged for a congressman to send my father, who was living off of his military retirement, a threatening letter. At the time, I thought (maybe I heard this from my mother) that my father sent money because he was afraid that the congressman could garnish his retirement checks. But he couldn't. My mother had already written to the Department of the Navy to ask for a portion of my father's monthly checks, and the navy responded, in a well mannered, bureaucratic letter, that it encouraged retirees to support their children, but it couldn't force them to do so. My mother split the $500 and opened two savings accounts—one for J.C. and the other for me. I went with her to the bank and watched her open the accounts.

My father returned to our house in Virginia Beach only once, shortly after he left on his business trip. He was with a friend. My brother and I were in school and my mother was at work. Grandma Mimi—my mother's mother—was the only one home. As it was told to me years later, my father wanted to see if an old pea coat were still in a chest in the attic. He searched but couldn't find it. Then he and his friend had a cup of coffee with Grandma Mimi and left. Years later, my mother told me how Grandma Mimi had described the visit to her. My father sipped on his coffee, talking with Mimi, his friend silent. Through it all, he never asked about any of us. This story helped me to write him out of my life.

I was twenty-four and in graduate school when my mother called, without any warning, to say my father had died. I expressed some shock on the phone, but I didn't really feel anything. No more than reading about the death of a celebrity or politician or hearing about

46

the death of a distant relative I had never even met. I can't say that the news disrupted my day. I don't think that I even told any of my friends. I certainly didn't take any time off from school.

He was buried in a national cemetery somewhere around New Orleans. At that time, J.C. was living at home, after four years in the Air Force, finishing college on the G.I. Bill, so the task of settling our father's affairs fell to him. The director of a funeral home in New Orleans called J.C. repeatedly to remind him that he was the next of kin and he was obligated to pay for the coffin and embalming. Our mother hired an attorney who told the funeral director that we had not heard from my father in sixteen or seventeen years and that J.C. was a boy of eleven when the old man left. The veteran who was planning the service also talked to J.C. He tried to shame him—all of us—into attending the service and paying our respects. It didn't work. I'm sure that it seemed odd to the vet that this man's family cared so little. The vet later sent us the flag from the burial service and a few of my father's personal belongings, which I didn't see until much later. My mother mentioned that the owner of the boarding house where my father lived also called, but I don't recall why. Maybe he wanted to know if he should ship his tenant's belongings to kin, no matter how distant. My mother said the man was kind. He told her he didn't have any idea his boarder had a family. He also said that, if we ever came to New Orleans, we should look him up. I'm not sure how all these people located my family. My father must have listed us as next of kin on some kind of document, maybe a hospital admission form. Odd.

For years after my father's death, I continued to tell myself the same story. The alcoholic was gone, I said over and over. My mother had saved us from my father. My father's drinking had not touched me. This simple story did not change for a long time. Then, at the age of thirty-five, I finally realized, in one of those moments of great insight into the obvious, that I had indeed grown up in an alcoholic family. My father had left but little had changed, at least, not immediately. From my perspective (and, at this time, that was the only perspective I would adopt), my brother, almost as soon as my father left, began to play the role of the alcoholic. His addiction was food, and he was moody and angry. He often hit me. I soon learned to be passive, a common strategy for children of alcoholics. If I put up a slight show of fighting back, enough for him to release his anger, he wouldn't hurt me too badly. My mother, as I eventually saw it, shed my father and then became co-dependent to my brother. His mood ruled the house. He was unknowable. A force. He was the person who made me feel unsafe in my own home, and he made my home feel like a practicing alcoholic was still living there. This is how I started to think of my family.

48 A few years later, when I was about thirty-eight, I finally asked my mother why she had never tried to stop my brother from hitting me. This was one of the few issues I ever harbored against her, so I thought it was time to deal with it. She told me, "I was afraid I would lose control." In other words, she was afraid that if she told my brother to quit and he didn't, then he would realize that he could do whatever he wanted. She would lose control, she thought. So she didn't try to control him and stayed in control. This is the kind of crazy thinking that only makes sense in alcoholic families, that special kind of nuclear family. Not a nuclear family in the sense of a nuclear unit, self-sufficient, self-contained. But a nuclear family in the sense of an isolated organism, a place where individuals go to self-destruct. Nuclear as in a neutron bomb. The bomb that can be dropped on a city, kill all the inhabitants with massive amounts of radiation and leave all the buildings untouched. In alcoholic families, the people leave or die, but the structure remains.

So I didn't hate my father. He wasn't there. I hardly knew him. I hated my brother instead. I only saw J.C. as he played the role of the alcoholic father. When my father left, there was a vacuum in the family. My brother filled the void, not consciously (for either of us) and hardly out of choice. He was sucked in by the laws of physics.

If all this sounds overly dramatic, like the ranting of a male hysteric, try to understand that this was all part of my new-found identity as a victim of alcoholism. I should have gone through this period of whining about the damage the alcoholic father inflicted on me when I was a teenager and dealing with all the other facets of adolescent angst, but my development was a little delayed. I was probably one of the few people in the history of humanity to experience adolescent angst, rage against the symbolic father, and mid-life crisis at the same time, and I probably needed to go through a period of blaming others and feeling sorry for myself. I eventually grew out of it in my forties.

Even more importantly, I eventually began to bring history to my family. I had always thought of my family as fixed at the moment of trauma, the break, the disappearance of my father. I felt that the family and the roles remained the same. I was convinced that nothing had changed for decades. I was wrong.

STUDYING ALCOHOLICS

BY THE TIME I WAS FORTY, I WAS MARRIED WITH TWO KIDS, LIVING IN MIS-
souri, and trying to deal with midlife issues. For men, midlife is supposed
to hit between thirty-eight and forty-two, so I was right on schedule. Does
this mean I was cliché about it all? Not at all. I didn't buy a red sports car
(I couldn't afford one), and I didn't have an affair (I'm a theoretician, so I
spent my time trying to figure out why other men had affairs). Still, I felt
confused and angry, and I didn't even know why. I wasn't a patient father
or an attentive husband. I felt isolated and imagined that my neighbors
gathered in small groups to talk about George's problems. This went on
for several years.

In 1993, about the time I was on the verge of moving from midlife
transition to midlife crisis, a friend, a recovering alcoholic who knew
something of my family history, suggested that I might benefit from the
Family Program at Hazelden, a treatment program based on the principles
of AA. For some reason, maybe I was desperate, I went. For five days, I
talked about my childhood with complete strangers, some who had also
grown up in alcoholic families, some who were living with alcoholics,
and some who were alcoholics in the twenty-eight day program. During
the days, we worked in small groups. At night, we listened to alcoholics
tell their stories. Some of the evening speakers had been sober for a few
months; others had been sober for close to thirty years.

At Hazelden, when I first heard a speaker describe himself as a "grateful alcoholic," I felt like I had been slapped in the face. How could anyone be grateful about being an alcoholic? But, as I listened to his story, I began to understand. The speaker was not grateful for the despair of his drinking days. He was grateful for the fellowship he found in AA, which he couldn't have experienced without being an alcoholic. So, at Hazelden, I made my first move toward understanding alcoholics, and it was there that I began to separate my father, the man, from my father, the alcoholic.

When I returned home, I began to read *Alcoholics Anonymous*, which members of AA affectionately call the Big Book, and I was struck by a particular passage:

> The alcoholic is like a tornado roaring his way through the lives of others. Hearts are broken. Sweet relationships are dead. Affections have been uprooted. Selfish and inconsiderate habits have kept the home in turmoil. We feel a man is unthinking when he says that sobriety is enough. He is like the farmer who came up out of his cyclone cellar to find his home ruined. To his wife, he remarked, "Don't see anything the matter here, Ma. Ain't it grand the wind stopped blowin'?"

The Big Book, it seems, had understood the effects of alcohol on a family long before psychologists. Alcohol alters the chemistry of a family. Even after the alcoholic has stopped drinking or boarded a bus for the West Coast, its effects linger.

The Big Book was about my family, too.

I even became interested in studying how alcoholics tell their stories in AA, so I began attending open AA meetings. In the rooms at churches, restaurants, and community centers, I found that I liked to sit in the back and watch the heads bob up and down. It's like sitting in an intimate café, listening to jazz, watching the crowd feel the swing. The speaker is telling his story or her story, a fragmented string of events, rarely a clear narrative with a beginning, middle, and end, but events held together more by a range of emotions that seem too disparate for a single talk, not at all like the story told in the room last week or that will be told next week, but the heads in the room keep bobbing up and down, saying in the language of the body, "I know how you feel. I've been there."

When the audience nods, the speaker knows that the audience knows because the speaker has also heard their stories. There is a sense of trust that has built slowly, maybe over years, as members shift back and forth from the role of story teller to role of story listener. One person tells her story and the listener says "I know how you feel" by telling his story. This is what the nods really mean. Nods are a shorthand for "Remember when I told my story," or "Remember, I went through the same thing," or "Know this, we are not so different."

This is communion. I began to commune with alcoholics, and at some point I began to care about my father. At AA meetings and later at Al-Anon meetings, I heard the fragments of my father's story, my mother's, and my brother's. I had learned that listening to stories can bring us together. It was only at this point that I started to dig through the chest of family artifacts, my mother's "papers."

As I began to draft a scholarly book on storytelling in AA, I started to learn that stories need to change. I began to understand how the stories of newcomers, those early in recovery, slowly evolve into the stories of oldtimers, those who have repeatedly told their stories in AA.

Listening to newcomers tell their stories is like being on an emotional roller coaster. They are crying one moment, rhapsodic the next. The story is fragmented, not coherent beyond the level of anecdote, and the anecdotes seem to be strung together randomly, out of sequence, without clear intent or moral. The talks of AA newcomers focus on the drunkolog, the section of the talks that recounts the speaker's drinking days. The events that led them to AA are only touched upon, and their story of a newfound life in AA is idealized, as if they are describing a self they want to become.

This is not to say that the talks of newcomers are unimportant. They tell their stories as they need to tell them at the time. One of the

GEORGE H. JENSEN, JR.

bravest talks that I ever heard was given by a woman who relapsed between the time that her talk was scheduled and the night she was supposed to speak. She decided that she should not cancel, that she should stand before her friends and say, "I am an alcoholic," and then honestly talk about how she had relapsed, how she struggles with the program, and how she keeps coming back. Most of those in the meeting gave her hugs and told her they were proud of her, but a few oldtimers later told her that she should have cancelled. Because she had relapsed, these oldtimers didn't think she had earned a right to speak. But I think she needed to speak to move past her relapse and make a commitment to the program. In the early days of AA, newcomers were often told—not asked—to stand up and speak after attending only a few meetings.

I have also learned from listening to oldtimers. The talks of oldtimers form a more organized narrative. They also speak in a voice that is not quite theirs. It is the voice of the program, a calm and serene embodiment of all of the program's values. Even when they speak of their current self, almost as if they were speaking of someone else, and their current struggles with the difficulties of life, staying sober, getting along with others, they transcend it all. They speak many voices— the voice of the program, the voice of their drinking self, the voice of their current self, and the voices of others who have taught them the program or had some impact on their recovery. And all of these voices have a life of their own, and they are clearly marked with boundaries, as if the speaker's intonation put quotation marks around the words of others. Oldtimers know that it is the words of others that force us to change.

One of the most amazing talks I heard was given by a man who had been in AA for about thirty years. He was dying of liver cancer. Word had gotten out that he was going to speak one more time, and the room overflowed with lives he had touched. He began to speak, and laughter erupted. We laughed with him for about twenty minutes; then he became serious and talked about how he was dying and how he was not afraid. The program had given him a good life and much courage. Just this. Serious, but certainly not sad, for about two minutes. Then he returned to talking about his life before AA, his coming to AA, and his life in AA, and we laughed with him for the rest of his story. About five weeks later, he died.

At AA meetings, in the stories of newcomers that evolved into the stories of oldtimers, I witnessed change. I saw men and women at their first meeting stand, shaking, hardly able to speak, say, "I am an alcoholic." And then they continued to attend meetings. They spoke of finding a job. Getting back with their spouse. Or getting a divorce and then meeting someone new. They spoke of becoming a better father or mother. Making amends to friends. I found reassurance in the change of other families. I could believe that the history of my family could have been different. I began to find possibilities reassuring. My father could have stayed in AA. He could have sobered up. Our family could have stayed together. In possibilities, alternative histories, I found hope. I saw something of my father's potential.

THE FAMILY ARCHIVES

IT WAS NOT UNTIL DECADES AFTER MY FATHER'S DEATH, YEARS AFTER MY mother's death, months after I began studying storytelling in AA, that I began to learn more about my father. Even though I initially learned only a few facts, a few fragments of a more complex family, my view of him began to change. I even heard his voice for the first time in letters scattered through boxes of my mother's belongings and papers, a collection of cancelled checks, recipes for dishes my mother wanted to cook someday, blank postcards, unlabeled photographs of people I couldn't identify, navy medals, newspaper clippings, Boy Scout merit badges, negatives, baby teeth, undeveloped rolls of film, identification cards, maps of cities we never visited, report cards, and just about everything else that had passed through her hands in a lifetime. My mother even saved the first nickel that my brother earned, when he was four years old, for helping a neighbor fill in a hole, and the ticket I received for surfing illegally when I was sixteen. These artifacts were scattered in file cabinets, desk drawers, chests, and tucked between the pages of a Bible. When my mother's Alzheimer's progressed, at the time we moved her to Missouri, the movers collected her "papers" into boxes and shipped them to my house. The boxes, eight or ten of them, sat in my closet for years before my wife condensed the "papers" into a single chest.

I might have left the family papers for another generation to explore, but Donna, when she was sorting through it all, found a letter my father sent to my mother. Donna handed it to me and said, "Read it." At that moment, I was writing in front of the computer, so I put the letter down on the desk. Donna said, "Read it. Now." So, I stopped and read. The letter was written in 1958, shortly after my father left our family. The other letters and postcards written by my father, the ones I found later, bore traditional punctuation. This one was filled with dashes that marked the points where he could not find a way to finish a thought. Each dash must have lasted for several minutes, and this is how it should be read, in short bursts of fragments, each separated by a long pause, more silence than words:

> Dear Louise,
>
>   Just a few lines to let you know I'm still among the living tho just barely—I ended up here with a borderline case of pneumonia, spent four days in Hosp on penicillin—at present am staying with mom—riding the Grub line so to speak—put in for rocking chair—the only thing I could do—I went down and put in for MSFS and a rigger job in Adak or Kodiak—not much hope on either—this area is all union so I'm lost unless I can find something non union—
>
>   I guess as soon as I can travel I'll hitch hike to Calif—probably no better but I can't stay here—mom just makes out as it is and the Hosp wiped me out but I'll get by someway—
>
>   I just about went to an AA meeting the other night but felt so lousy I couldn't make it.
>
>   I just read two articles in Sat Evening post on marriage counseling—you should read them, we lost something some place—me I guess but both of us too—
>
>   But I do love you and believe me I miss you so much, I've lost about 20 pounds—I can't sleep eat or do anything when I get to thinking of you—I guess I didn't tell you or show you often enough—sometimes I tried and felt kind of rebuffed in my attempts maybe my methods weren't right—anyway I felt hurt and baffled at the rebuffs or what I thought were—

I would like Rev. Farr's address. I'll write him, I feel like pouring out everything that seems to have built up in me and maybe he can straighten me out on some of it. It might help me—and maybe help him counsel you or try to explain me to you.

Louise my life without you and the kids is not worth living—I came very close twice to closing it out in the past two months and there is no guarantee on it yet—this is the lowest mental state I have ever been in my life.

Well I hate to burden you with my troubles—all that I started to say was that you are the only woman in the world for me and that I love you very much—I think you know that—I still respect my marriage vows and always have and always will until you decide to cancel it out—I'm still married to you and hope to be for the rest of my life—I wish you felt the same—

All my love,
George

I couldn't even take in the entire letter at once. I had to reread it, spacing out my readings over years. Even then, it was hard for me to process. My father was a good writer, yet, in this letter, as he describes his life falling apart, his prose rambles, his thoughts break under their own weight, his sentences trail—

He was "riding the Grub line." This is a cowboy phrase that means moving from place to place while working odd jobs for a meal and bed. I was surprised to read that he thought about attending an AA meeting, that he considered suicide, that he thought life without us was "not worth living." He wrote that my mother was "the only woman in the world" for him. What I found most striking was that, at this moment of deep despair, "the lowest mental state" of his life, he was unselfishly thinking about my mother. He wanted to write Reverend Farr, our minister at the time, so that the Reverend could better counsel my mother.

I wonder how my mother read the letter, because her reaction is also part of my family's history. Did she feel that he was trying to manipulate her? Draw her back into a marriage she had struggled to escape? Or, did the letter make her feel what she was trying to forget, that she loved him and wanted to be with him, that she needed him? Maybe she read it while repeating to herself, "I wish he would just let this thing die." But she kept the letter. All those years, she kept it. Maybe, she wanted to try to unravel it, as I do. Imagine his intentions. I am sure she wondered what she might have done to make him feel "rebuffed."

In the letter, my father asks my mother to read the *Saturday Evening Post* article on marriage counseling. He meant something by this, but what? At the university library where I taught, I started trying to track it down. In the *Readers' Guide*, I found a series of three articles in the *Post*, but the library did not have those volumes. I ordered them on inter-library loan and waited three weeks for them to arrive. When I picked them up at the circulation desk, I began to read them as I walked back to my office.

The series, entitled "Marriage is Our Business," ran for three issues. It presents case studies "from the files of the Marriage Council of Philadelphia" that "show that even a wife-beater may have his side of the story." I believe that my father had read the first two installments and then wrote my mother before the third came out.

The case study that is most like my parents tells the story of Bessie Jacobs (as she is called in the article) and Mr. Jacobs (who is never given a first name). The wife, like my mother, had a college degree; the husband, like my father, only finished high school. During the first session with a male counselor, Bessie says that she does not know if her husband will show up. She says that her husband has "had a complete personality change." He used to be "sweet and helpful." Now he is "ugly and downright brutal." He has been "drinking secretly," and she found "a bottle in his closet."

Mr. Jacobs shows up "an hour or so late" with a note in his hand. His wife, he says, had begged him to come to counseling, then she wrote him a note and left for the appointment. The note said: "If

---

you don't appear you can pack your things and get out." He begins to complain that his wife "felt superior because he only had a high school education." She had even "once thrown his week's earnings in the street in scorn." Interestingly, these words run parallel to an advertisement for Hamilton watches, "the reward for love," a great graduation present. Remember that Bessie has a college degree, her husband does not. The opening line of copy reads: "Hamilton is the watch worthy of your love, worthy of resplendent pride." In the 1950s, we were already being told that money, respect, possessions, and love were somehow all connected.

As the session continues, the counselor asks Mr. Jacobs if his personality has changed. His answer, as paraphrased by the author, reads:

> Maybe he had changed, but he was tired of being treated as a doormat. His wife used sex as a weapon. She hadn't let him near her in years. Even the children had taken to picking on him and making fun at him. Drinking? Who wouldn't take a drink, when things were this bad? One drink and she called him a drunkard.

The couple clearly had communication problems. Bessie claimed that she sent him a postcard when she was "at the seashore with some friends." She made what she felt was an innocent comment about how "it was pleasant to breathe clean fresh air" and Mr. Jacobs used this as an excuse to "walk out and stay away for a month." Mr. Jacobs had saved the postcard. It was actually addressed to the children, and Bessie's words were not what she had remembered. She really wrote: "It was good to get away from all of the ugliness and tension." This must have resonated with my father, the man who felt "rebuffed."

The turning point in the therapy comes when Bessie realizes that she had "been pretty selfish and arrogant" and had "been using her husband as a scapegoat for her disappointment at not achieving the glamorous, luxurious life she had dreamed of." Then, on the pages of *Saturday Evening Post*, the magazine of Norman Rockwell covers, the magazine sold by young boys on street corners, we have our happy ending:

> From then on, each week they made remarkable progress. They went back to taking walks together. They went back to making love. The children began reflecting their mother's new attitude and treated their father with new respect and affection. Mrs. Jacobs even began offering her husband a drink in the kitchen before dinner. When they left us they were happily bewildered by the change in their lives.

The article, to be fair, does not claim that marriage counseling is always successful: "About 5 percent of all the cases we work with are flat failures–that is, the relationship is even worse when the clients leave than when they came." Still, the case studies leave the reader optimistic—couples can learn to understand each other, marriages can be saved. My father, who had recently considered suicide, clearly needed this optimism. It would be easy for me to say that he wanted to believe that he was not really an alcoholic, that he could return home, get a job, maybe even have a drink every evening in the kitchen as my mother cooked dinner and listened to stories about his day at work. But I am not so sure this is how he read the articles.

My father was trying to communicate something. But what? That he still loved my mother and he wanted to save their marriage? That there was still hope? I don't know if these messages would have been heard. My father's letter may have represented the kind of communication problems that often cropped up between my parents, problems clouded by alcohol. I am certain that my father's drinking complicated my parents' marriage enormously, but that doesn't mean that he was always at fault.

Still, if my mother did read the article, I suspect she would have felt blamed, as if my father were saying that her "rebuffs" drove him to drink. I don't believe that my father was trying to say this. I think he was trying to say that he still loved his wife, the "only woman in the world" for him, that marriage counseling might bring them back together.

But, even if my father were trying to say that her "rebuffs" drove him to drink, this conclusion would not have been unusual in the 1950s. Many therapists, novelists, and ministers considered excessive drinking to be a man's natural reaction to a wife who had taken over the man's role. Later in the *Saturday Evening Post* article, I read: "Some men react to a domineering wife by fighting ... or alternately submitting and rebelling—like Mr. Jacobs." Then an ominous warning: "We see many husbands act in a far more devastating way. If their wives don't respect them as men, they simply lose their capacity to act like men." A female therapist related this very male perspective to a female writer, who then shared it with the American reading public.

We can see the era's gender issues of alcoholism in novels like Harlan Ware's *Come, Drink the Cup*, which was published in 1957, a year before my father's letter. In the story, Lew Marsh is a reformed drunk and the city editor for a Chicago newspaper. His boss asks—demands—that he try to sober up Boyd Copeland, the son of a close friend. Lew believes that there "are no orphan-bachelor drunks." He adds, "It's axiomatic that they have a wife, or a mother, or an indulgent aunt." As the novel progresses, we learn that Boyd's problem is not really "the jug" so much as it is his mother who wants to tuck her grown son into bed. She is why he drinks. Lew says that drunks must sober up alone (that is, away from women), after they hear "angel feathers in the county hospital." He later advises one of his reporters, who is too concerned about keeping his wife happy, to kick her "pretty ass." Why? Lew says, "It's a man's world, pal—didn't you know?"

By the standards of the 1950s, my father probably felt he was a complete failure as a man. He couldn't keep a job. He was also, I believe, a gentle and sensitive man (although I am not sure how I came to believe this); he may have felt he was not a tough guy like other men. He might have believed, even though his courage was repeatedly tested in the Pacific campaign of World War II, that he felt things a little too deeply. He might have found it even more difficult to be without work, supported for a while by his wife. He might have suffered from Post-Traumatic Stress Disorder, but even psychologists would not understand this affliction until long after the Vietnam War. He probably felt out-of-control emotionally long before he felt powerless over alcohol. I don't think he could understand himself or what was wrong with his marriage. I'm sure that my mother, at some point, gave up trying. Maybe she gave up long before she asked him to leave, and that is why he felt "rebuffed."

62

ENOUGH OF PARADISE

IT WAS AA THAT HELPED ME TO CARE ABOUT MY FATHER, AND IT WAS HIS letter that encouraged me to delve deeper into the family papers. In my first dig through the chest, I was struck by the photographs that seemed separately and together to say something about my family. I was struck, in particular, by how few pictures I found of my father and mother. Even early in their marriage, they didn't seem to be a couple. I found wedding pictures. A simple ceremony conducted by a navy chaplain. I found a few pictures of them before their marriage, when he was in the navy and she was working with the Red Cross, grouped with friends, drinks in the foreground.

Most of the photographs were of my mother and her sons, my father and his boys, my mother and relatives, family friends, but only two or three of my mother *and* father. At some point, they just stopped being a couple.

As I continued to dig through the chest, maybe even months later, I found another letter from my father to my mother, probably written late in 1947, about a decade before my father left, before he felt "rebuffed." He had been transferred back to Pearl Harbor. My mother, who had just given birth to J.C., stayed behind for a while. The letter, typed on "FOURTEENTH NAVAL DISTRICT" letterhead, addressed "Hi Darling," begins: "Just got the good news that you are on your way." Then he writes:

I'm so damn excited this will probably sound very confusing. But Baby I have waited so long for you and longed for you so much—every day—that when I did get that word that you are on the way I'll just be jumping from now on. Don't worry about my time. Your little trundle bed will be made up and all ready for you. I'm going to take the day off and just baby you from then on.

He comes across like a love struck school boy, giggly and giddy. This letter makes me happy. To think that they were once in love, really in love. Then something happened. My mother later told me that his drinking was particularly "bad" when they were in Hawaii, stationed back at Pearl Harbor, where he had witnessed the Japanese attack. He had frequent nightmares of the war. She said he beat her. She was so glad to leave Hawaii that she stood against the rail of the transport ship, full of families returning to the mainland, holding her lei of flowers until she could no longer see land. Only then did she throw it into the sea. If the lei had drifted back to shore, the legend holds, she would have returned. I don't think they ever recovered from paradise.

I would guess that my father's drinking progressed and my parents' marriage deteriorated. It is in a memory from around 1956, maybe shortly before my father left, that I see them sitting at the kitchen table, in our house. He was drawing something on a napkin, probably trying to explain his latest get-rich-quick scheme. He always had a big idea working. One of his ideas was about heating vents. In the houses of Aragona Village, the heating vents came up from the floor, usually right under windows. The heat, my father reasoned, either went straight up to the ceiling or became lost in toasty warm curtains. He and our neighbor, Ben Smith, who was a sheet metal worker, developed a cover for the vents that shot more of the heat into the room. Ben manufactured the vents on the sly at work, and my father left many evenings to sell them door to door. He would leave with a box full of vent covers and return home, hours later, pretty much with a box full of vent covers.

In this memory, as my father and mother sat at the kitchen table, he was explaining a different idea, his newest one. I never quite caught the gist of it. My mother, as I remember it, was trying to feign interest. She wore one of those plastered-on smiles, her eyes wide with panic or confusion. I remember that look, the visual image. It was later I interpreted it. Many of my memories are like this. Cryptic events, sounds and sights, that later take on meaning. I have come to think she was really trying to understand, encourage him. But maybe she was saying to herself, "This is just another one of his stupid ideas that never goes anywhere." I'm sure she just wanted him to stop drinking and hold down a job, any job. And there he was explaining the idea of the century. After a while, he gave up. He wadded up the napkin and said something like, "I can see that you're not really interested." He seemed like a hurt child, ignored by the one person he wanted to impress. I thought of this scene when I read that my father had felt "rebuffed." It is only a single word, one that hardly changes the material facts or the chronology of my father's story, but it does help me to see the man, imagine what he might have felt. I have come to understand how difficult the last years of their marriage must have been—for both of them.

Now, in Missouri, in the house of my current family, we have my mother's bed in our guest room. It is the bed that my parents shared until my father took his bus ride to Washington. I sometimes sleep there, when I am tossing and turning or when my allergies are bad, so I won't bother Donna. It is a traditional double bed, and I have trouble getting comfortable in it unless spread out diagonally. When I am struggling to find a tolerable position, I wonder what it was like for my mother and father to share the bed when he felt "rebuffed" and when she asked herself, "How long can I go on like this?" They must have bumped into each other all night, every night.

The letters my father wrote to my mother help me to see his side, to see his place in our family, and, at some point, I started to realize that *my* story—the simple story I told myself repeatedly—was in its own way keeping my father, mother and brother, even me, in roles. My simple story—the string of statements that were not even arranged

65

sequentially—was merely a loose collection of thoughts I repeated to myself over and over, a talisman to ward off other thoughts. At some point, I realized my story bore some similarity to the Annals School of history, not really a school of history at all, but more how the rare literate stumbled into something like history in the Middle Ages. In the Annals School, events were not narrated; they are only cataloged year by year:

709. Hard winter. Duke Gottfried died.
710. Hard year and deficient in crops.
711.
712. Flood everywhere.
713.
714. Pippin, Mayor of the Palace, died.

This list could be interpreted. Hayden White argued that it "located us in a culture hovering on the brink of dissolution." But the list hardly helps us to understand that culture. I find it hard to empathize with the death of Duke Gottfried in the Year of Our Lord 709 or the horror of floods in Year of Our Lord 712. It could be argued as well that the list only raises questions: Who compiled it? Why are some years merely place holders? Why does this culture feel that little of significance happens, so little deserves to be recorded? How did these events affect the lives of ordinary people? The list says so little, yet it assumes great authority. It seems to say, "This is all that happened of importance. This is all you need to know."

As I continued to work through the chest, which didn't happen in a single day, but many days, spanning several years, I soon began to feel like Henry Schliemann, the amateur archeologist who excavated the site of Troy. Schliemann was certainly excited about finding Troy, but he was probably equally distressed that he continued to excavate one Troy after another—nine in all. Then he had to ask: Which was the *real* Troy, the Troy of *The Iliad*? I didn't look through the chest of my mother's "papers" once. I kept going through it, unearthing level after level of family documents, finding different documents and a different story with each foray.

I had always thought that my father only sent a couple of letters after he left, and those only to me, not to J.C., my brother. Yet, I found a number of postcards to J.C., also a letter to J.C. and me, probably written about the same time as the rambling, disjointed letter to my mother. In the letter to his sons, he also mentions being in the hospital with a "bad cold" and the *Saturday Evening Post* articles, but the letter is more upbeat, at least on the surface. He mentions that grandma, his mother, is going to send us "some real buffalo" horns that our grandfather "bought from an Indian years ago in Colorado." He says, "you can take them to school and show them to your classes." Then he starts to close the letter:

> I don't know when daddy will be back to see you but you can believe he loves you very much and your mother too— I miss you so much but things may work out sometime and we can be together again.

> I want you guys to do everything you can to help your mother and be very good to her—you are lucky to have such a wonderful mommy—don't forget that—

> I can't think of any more to say but I want to hear from you, what you are doing and what grades you get in school—and how mommy is—will you write to me? Please do because I do miss you all so much.

> All the love in the world
> Daddy—

J.C. and I must have read this letter when it arrived, but I didn't remember it. I don't think that J.C. remembered it, either. I have only a vague recollection of reading some letters from my father and writing a few to him. At some point, the correspondence stopped, but I don't

---

know when or why. Maybe one of my letters was returned, stamped with "ADDRESS UNKNOWN."

The Loss of Certainty

When I was six, after we moved to Virginia Beach (before my father left), I remember running into the bedroom that I shared with my brother, frightened, jumping onto my bed, cowering close to the wall. My father followed close behind. I can still see his face, tense, angry. He grabbed my ankle with one hand and raised the other to spank me—then stopped. He released my ankle, lowered his hand, and walked away, without a word. Until I read my father's letters, I hadn't thought of this episode. Now, this single event, the stuff of ordinary life, what would never be recorded by the scribes of the Annals School, seems important. It seems to say something important about the man. Something simple. Just this: He was kind. This memory is a glimpse into how my father was then, in moments without alcohol, and how he might have been as a father if he had stopped drinking, if he had stayed, if he and my mother had worked through their problems. As I learned more about my father, I became fascinated by what happened beyond my memories, how my father felt as he tried to control his drinking, as he saw his life falling apart. I also became fascinated with possibilities, how his life might have turned out differently, how his sobriety might have affected our entire family. I wanted to imagine a man who wanted a different life for himself, a life with his wife and kids.

On one of my digs into my mother's papers (one of the last, I think), I found a typed letter, dated October 19, 1958, from my father to "R.C.

Stackhouse," who was apparently my mother's attorney. Stackhouse had written to my father to ask for child support. The last two paragraphs of my father's reply read:

> In regard to support of my dependents, I fully realize my responsibility and expect to be in a position to not only meet them but to repay the back payments within the month. I have been unemployed since last February 22, with the exception of commercial fishing a venture on which I lost money.

> I expect to return to Norfolk about the first of the month where I have the promise of work. I will contact you upon my arrival and work out with you a suitable arrangement for meeting my obligations.

At the bottom of the letter, my mother's attorney penned: "Rec'd this in todays mail. Quite a surprise." The return to Norfolk on "the first of the month" might have been when he came to our house looking for his old pea coat, but I am fairly certain that he never found steady work or remained in the area long. I am pretty sure that he didn't send money then. My mother was insistent that he had only sent money once. Still, I have come to believe that he loved us, that he meant well. When I was growing up, when I needed a father, I don't think those expressions of love or good intentions would have meant much. I needed the actions—the presence—of a father. Now, it helps. I'm not sure how or why, but it helps. It might be, and this is but a vague idea, that seeing my father as more than an anecdote brings him into my life even as this new, fuller story releases me. My father is no longer a still point, a stark value, that I used to move into adulthood even as it kept me a little boyish. As I was leaving my teen years, I often said to myself, "I will be a better man than my father." I knew that I wanted to move past the man that I believed my father to be, but I found that the still point was always with me, defining me. As I opened to accept my father, I allowed him to become a full person. As I considered his potential, I was no longer a son, a child. And being a man was not so simple, either.

In another trip through my mother's "papers" (a late trip, I think even after I found the letter from my father), I found my father's wallet, the one he was carrying when he died. Because I was away in graduate school at the end of his life, I had not seen the few personal effects sent to us. In the wallet, I found a few bits of identification, a social security card and a merchant seaman's license. For me, the license first triggered images of Eugene O'Neill's travels as a seaman on a "tramp" liner. I had read several biographies of O'Neill when I was in graduate school, and O'Neill's days at sea seemed particularly romantic, especially when read through the lens of his early plays and Edmund's descriptions of sea life in *Long Day's Journey Into Night*. When I read the O'Neill biographies, I was about the same age as O'Neill was when he shipped out for Brazil. Now, much older and a father, I think of O'Neill as fleeing or abandoning responsibility rather than exploring. He already had a son. He was drinking heavily and living homeless, hand to mouth, on the docks of Buenos Aires.

The more I looked at my father's license, the more uncertain I was about the photograph, which was taken in 1968, six years before his death. To others, the image, the eyes here, might bear little more than a glance. They might think this is the kind of institutional picture that typically accompanies a driver's license or passport. Or they might even see an old sea dog. That's not how it is for me. I don't like to look into the eyes of this man.

But it's also hard to turn away. Sometimes photographs, no matter how carefully staged, reveal something of the feelings that usually remained hidden. In this way, photographs are lyrical, capturing a single and pure emotion—the joy of new love, the pain of rejection, the torment of desire. In this photograph, a candid shot, meant only for identification, something comes through. Maybe despair or loneliness. But also something else.

From being around alcoholics, I have learned that their drinking, as it progresses, ceases to be fun. They learn to hate themselves. They don't yet understand the power of alcohol. They think that they are the person that drinking has wrought. This might be what I see here in my father's eyes. Self-loathing.

The face on this photo is much different than the face on the photos taken earlier, when he was still in the navy, before his drinking had progressed, before he had lived alone for so long. In the old photos, I can still see hope. Or, I see a man happy with his drink, as my father was in the pen and ink drawing sketched some twenty years earlier.

The photograph on a Merchant Seaman license is the only glimpse I have into my father's life long after he left the family. A photograph, Roland Barthes says in *Camera Lucida*, is a kind of document that "authenticates the existence of a certain being." This photograph "authenticates" the man that my father had become close to the end of his life. When I first looked at it, I felt like he had appeared on my doorsteps.

As with my father's letters, the photograph is a way of hearing his voice, but a few letters and an image, passing particles of light caught on film, leave gaps. In AA meetings, as I listened to recovering alcoholics tell their stories, I also heard his voice. Their stories helped me imagine what happened in the gap between my father's letters in 1957 and the ID photograph taken in 1968. I remember, in particular, listening to a woman who had bottomed out in New Orleans, where my father spent his final days. I had always wondered why he ended up there, in a boarding house in the heart of the French Quarter. New Orleans had struck me as a place for college students, drunk frat boys and girls gone wild—not weathered seamen. Then, as I listened to the woman speak of what it was like to be an alcoholic in the French Quarter in the 1960s, I began to understand. She spoke of how a person could pass out in a bar, and the bartender would put him in a cab, the cabdriver would take him home, carry him inside, come back the next day for his fare. It was a safe place to drink, and, in an odd way, it was home. Alcoholics took care of alcoholics, and alcoholics fit in.

From listening to talks like this, I began to understand a few more fragments of my father's story and I found more of my simple story in shards. Even more importantly, I have listened to many talks where speakers tell of the power of alcoholism, how the bottle becomes their best friend, how they are consumed with their habit, how they came to AA, started to work the program, how they could begin to find time for their family once they sobered up, how they could rebuild their marriage, and their relationships with their kids. The talks have helped me to care. My childhood no longer seems unusual, so I don't take it so personally. I know that my father's drinking must have brought enormous problems to his marriage and that my mother did her best to hold the family together. When I think of my family, I feel loss and sadness, but not anger. Things have not, however, settled down. I cannot rethink my father's story without changing, and I cannot change without rethinking my father's story. In yet another dig through the layers of papers in the chest, I again looked through my father's wallet, the one sent to us after his death, this time more thoroughly. Earlier, I had found his merchant seaman's license. I had seen the photograph on it, taken in his last years. This time, in a more recessed pocket of the wallet, I found an dog-eared AA card, with the Twelve Steps on one side, the Twelve Traditions on the other. My mother, my brother and I had all missed it. It was a shock, one that again forced me to rethink my simple story about my father. As *I* told *his* story, he went to AA for six months, he came home, told my mother that he was not an alcoholic, then he drank himself to death. How could this card fit with that story? Now I had to consider that he might have been attending meetings in his last days. Maybe he had even stopped drinking.

Even now, years later, I cannot settle on a single emotion to sum up how I feel about that AA card. Most of the time, I hope the card means that he found some peace at the end of his life. At other times, I feel a loss. If he were in AA, if he were working the steps, why didn't he contact us? Why didn't he attempt to make amends? At open AA meetings, I have heard men speak of reunions with their children. I have also heard of men who attempted to make amends to children, but their grown children returned their letters or refused their calls. To be honest, I don't know how I—or my mother or my brother— would have reacted if he called or appeared at our house—his house— in Aragona Village. I might not have wanted him in my life, even if he were sober, but I do believe that even an awkward attempt at amends,

---

a simple "I'm sorry I hurt you," would have helped my brother and me to move on sooner or more completely. I have to think it would have helped.

After finding the AA card, I even entertained the notion of going to New Orleans, hanging out at AA meetings, talking to oldtimers, to see if I could find out something of my father's last days. I tried to imagine how my father, if he were alive, would feel about this. Would he want me to know more about his life? Would he see this as caring about him? Or would he think I was violating his privacy?

I also wonder what is missing from the chest of my mother's papers. Maybe nothing of significance. My mother was a packrat. But what if she had thrown out my father's letters—the ones I have quoted here—in an act of anger? How could I have come to know what I now know? How could I have ever moved past my simple story?

By thinking the unthinkable?

Maybe my father wasn't even an alcoholic.

Shortly after the HBO special *Band of Brothers* came out, I was talking about the show with Sheryl Gowen, a friend and former colleague. She said that many World War II and Vietnam veterans suffered from Post-Traumatic Stress Disorder and developed drinking problems or addictions. These veterans, she conjectured, might not have had addictive personalities; they might not have become drinkers or addicts if not for the trauma of war. I have known drinkers like this. They appeared to be alcoholics when they returned from Vietnam or when they were going through a difficult divorce, then their lives settled down, and they returned to moderate drinking. This is not a story one hears in AA.

Many of the pictures of my parents when they were apparently dating were filled with sailors and Red Cross workers, surrounded by drinks. I even found pictures of couples passed out on couches. I would guess that many vets drank a great deal during the war and in the years after victory. Apparently, my father's drinking was worse when he was stationed in Hawaii after the war, around 1948, when he had to return to Pearl Harbor. Maybe he was trying to find some way of dealing with the trauma of war.

Apparently, my father's drinking didn't fit into the pattern of most alcoholics. He was a binge drinker. My mother said he could go for a while having only a few drinks every night, then he would start a binge and be gone for weeks. I can see why he thought he wasn't an alcoholic. The six months that my father spent in AA probably happened around 1956, shortly before he left our family. If he read *Alcoholics Anonymous*, he probably would have read the second edition, published in 1955. I read through the stories in this edition, trying to imagine how my father might have read them, looking for a story that described the way he drank, at least, as well as I understood it. In the second edition, I didn't find any stories that described an alcoholic who could drink normally for months at a time and then launch into horrific binges. Unless the way my mother described my father's drinking was an early stage of his alcoholism.

In a story entitled "Desperate Drinking," Pat wrote: "A former employer of mine said to me a little over ten years ago, 'Pat, you seem to be one of those unfortunate people who at least every six months must go out and roll in the gutter.'" Pat goes on to share how the "intervals" between his binges "grew shorter," and "binges were longer." Maybe my father might have identified with Pat's story, if he read it. The more typical story told in AA is about drinkers who always lose control with the first drink, who never have periods of "normal" drinking. This might be why my father told my mother, "I don't think I'm an alcoholic." I can *almost* convince myself that he was right.

Then I think about how alcoholism runs in my father's family. My great-grandfather (Grandma Musa's father) was a drinker who terrified his family and the guests at his hotel in Bruel, Nebraska. Grandma Musa was determined that none of her sons would be drinkers. She wouldn't allow alcohol in her house. Even after her four sons married and moved into their own houses, she would search for alcohol in *their* cabinets, *their* closets, or *their* chest of drawers. Despite her efforts to keep them away from alcohol, all of her four sons were drinkers. Dale never married and simply disappeared one day. He was never heard from again. Forrest, Vicki's father, married, divorced, and *drunk himself into an early grave.* (Here I find myself slipping into the language of the late nineteenth century temperance movements.) My father may have done the same. Russell, the one brother who was not an out-of-control drinker, had two daughters. One of those daughters *drank herself into an early grave.*

My father's family came from Denmark. Shakespeare's Hamlet says that "heavy headed revel" makes Denmark "traduced and taxed of other nations." In other words, his countrymen are chastised throughout Europe for being drunkards. In *Havoc,* Danish novelist Tom Kristensen calls drinking the national disease of Denmark. When I visited Denmark in 1983, I was struck by how much beer is a cultural focus. Tuborg and Carlsberg brew lunch beers, with low alcohol content, and heavy beers, which contain around twelve percent alcohol. The nation produces beer for every occasion. As my cousin Vicki says, "It's in the blood." The Danish culture and my family history seem to say that my father was an alcoholic, but I cannot even say this with certainty. And I'm not so sure I even want certainty any longer. Certainty brings judgments in its wake. Judgments preempt change. All I know for certain about my father is that, at this point of my life, I have come to care about him. And I am okay.

I am learning to focus more on the fragments of *my* story, the effects of *my* memories, the memories that I carried with me from childhood and the memories that I have created from my mother's papers. There are other memories, too. The ones I feel in my body. I have no images or words for these. Just feelings. When I am at loud parties, I find it difficult to relax. I have trouble talking to others. I want to run. When people bring alcohol into my house, I feel angry. I am frightened. I do not even like to be around sober people who act like alcoholics, even a ten year old kid who talks loudly, tells wild stories, brags, tries to brown nose me—a kid who wants desperately to be accepted. I become angry, irritable, rude. I cannot recall specific events that would explain these feelings, but these are memories nonetheless. They are the hardest memories.

A MOTHER'S SENSE OF PLACE

APPALACHIA

MY MOTHER GREW UP IN APPALACHIA, A QUAINT COAL MINING TOWN IN THE southwestern corner of Virginia. It was still quaint in the 1960s when those who remained in my family—she, J.C., and I—occasionally visited from the growing, sprawling city of Virginia Beach. When I was ten, a few months after Grandma Mimi died, we spent Christmas there with the Youngs—Uncle Billy, who was Grandma Mimi's brother, Aunt Anna, and cousin Doris, who was my mother's first cousin.

The trip began with a series of bus rides that crept westward from one end of Virginia to the other. I don't remember how long the trip took, probably about eighteen hours, certainly a long time to huddle with thirty or forty strangers and their smells. (Riding for a long way on a Greyhound bus is always about smells.) After a night and the better part of a day, we walked into the front door of the Youngs' house, which seemed even more wonderful after our time in bus reality. I smelled evergreen even before I saw the tree and presents spread across the living room floor. Once we walked into the dining room, I saw an entire bowl of candy bars. J.C. and I grabbed one right off, even though Aunt Anna, who was a great cook, was preparing a meal: ham, scalloped potatoes, cornbread, green beans, and chocolate cake.

The next morning, while walking around the snow covered streets, I picked up a lump of coal and carried it back to offer it to my mother, in my open hands, as if it were a present, as if I were much younger than ten years old, more like I was five or six. My mother pretended to share my excitement, but I'm sure she was chagrined by my grand discovery of coal in a town surrounded by coal mines and heated by coal stoves. If, earlier that morning, before walking outside, I had followed the stairs of the Youngs' house to the basement, I would have found a few tons of coal and might have even seen Uncle Billy shoveling coal into the furnace and then banking the fire so it would burn more slowly.

That afternoon, I was walking around town and found a small hill. I climbed it. I wanted to tell my friends, once I returned to Virginia Beach, that I had climbed a mountain. The next day, I took my mother back to the same hill and we climbed it together. Again, she seemed to share my excitement, even though, as I know now, it was only a small rise in the Appalachians, certainly not anything like a peak.

Most nights, J.C. and I rode around with Jim. He was Doris's fiancé and had been for about ten years. (The pace of life in the town of Appalachia was obviously slower in almost every respect.) From the back seat of his VW Bug, we watched him drive and shift gears, light Cherry Bombs and throw them out the window. Jim was in his late thirties, maybe his early forties, and everyone in town must have known the sound of his VW, which was probably the only German car within three counties. They must have wondered why this grown man was acting like a teenager, but J.C. and I thought he was just about the coolest adult in the entire state. He even let us light some firecrackers, but he insisted that we put them on the road, light them and then run like hell. We weren't old enough to throw them from the car.

I spent the bulk of most days pretending to work in Uncle Billy's hardware store, which was in a brick building with a patterned tin ceiling. I was fascinated by the range of tools, knives, and guns. Some of Uncle Billy's stock—such as bear traps—must have been on the shelves for decades. I was intrigued by people who bought an alarm clock or a washing machine and said, "Put it on my bill." I was astonished when my uncle's customers came in on Friday afternoon or Saturday morning and made a payment on their bill and said, "I'll get the rest of it paid off as soon as I can." Uncle Billy always replied, "Don't worry about it. Just when you can." I asked Uncle Billy, "How do you know they'll come back and pay?" He seemed surprised at the question. After a pause, he said, "I know." Appalachia was the kind of community that was disappearing all across America. At the time, many of us Americans, even if we had not grown up in a small town, watched *The Andy Griffith Show* and felt nostalgia for a time and place beyond our memories, a place like Appalachia.

My mother and I returned for a short trip at Thanksgiving in 1966. J.C. was already in college and decided to stay home. We drove up with the Smiths, who had relatives in nearby Big Stone Gap. This trip was easier than the Greyhound bus ride six years earlier, but it was still cramped. Five of us were in their car. We didn't have to endure the smells of strangers and their food, but it was still a long trip, about ten or eleven hours, much of it on windy mountain roads. During this stay in Appalachia, I enjoyed hearing Aunt Anna's stories about how she hunted with her World War I, army issue, M-1 rifle and how she had designed their house. At the time, I was taking drafting in high school and wanted to be an architect. On Friday morning, I was hanging out with David, the son of one of my mother's old friends. He needed a haircut, so we went to the barbershop on Main Street, which wasn't like the barbershops back home where the goal was to get in and out as quickly as possible. Men often came in to visit, trade jokes, and catch up on town news, even when they didn't need a haircut. While we were sitting there waiting for David's turn, the barber glanced toward the street and said, "There he goes. Every day at the same time. You could set your watch by it." It was my Uncle Billy, mayor of Appalachia for over thirty years, walking up the street with a sense of purpose. I later learned that he left his hardware store every day at 11:30 to walk up the street to the drug store, where he sat at the counter and waited for his milkshake with one raw egg in it. He didn't have to order it. He could just say hello to the soda jerk and talk about the weather until his shake was ready. Then he could drink it, chat with a few friends, and say, "Put it on my bill." Every day he made the journey. And every day, I am sure, the barber said, "There he goes. Every day at the same time. You could set your watch by it."

After the barbershop, David and I went to the local diner for lunch. While we were eating, a woman came up to me and asked, "Are you Louise Caruthers' son?" I nodded. She said, "I read in the newspaper that you and your mother were in town. You look just like her." During the trip, this scene was repeated several times. Strangers came up to me on the street and asked, "Are you Louise Caruthers' son?" My mother had not lived in the town for thirty some years, and people could still recognize her in the face of her son.

By this time, Jim and Doris were no longer engaged, so I couldn't ride around with him. A loss, certainly. I was old enough that he might have let me throw the Cherry Bombs from the car window, but this lost rite of passage was still a small disappointment in an otherwise pleasant trip.

One evening, I was sitting in the living room, working on some designs for my drafting class. Uncle Billy was staring out the window, watching the sun drop into the mountains. He turned to me and said, "It is a shame that our boys have to die in that war, half way around the world." He didn't say anything else, not even "Vietnam," yet that one moment—or that brief insight into Billy's character—had a profound effect on me. He was a gentle man comfortable with his gentleness. These trips helped me to understand something of my mother's family and something of her childhood in Appalachia. It must have been a good place for her childhood to unfold.

All of this might sound overly nostalgic, like a passage from one of Laura Ingalls Wilder's stories, but that's how I remember the town. As a grown man in my early fifties, a professor well schooled in skepticism (I really believe that the most hurtful insult to hurl at a college professor is "you're naive"), I feel obligated to look for the town's dark side, but I could only find a shadowy side, not even that, more like a dusky side.

My mother once told me that, when she was a young girl (I imagine she meant about twelve or so), a gunfight broke out on Main Street. She said that she crept closer and closer to the action, hiding behind buildings, telephone poles, and trash cans, to catch a glimpse of the action. Typical of my mother's stories, she never said who started the fight, how it ended, or whether she was caught in the crossfire. I don't think any of the James boys were involved; it was probably a brief skirmish between two drunk miners who never came close to hitting their intended target. And I doubt that anything like this happened on a regular basis.

The town did apparently have homeless people, or (to be honest) one homeless person. Her name was Crazy Alice, or something like that. She walked in front of the Youngs' house one night, during our 1966 visit, and my mother ran to the window like a little girl (more in the range of eight years old) to watch Crazy Alice until she disappeared down the street. As a reminder, this was about the time that LBJ's Great Society began to institutionalize people like Crazy Alice (at least, in big cities), but before Reagan's Not-So-Great Society cut social programs and put them on the streets again (at least, in big cities). In Appalachia, I would imagine that Crazy Alice slept in a small shack with a coal stove, so she probably wasn't a certified homeless person. She probably received regular handouts from the local diner and a few kitchen doors. And her life probably didn't change at all from one presidential administration to the next.

The Ku Klux Klan made a brief appearance in the WASPy town, around the 1930s, I would guess. A number of townsmen, including my Uncle Billy, were drawn in by the fine speeches about America, God, and morality. They joined up, but then they didn't have a whole lot to keep them busy. The men, my mother told me, escorted a young woman, a secretary who was having an affair with her married boss, to the train station and made her buy a one-way ticket to Richmond, Kingsport, or some other evil city. I could say that the town was patriarchal (after all, they didn't make the married boss leave town) and racist (even though I am fairly sure not one black person lived within a hundred miles, so race wasn't really an issue that most people even thought about). According to my mother, as the men in the town listened to more KKK speeches, they didn't like what they were hearing. They started to drop out, one by one, including my Uncle Billy, and soon the Klan leaders moved on to Richmond, Kingsport, or some other evil city. The men of Appalachia seemed to have been rather unmoved by the Klan's ramblings about Jews, minorities and foreigners.

Appalachia was, however, an American town, and it was affected by sweeping changes in the American landscape, such as the Great Depression. When my mother was young, her parents prospered, owning a couple of clothing shops and some apartment buildings. They lived in a large house and had a maid. Then, when my mother was sixteen, the Depression hit, and they lost everything. Like many of her generation, I don't think that she ever recovered from the shock. For the rest of her life, she dried out and reused paper towels; she used a single tea bag to make three or four cups of tea. When I was about fourteen, she said, "I haven't bought a new dress in three years." I don't think she expected pity. She seemed proud of her ability to scrimp and save. By the time J.C. and I were grown, we often joked with her about how she squeezed a penny so tight that she assassinated Lincoln all over again, but she was actually one of the most financially rational people I have ever known. She didn't buy new gadgets or name brand clothes. She drove cars into the pavement. When she was done with an automobile, the machine was used up and even the junk yard would not buy it for parts or scrap metal. She used an old bed as the couch in our family room, actually just a cramped 8' by 10' bedroom where we watched our black and white television, years after most families had a color set. But she never complained about spending money on necessities: decent food, functional clothes, dental checkups, and school supplies. From the depression and her family's losses, she learned that frugality meant security. At a time when many Americans were beginning to live beyond their means by taking out second mortgages, she was never in debt. She even paid for her used automobiles with cash money.

In the wake of the Great Depression, after her family lost their property, they moved to Lexington, Kentucky, for the job opportunities of a large city, but my mother stayed behind in Appalachia and lived with friends so she could finish high school. Betty Sue, her sister, ten years younger, left with the family.

Once relocated, her father hit the road to sell ties, shoes, and kitchenware, representing a number of companies. A few of his letters from the road survive. They were written in 1951, after both of his girls had finished college and moved away, a year after I was born, and shortly before his fatal heart attack in a hotel room. He addressed his letters to "Mother," his wife, and signed them "Dad." The content of the letters are of little substance—simple details of a routine life. It is the feel of the letters that draws me in—the weight of years on the road to support his family, how much he missed his wife and his girls, his single, consuming desire to be home, as soon as possible. He wrote about driving from town to town—Chattanooga to Lenoir City to Athens, Cleveland to Harriman, Dayton to Harriman to Springfield. And he wrote about being bored in hotel rooms. It must have been hard for my grandmother's letters to find him, but he always longed for them. On April 6, from the Hotel Humboldt in Humboldt, Tennessee, he wrote: "I was disappointed when I arrived here and no letter. I got off regular staying places last night as I stayed at Delmar and I guess you couldn't have located me, but I thought sure I would have a letter here." Three days later, he wrote again from the Humboldt: "Well I finally heard from you today after I had given up. It was just an accident I came back here." It is clear that they deeply loved each other, and I believe that they gave my mother and her sister a healthy and normal childhood when the entire country was in crisis.

The few, brief stories that my mother shared about her family recounted what many families must have experienced during the Great Depression. She told me that they often had only beans for dinner, for days at a stretch. Her parents scrimped to send her to college because her father thought education was important, even for girls. She had to borrow books to study. Her short, truncated stories were about a family struggling through tough times.

In her brief recollections, I only remember my mother speaking about her parents in warm terms. When her father began to teach her to drive, a privilege not then afforded to all young women, he told her that he didn't care if she wrecked the car, the Ford that he drove through a blur of towns. He could get it fixed, he said. She told me that

---

he was quick to anger, but his outbursts passed in a moment. And this she said with understanding. I never had the sense that his outbursts disrupted the family routine for long. After he passed away, Grandma Mimi began the cycle of spending six months with Betty Sue and her family, then six months with us. My mother drew strength from her mother and felt lost when she passed in 1960. Then, I am sure, she felt even more alone raising her sons, more thankful that she had loyal friends. Even well into my teens, it seemed important that I accompany her on visits to her friends in Norfolk, most of whom she had known from my father's navy days. I hated the tedium. Even more, I hated the way she fought back tears when these friends gave her some old plates or used dresses. I don't think that we really needed the handouts, but she needed the feel of an extended family, the safety of a small town.

The Separation

My mother once told me that she wanted to marry a man with a steady job. A man she could lean on. A man who would provide security. She married my father, she said, because he was in the navy and she thought that he would always have a job. When she told me this, maybe I was thirteen or so, she certainly saw the irony, but I didn't sense any bitterness. Her words had more of the tone of sadness and loss.

My parents met a few years after World War II while my mother was working in the Red Cross and my father was in the navy. That was *when*. I never heard the story of *how* they met. The *how* story is, I guess, the kind of anecdote that couples tell their grown kids when they celebrate a silver anniversary, a way of saying we've stayed together for many years and we're still in love. Kids, grown or not, do not hear about the *how* story from parents who have split.

They were together for about fourteen years, living in Delaware, Hawaii, New York, South Carolina, and Norfolk, where my father retired from the navy. Then they bought their house in Virginia Beach and planned to settle into a normal suburban life.

Shortly after we moved in, my mother took me to register for my first year of school. Almost as soon as she turned in my paperwork, the principal noticed that she had a college degree and a teaching certificate. In 1956, the population of Virginia Beach was mushrooming, Baby Boomers were crowding schools, and teachers were in short supply. Most schools were forced to run classes on split shifts with one group of students in the morning and another in the afternoon. So the principal pulled my mother aside and begged her to return to teaching. In a matter of days, she was teaching fifth grade at Thalia Elementary School. My father was in and out of work, but my mother had a secure job because her father had insisted she go to college. She had a means of supporting her family, and, in little over a year, she would ask my father to leave.

I don't know much about the event. She said, "We can't go on like this." My guess is that my father quietly agreed. They talked about how to handle his departure. I'm sure he said he would travel to the West Coast, find a job and send money. Then they noticed that J.C. had been listening through much of the conversation. He ran off and hid. My mother went to comfort him. They would have to work out the other details later, maybe at night, before they went to sleep, still sharing the same double bed.

I marvel at how my mother found the conviction to raise the issue of separation. She must have feared that her husband would erupt, that the barely controlled tension in the household would surface, that he would argue with her, try to manipulate her, that she might not be able to remain strong, navigate the course from "We can't go on like this" to separation to divorce. After her husband left, I wonder how she remained firm. When she read his letter, when he wrote that he thought of suicide, that she was the only woman in the world for him, I wonder how she kept from writing back, "I can't raise these kids alone. I'm too frightened. I'm too lonely. Come home. We'll work things out." Yet, she held fast. Although I only thought of this recently, my father needs to be given some credit for leaving without a fight. Many practicing alcoholics refuse to leave or manipulate their wives into letting them stay. Many stalk their wives for years. For so long, I wondered how he could stay away, how he could abandon his kids. Now, I think that it took considerable strength on his part to leave us alone and let us get on with our lives.

In the years following my father's "business trip," my mother struggled to be a mother and a father, a cleaner and a provider, a disciplinarian and a nurturer. I am sure that she had moments when she longed for a man, any man, to take care of her, or at least to take on some of the responsibility. About this time, I remember us looking through old photographs. She pointed to a photo of a young man, handsome, well dressed, swinging a golf club next to a new Oldsmobile, on a scant strip of grass between the sidewalk and the street. She said, "This is the man I should have married." This man, whoever he was, would have given her a better life. Even I was drawn into the fantasy. If she had married him, I would have had a father, he could have taught me to play golf, we would have had more money . . . Then it occurred to me. If my mother had married him, I would never have been born. She would have had different children.

This photograph and this man were a brief daydream for her, also. It lasted about as long as a sigh. After my father left, I think my mother decided she would never depend on a man again. Instead, she tried to create a sense of security by building her savings account and buying life insurance. She even bought a $500 policy for both J.C. and me. The Policy Man (this was a Southern term for the insurance man who specialized in selling policies to poor families) visited the house every other month to collect a payment of $7.50 on each policy. Sometimes, he sat and had a cup of coffee and chatted about the importance of insurance and how you could never have enough of it. My mother paid on those policies for years, probably close to $1,000 on each policy, and then she was surprised that the fully matured $500 policies were worth less than $500. When my mother realized that she had been cheated by the nice man who drank coffee in her living room, she was more angry than I ever saw her.

As the years passed, as she continued to raise her two boys, she dated a few men from time to time. I don't remember any of their names. One of these men—he was in the navy, I think—once played catch with me, probably when I was about ten. He threw the ball high in the air, really high, so that I could practice catching fly balls. He threw so hard that he split open the back of his plaid, short-sleeved shirt. It is the only time I remember any of my mother's "dates" doing anything with me. J.C. wasn't there. At least, I don't remember him being there. I have too many memories like this, memories of an event where J.C. should have been there, but wasn't.

Later in the evening, I was lying in the floor at the top of the stairs, which led directly to the front door. I think I was drawing or looking at a book. My mother said goodnight to this man and kissed him. I looked away. He opened the door, said goodnight, and left. I heard the door close. I looked back and saw my mother turn and lean against the door, cover her heart with her hands, and sigh like a schoolgirl.

The event was disturbing. I don't think I felt any anger about the man possibly replacing my father or stealing my mother's affection. I felt more confused. I had never seen my mother with any man in this way. At this moment, she probably seemed vulnerable. But she wasn't. This man, like the few others she dated, was around for a while, and then he was gone.

She never seemed to allow any of her relationships to develop. Maybe she just never met the right man. Maybe no man could be right enough. When I was about fifteen, she took a trip to the beach at Nags Head with Lorraine, an old friend visiting from New York. She and Lorraine were sunning by the pool when the man my mother was dating at the time, who was a member of AA, appeared to surprise her. I guess that he thought he was the light of her life and that she would be overjoyed. Annoyed, she told the man that she was on vacation and that she wanted him to leave. Shocked and hurt, he told her that he had come down there to ask her to marry him. Vexed, she told him that she had no intention of marrying him. Angry, he said it was over. Triumphant, she said good. The could-have-been-fiancé turned and headed for the parking lot, probably trying to count in his head the number of liquor stores he had passed on the trip down.

My mother later told me about the incident without any sense of loss. She was as kind a person as I have ever known. If someone severely wronged her, she might say, "He's an . . . ick" With a long pause between "he's an" and the nasty word she could only force herself to say once she lowered her volume and softened her tone. By the time she muttered "ick" the word almost seemed like a compliment. Still, she seemed to have enjoyed telling this man, who must have been rather harmless, to get lost. She even seemed to enjoy telling me about the brief repartee by the pool. Then she asked me if I wanted a father. She said, "I always felt bad that I denied you a father. I would marry him if you feel like you still need a father."

"I don't need a father," I told her. I certainly didn't want a moronic step-father. I don't think she wanted a husband, either. She probably was lonely and wanted companionship, but she couldn't chance a man coming through her life—and the lives of her sons—like a tornado.

When I was in college, she dated a different man who was in AA. I never heard how they met. One Sunday afternoon, I went with her to a cookout at his house. She seemed to like him and his grown children. Then it ended. She later told me that he had relapses and expected her to nurse him back to sobriety. To her credit, she would have none of it. So he ended it and found some woman who fawned over him after every little binge. This breakup seemed more like a loss.

Years later, when I read Tobias Wolff's *This Boy's Life*, I thought of my mother's reluctance to jump into another marriage. Wolff's book says little about his father (*The Duke of Deception*, by Geoffrey Wolff, Tobias's brother, treats the father more fully); instead, Tobias writes about his mother's need to be with a man and her inability to find a good one. My mother never felt like she had to have a man, which I am certain saved us all a lot of pain. When I was a teenager, we visited one of her friends, a woman who taught in her school. The woman's husband was frequently abusive. On our drive home, my mother said, "She believes any man is better than no man. We've had long conversations about this." She didn't have to tell me her side of these conversations. I knew that my mother believed that no man is better than one with "icky" baggage.

We all, in our own ways, slowly began to adjust to being a family without a man. In one of the postcards I found in the chest of family papers, my father wrote to J.C., "You're the man of the house now." But J.C. was only ten, and he was deeply wounded. There was no man in the house. When my mother needed to talk about her frustrations and worries, she came to me. She would cry or say she was worried about money. Then she felt better. I listened and thought, "How can I fix this? How can I make her feel better?" She had a lot on her shoulders and no husband to lean on. I later learned from visiting AA and Al-Anon meetings that all I had to do was listen. That was all she needed. But, then, I felt panic. I wanted to make things better and didn't know how. These occasional and minor meltdowns disappeared after a few years, after she had some savings and a bit of a track record, so to speak.

Those who knew my mother before the separation probably thought that she was kind and sweet, easy going, graceful with others, empathic. They wouldn't have thought, I imagine, that she was independent and strong. She struggled with decisions, and the complexity of her life always seemed to exceed her ability to organize it. She usually deferred to others, even to her mother long after she was an adult, after her mother was living part of the year with us. Grandma Mimi, who thought that her daughter was too lenient as a parent, occasionally advised her to spank us. One day, I must have been eight or nine, I did something wrong. I don't even remember what. Mimi was there, so my mother took me into her bedroom and spanked me with a belt.

So much of my mother's gentleness is in this story. She only spanked me so that her mother would think better of her parenting. Somehow we both tacitly understood the game. She spoke stern words, loud enough for her mother to hear. Then she told me to bend over and she whacked me a few times. It didn't even hurt, but I yelled as if I were being tortured. After this charade, Mimi was satisfied, or maybe she herself understood the ruse and decided that her daughter was hopeless. I don't remember Mimi offering advice on parenting again, and I am fairly sure that my mother felt silly about the whole affair. She never spanked me again. This at a time when most parents spanked their children, many slapped their kids across the face, and even teachers were allowed to spank their students.

My mother's character—her gentleness, her desire for security, her struggles to make decisions, her piles of unfinished tasks—makes her accomplishments in raising two boys on her own even more astonishing. Even today, when news of a divorce hardly raises a yawn, so many women feel trapped by the security of living with a man, but my mother asked my father to leave in an age that recognized only the normal. It was the time of *Leave It to Beaver* and *Father Knows Best*, sitcoms about nearly perfect nuclear families. These shows, of course, had their own moments of tension. The kids might stray into trouble during the day, all of it pretty tame by current standards. The kids might leave wet towels on the bathroom floor, use Dad's tools without putting them back, or break into their piggy bank to buy some candy bars. But, as soon as Dad came home, he restored order. Evenings were a time of tranquility. The kids did homework or cleaned their rooms. Dad read the evening edition of the newspaper and smoked a pipe. Mom cooked in a starched dress with a spotless white apron. In our house, it was my mother who came home from work and rushed to cook a quick meal. The sitcom families had sit-down dinners in the dining room—every night. We didn't even have a dining room. They had fresh pie for dessert—every night. My mother never baked a pie in her life. I think that the only reason I watched *Leave It to Beaver* was to see June walk from the kitchen into the dining room with a hot pie in her hands. Of course, a few 1950s shows presented alternative families. In *My Three Sons*, the father raises his three sons with a little help from a bitchy uncle, who could cook and clean pretty well but was otherwise absolutely useless, probably because he took too many hits from the cooking sherry. *The Andy Griffith Show* was about a widower raising his son with the help of Aunt Bee, who could cook and clean as well as June Cleaver, but even the small problems of Mayberry left her frazzled. These shows seemed to say that mothers are more easily replaced than fathers.

How did my mother find the courage to depart from such clear norms? Some strength, I am sure, she mustered from her normal parents and her normal childhood. She had seen how much her parents loved each other, and this must have provided a reality, a perspective, for grasping what was wrong with her own marriage. Attention was paid as her parents made sacrifices to raise a family during the Depression.

She had known a strength in families. Her friends and neighbors soon saw strength in her.

Drawing from the continuing presence—the script—of her ordinary and normal and extraordinary parents, she often worked two jobs to support us, teaching during the day and tutoring or teaching adult education courses at night. During the summer months, she worked as a playground supervisor. She even cooked and cleaned. She didn't do either particularly well, at least by 1950s standards, that is, when compared to mothers who stayed at home. I'm sure that stay-at-home moms probably realized that she didn't clean corners, wash windows, or vacuum under the couch very often, but I never heard them openly criticize her. J.C. and I, however, often teased her about her cooking. She could make a pretty good pot roast with a little help from Campbell's Cream of Mushroom soup, but most of her dishes were unintentionally exotic or mysterious. She was particularly proud of her boiled (not broiled) spare ribs, which she served vertical (that is, with the ribs planted in a bowl of Uncle Ben's Rice). This dish tasted pretty close to how it looked. She often cooked salmon croquettes because she hated to waste leftover mashed potatoes and the recipe was simple. Mix a can of salmon, leftover mashed potatoes and chopped onions, form into little logs, roll in egg wash, bread with cornmeal or cracker crumbs, fry in a pan until golden brown and crunchy. J.C. and I had a special name for this item: Fish Turds. She even failed to master a number of simple dishes, like grits. Her grits were more singular, more like a grit, a breakfast (or sometimes dinner) side dish that had to be cut with a knife. Whenever we teased her about her cooking, she always laughed with us.

My mother could have learned to cook. Grandma Mimi, her mother, was an excellent cook. When I was seven or eight, I loved to tell other kids how she could make whipped cream from scratch. I thought this was close to a culinary miracle, because the only whipped cream my mother ever served came in an aerosol can. Betty Sue, my mother's sister, was also a good cook. I think that my mother liked the idea of others cooking for her. Shortly after I was married, Donna noticed that her new mother-in-law pretended that she could barely manage to boil water for her tea. When she came to visit, she never even made a sandwich. She wanted someone to take care of her.

THE MANHOOD PROJECT

MY MOTHER, I'M SURE, KNEW SHE COULD NEVER BE A FATHER, BUT SHE DID try to nudge J.C. and me toward the world of men. It's almost like she had a plan, a manhood project, which included baseball, Boy Scouts, a job, religion, and a lecture about ... well, you know. I'm not saying this plan was written down, verbalized, or even consciously mapped out. It just seems that way, looking back on it. The gist of the plan (and, again, this is just my post-hoc assumption, being a man of fifty-something, looking back on the lost world of a child, ascribing intentionality to a string of events that probably just fell into place rather haphazardly) was to situate my brother and me around men who were fathers and then hope that something would rub off, or these men would share some fatherly approval, stand as role models, or even tell us to quit whining, suck it up, be a man, live with the pain, kick some ass, or something like that. Basically, looking back at it all, understanding that it didn't quite work out as expected, I would still have to say it was a pretty good plan. My mother did her part. She set up the contact with men. It's just that most of the men didn't quite stand in for the father, or maybe I wasn't easy to reach. I probably came across to the men around me as being self-sufficient and independent, as a kid who was doing just fine.

It began about a year after my father left, when my mother decided I should play baseball on a real team. I assume she had read in the newspaper about a new league forming and signed me up. One day, I must have gone with the little kiddie glove my mother had bought me—no bat, no ball,

96

no hat—and tried out, but I don't remember it. So here is what I think happened. On the first day of tryouts, we were already split into teams. I was selected to try out for the Orioles because my mother taught at the same school as the coach's wife. During the tryouts, I didn't catch even one grounder, but my coach had more uniforms than competent players and his wife spoke on my behalf.

I made the team by default, but I rarely played. This was long before kids expected (or parents demanded) equal playing time, long before the era of feel-good sports experiences. Besides, the league, which was a local organization, not Little League, had only four teams and no levels. This meant that some of my teammates were three or four years older. Mostly, I remember sitting on the bench, in my clean Orioles uniform, a little worn in the butt, watching some other kid cry because he had allowed too many hits or cuss because he had struck out. Occasionally, one of my crying or cussing teammates turned in my direction and said, "What the hell are you looking at?" I only remember playing in two games.

In one, I was subbed into center field for half an inning. After my teammates moved me around ("farther out" and "over that way"), I watched the game with a sense of detachment. In other words, as if I were still on the bench. Then a fly ball sailed past the infield but not quite to what I considered the outfield, my area of responsibility. The other guys will get it, I thought, but they just turned and looked at me. I watched the ball hit the dirt, some twenty feet in front of me. A puff of gray dust rose and hung in the air. The ball bounced and landed once more. Another puff of dust. Hiroshima, I thought. Nagasaki. I'm as doomed as doomed can be. Then my coach, my teammates, maybe all the parents in the bleachers as well, started yelling, "Get the ball! Get the ball!" I detected a general sense of panic, like when the stock market drops a few hundred points. Eventually, after a slow eternity, my feet moved, almost as if apart from my control. As with those reports of near-death experiences, I seemed to float above my body and watch myself move toward the ball. I grabbed the ball and made a weak throw to second. Then . . . I honestly can't say. I have no memory of what happened after my throw. For all I know, I could have been the key to an inside-the-park-blooper-just-past-the-infield-home-run coupled with an error-by-severe-neglect-rather-than-any-kind-of-honest-attempt-to-get-the-friggin-ball.

In the other game, I was subbed in and allowed to walk to the plate with a bat in my hands. We must have had a large lead. An insurmountable lead. The pitcher for the other team looked huge, much older, like a grown man, but without a bulging stomach. As I remember it, he had a four o'clock shadow and sipped on a beer between innings. I stood at the plate, petrified, and watched four pitches whiz past. All balls. I didn't move until the umpire leaned toward me and said, "Son, you have to run down to first." Then he pointed me in the general direction. It was hardly a moment of triumph. The pitcher probably wasn't used to such a small strike zone. I was like the midget that Bill Veeck, owner of the St. Louis Browns, once sent in as a pinch hitter. The midget, like me, reached first base.

After the game, the coach's wife said to her husband, loud enough so that I could hear, "Wasn't George brave to stand up and take those pitches?" The coach, for the sake of marital harmony, nodded. Even then, I knew I didn't deserve the praise. I had no intention of swinging. I even remember feeling a little sorry for my coach, who didn't know what to do with me. I still remember the only bit of advice he gave me: "Get a rubber ball. Throw it off your house. Catch it." I tried to follow his advice, but the rubber ball got stuck in the gutter.

When I look back on my time in sports, I don't ever remember my incompetence bothering me. I can't say that sports were particularly formative, nor can I say that sports were particularly painful. I never expected to do well, and my mother never put any pressure on me. It was okay, quite different than my sons' experience. As I watch them play sports, I see joy, exaltation, comradeship, frustration, embarrassment, and disappointment. I don't remember feeling particularly bad about errors, excited about wins, or even especially upset about losing. Yet, oddly, I came to believe that, if I had a father, I would have been good at sports. And, if I had been good at sports, my entire life would have been immeasurably better, especially high school. In recent years, I have decided that the best thing about sports is that, as one ages, they become less and less important. J.C. never played organized sports. He was always the smart one.

Boy Scouts was a different deal. Competence was not such an issue, except for those kids who were driven to become Eagle Scouts, a goal I abandoned after a year or so. Mostly, Boy Scouts was a time to be with friends and learn how to handle an ax, pitch a tent, build a fire, and cook in the woods. My mother couldn't do much to help me in Scouts, except drive me to troop meetings and camping trips, buy me equipment, and sew patches on my uniform. She did all this. Scouting would have been a pretty good experience for me, except I just didn't relate to the troop leaders too well. Because we were in a military area, most of the troop leaders were military men, and Boy Scouts became something like a militia, not of the looney survivalist ilk, but paramilitary nonetheless. When I was thirteen, my last year in Scouts, I went off to Boy Scout camp expecting to share a tent with Jeff McCain, then my best friend. Once we arrived, Mr. Johnson, the Scout leader, told me that I would be sharing a tent with Paul Johnson (who was not my best friend, by a long shot), because we were the highest ranking members of our troop and our tent could be a command post. I told him I wasn't going to do it. He blathered on and on about "being a leader" and "the good of the troop" and "falling on a live grenade to save your buddies" for a long time; then, he looked at me and asked, "So?" I responded, "So what?" He threw up his hands and walked off. I bunked with Jeff, as planned. We didn't have a command post, and no one seemed to comment on major SNAFUs or serious lapses in logistics.

The rest of the week was more of the same. I tried to earn a merit badge in canoeing with sixteen other kids. Every day, for two hours, we met at the James River, listened to a fifteen minute lecture on the shore, and then launched our canoes and paddled around in circles. The instructor, one of those grown men who was a professional Scout leader and wore his Boy Scout uniform most of the day, even when he went to the Piggly Wiggly, sat on the shore and talked to other grown men, who were also professional Scout leaders. At the end of the week, he awarded a badge to only one of us. I wasn't the one. I also tried to earn a merit badge in cooking. Two other Scouts and I built a fire and cooked campburgers and biscuits in tin foil while a pimply sixteen year old camp counselor, who should have moved on to girls a long time ago, evaluated us. We then sat down and ate. I assumed that anyone who could eat his own cooking would automatically pass, but I was wrong. Mr. Pimply failed the other two guys right off the bat because they burned everything. My meal was, in comparison, pretty good, except my biscuits were a little black on the bottom. So Mr. Pimply thought about it for a while, then failed me. I protested long enough that he asked an older camp counselor, who just happened to be walking by, what he thought. This guy noticed that I had leaned my fork, after the entire meal was eaten, against a piece of used tin foil, which was on the ground. He said I shouldn't have placed my fork on the ground, which meant that I deserved to fail. I protested again: "In the first place, I have finished eating. In the second place, I leaned the fork against some foil so that the part that goes in my mouth was not on the ground. In the third place, we don't have a table or chairs here, so I didn't have anywhere else to put it." He said, "You should have put the fork on a tree branch." That was it. I was done with Scouts, which I decided, at that very moment, was nothing but a socially sanctioned form of child abuse. To this day, I still hate Scouting, and I discouraged my sons from having anything to do with Cub Scouts or Boy Scouts. For some reason, J.C. loved all of it.

Then came the job. When I was about twelve, my mother said to me, "I want you to go around to the stores at the front of the village and ask about work." So I went off to the strip mall near the main entrance to Aragona Village, and, deciding to start at the west end and move east, I asked for a job at the drug store. I skipped the fabric shop and asked for work at the hardware store, the grocery store, then Woolworth's Five and Dime. They all said they weren't hiring. When I asked the short, plump, bald man at the hobby shop, at the very east end of the strip, which means this was my last chance to make something of myself, he looked down at me, over the top of his glasses, and said, "I couldn't hire you if I wanted to. It's against the law." Even though I didn't ask for an explanation, he launched into an extended lecture on child labor laws, which was all news to me. And then I felt a little better, like I had a reason for not landing a job, so I went home and told my mother about kids and factories and coal mines and sixteen hour days. She didn't seem surprised and said something about having a B.S. Ed. in History, but the job issue was put to rest for a while.

After another year of being unemployed, I took over Terry Tereskerz's paper route. Terry was Elsie's son. Elsie was my mother's best friend, so it was all arranged between moms. Most weeks, I didn't break even, partly because I kept delivering papers to subscribers who didn't pay me and partly because Terry, who was seventeen, driving, dating, and now unemployed, continued to collect money from my subscribers whenever he needed gas money. (To be fair, Terry still denies it all, even to this day. He claims he was collecting for weeks of papers that he delivered before I took over. What I remember is that we met the route manager the day I took over, looked over the payment stubs, figured out how much money was on the books, so to speak, what I owed Terry for his official paperboy bike basket, which we had transferred to my bike, and settled up, all under the supervision of the route manager.) The only significant money I earned off the paper route was from Christmas tips. As soon as I collected them, I told my mother that I was quitting. She was disappointed. Severely so. It looked like it was going to be a dismal January until J.C. decided to take over the route. By summer, he had won a bike for selling new subscriptions. He also turned a profit. Every week. If a subscriber didn't pay, J.C. cut them off. No papers.

The final phase of the manhood project was a birds-and-bees lecture; this is the only part of the project that my mother took on by herself. When she broached the subject with J.C., he told her that he didn't want to hear any of it and walked off. I, on the other hand, dutifully sat and listened as she pulled out a few library books, with illustrations of sperm and ovary tubes, and told me about reproduction—not really sex—in the most general terms. It was almost as puzzling as my father's "neck-ed ladies" lecture. I learned about how the male emits two kinds of sperm, one had a pointy head and made a boy baby and the other had a rounded head and made a girl baby (I heard this as "male sperm" and "female sperm," knowledge that I later used to embarrass myself in a high school biology class), how women release eggs (scrambled, the way I like them? I wondered, because I was really thinking that these eggs had to come a dozen at a time, maybe even in little cardboard containers), and how women bleed once a month and need tampons (I already knew this because I was with my father once when he bought a box for my mother, the box was gray and had "Generic" on it in big red letters, so I asked him what was in the box, and he said something about "women" and "month" and "stopping blood" and "they're cheaper than the name brand kind," and I said "oh" like I understood, but I didn't really, because for a long time I thought that menstruation was somehow generic, maybe I still think that). It went on and on like that, the text of her lecture interrupted by the subtext of my confusion.

The entire twenty-one minutes of the lecture, give or take a few moments, was awkward for both of us. I heard nothing about intercourse, penises, vaginas, friction, lubrication, or even respecting women, being gentle, and using birth control. Nothing that would prove useful. The "talk" was a complete failure, but I admire her for trying. And it didn't mar me for life. I was eventually able to have children.

In fact, I weathered all this manhood instruction pretty well, without any of it harming my relationship to my mother. It was religion that proved more of a sticky issue. A Southern Baptist, my mother believed in going to church on Sunday mornings and evenings and prayer meeting on Wednesday night. On a good week, she could also fit in a potluck dinner and a circle meeting. I'm not exactly sure what a circle meeting is, but I think it's a group of women who get together at someone's house once a month to pray, talk about the Bible, drink coffee and eat feminine snacks, more finger sandwiches and cake than salami and chips. (This is all a guess on my part. When my mother's circle group met at our house, I hid upstairs and peed in an old peanut butter jar so I wouldn't have to walk through the living room, crammed with women, to use the only bathroom in the house.)

GEORGE H. JENSEN, JR.

For a few summers, I also attended Bible School. Through all of this, I somehow managed to grow up without learning the books of the Bible in order, memorizing long passages from the Bible, or knowing anything about the river Jordan, except that it was somewhere near the country of Jordan, which wasn't a country in biblical times. But it wasn't my failings as a student of the scripture that was a problem; it was more my loss of faith.

I remember the moment it happened. I was about thirteen years old, sitting in a Sunday school class. The father who was teaching the class said something about having to believe in Jesus to enter the gates of heaven. I asked, "What about the Jews?" He said, "That's for God to decide." His answer was politic enough, leaving some hope for the afterlife of the Chosen People, but I didn't believe that he believed what he was saying. Right or wrong, I felt that he was thinking, in the privacy of his own mind, "Of course, the Jews are going to hell." My loss of faith came down to a simple syllogism: God is a better being than I am. I would not want my worst enemy to go to hell; therefore, I don't believe in a God who would send anyone to hell. The conclusion, as any student of logic has already figured out, does not follow from the major and minor premises, but I had not yet had a course in philosophy. I was just winging it on my own. Logical or not, I was done with being a Southern Baptist. (It is interesting that I later was married to a Jew by a reformed Rabbi.) I was smart enough to keep my syllogism to myself, but I did start to complain about going to church. My mother said, "You have to go until you are sixteen, then you can decide on your own." I went until I was sixteen and then I never went again. It wasn't until I started attending open AA meetings and learned that I could create my own Higher Power, one that made sense to me, that I started to pray again.

While she never tried to shame me into rejoining the flock, I am sure that my departure from church was a major source of worry for my mother, who was concerned about the afterlife, but even this was not a major problem. My mother was not dogmatic like those who are convinced that they have already been saved. Once, she even told me, "I'm not sure I'm going to go to heaven." I remember thinking, "If my

103

mother doesn't make it to heaven, then there's no hope for the rest of us."

Maybe my mother doubted her salvation because she was not a rigorous Baptist. She didn't believe that dancing was a sin (she forced me to attend ballroom dancing classes), and she even drank from time to time. She usually kept a few beers in the Lettuce Crisper, safely hidden in case some friends from Thalia Lynn Baptist Church visited. My Uncle R.T. used to tease her about her "Southern Baptist drinking." R.T. was fairly deaf from a long career as high school band teacher. Even in a quiet location and during an intimate conversation, he almost shouted. When he had a few drinks on Friday nights, he resuscitated the persona he had developed as a trumpet player in a Big Band in the 1940s. Standing in our kitchen in his boxers, he talked loud enough for the neighbors to hear, and everything was "ring-a-ding-ding." He would tell my mother: "Southern Baptists drink, ring-a-ding-ding. They go to their conventions and they pull out a bottle in their hotel rooms, ring-a-ding-ding." My mother didn't think this was funny at all, which is why Uncle R.T. thought it was hilarious and repeated it two or three times a night, whenever the Kirks were visiting.

I only remember seeing my mother intoxicated a few times, during neighborhood parties. Each time, it scared the hell out of me.

The Image of the Mother

IT SEEMS LIKE THE EFFECTS OF MY FATHER'S LEAVING WOULD HAVE BEEN immediate and intense and then lessened as months and years passed. Soon after my father left, I do remember my mother and J.C. yelling at each other, which was part of the tension and anger lingering from the days when my father's drinking kept the family off balance. I don't remember yelling, but I would guess that J.C. expressed much of what I was feeling. This tension and anger lessened with time. But other effects seemed to emerge later or become stronger. When my father left, I assumed he would be back any day—for years. Once I accepted he was gone for good, I began to realize, although not consciously, that it was my mother who provided everything I needed. Not surprisingly, I began to idealize her.

I relied on my mother, and I believe she even relied on me. When she felt overwhelmed and frightened, she came to me in tears. She let it out and she felt better. Less alone. More able to return to the tasks of raising two boys. When I was about fifteen, she told me that she didn't know how she would have made it over the last eight or ten years without J.C. and me. I didn't know what she meant at the time, because we didn't have jobs or make repairs. She apparently relied on us more than we realized.

I even believe that she was ambivalent about my dating. When I was in the seventh grade, I had my first girlfriend. The girl—I can't remember her name, so I'll call her Martha, because I never liked that name–had just broken up with some other boy—we'll call him Bubba. Through one of Martha's friends, we established that we liked each other, and, through the same friend, I sent her a friendship ring, which I bought for 57¢ at Woolworth's. I walked Martha home a few times and we held hands. We sent notes and met at a dance. The relationship, if it could be called that, lasted about ten days. Then Martha decided she would rather "go with" Bubba again, who now wanted her back because some other guy (this would be me) wanted her. She sent the ring back through Mr. Thompson, my teacher. He approached me when I was talking to two of my friends, offered the ring to me in the palm of his extended hand, and said, "Martha asked me to give this back to you." It was almost as if the two of them, Martha, now my former sweetheart, and Mr. Thompson, my teacher who claimed to be a man but was clearly behaving like a school girl, had conspired to find the most embarrassing means for ending my first relationship. My face burned. After the initial humiliation, the aftereffects of this negligible adolescent tragedy were quite pleasurable. My friends rallied around me and offered up a string of platitudes: "She'll want you back soon." "She's not so good looking." "Her boyfriend is a sissy." "You'll get back together." "As my dad says, there are plenty of fish in the sea." It wasn't the platitudes I prized so much as having friends who consoled me about the kind of pain that every kid feels. For a few days, I didn't feel any different than the rest of my classmates.

I was, however, a little puzzled by my mother's reaction to the breakup. She taught at the same school Martha (or whatever her name was) and I attended, and she had seen us together, walking down the hall before classes began. After she found out that the girl dumped me, she said, "You didn't like her much anyway, did you?" The statement shocked me, partially, I'm sure, because I wanted to wallow in the misery of it all. If I didn't really like her, I couldn't justify being so wounded. But, in my mother's statement, I also heard something around or between the words that made me think she didn't want me to have a girlfriend. Of course, this was just my interpretation of a short, simple statement, but I carried it with me for a long while. And, of course, I never bothered to ask my mother what she really meant. Maybe she was, like my friends, trying to console me.

GEORGE H. JENSEN, JR.

After this brief romantic fling, I was slow to date and late to marry. For a long time, I told myself that this was because I was quiet and shy or because I never had anyone model a relationship for me. I didn't know how to flirt, ask a girl out, chit-chat. Throughout high school, I had a crush on the same girl. I knew that she liked me, but somehow I could never ask her out. I was Dante gawking at Beatrice from afar. When we passed in the hallway, I stared at her and she stared at me. She waited for me to speak. I never did. We just exchanged protracted, all-too-obvious stares. This went on for about two years. She probably wondered—maybe still wonders—what was wrong with this guy. I am sure she asked her friends, "What do I have to do to let this guy know I am interested?" Now, I think it was the image of my mother that kept me distant. As I idealized my mother, I idealized women. If I approached women, they could not remain ideal. If they—and my mother—did not remain ideal, I would not be safe. Dante could revere Beatrice for the rest of his life, through *La Vita Nuova* and *The Divine Comedy*, because he never approached her. It was a grand boon to western literature that Beatrice died young.

Even after I started to date, occasionally and sporadically, I could not date casually. I would not ask a woman for a first date unless I could look weeks, months, years ahead and convince myself that it would work out, unless I could make a commitment. Unlike many men, I was not afraid of commitment; I was afraid of failing *the woman*. Developing a relationship was equally disquieting. A relationship felt like a betrayal of my obligation to my mother, not in a clearly conscious way, but vaguely, felt only as a general sense of unease. If being in a relationship was uncomfortable, then ending it was horrifying. To end a relationship meant that I became my father.

Even after I was grown, I never talked to my mother about my relationships. I had some sense that it was a touchy subject. Though I was thirty-three when I told her that Donna and I were engaged, I was apprehensive about how she would react. And she was reserved. She seemed shaken. She asked, "Are you sure about this?" She eventually came to know and love Donna, and she was very happy at my wedding. At first, however, I think she was afraid that she would lose me. Through the difficult years, we had relied on each other.

Coming of Age

Parents worry, I now know from my own experience as a father, about their kids constantly and obsessively, and they have their own special set of worries for each child. With J.C., my mother worried mostly about his weight. With me, she worried about schoolwork and grades. As I began high school, she had some concerns about my lack of friends and later, as I was finishing high school, she had concerns about my choice of friends. For a short time, I think she worried about me being depressed, possibly even suicidal.

My mother claimed that I was in the fifth grade before I learned to read. I don't think this is entirely accurate (my transformation from an illiterate to a PhD became something of a family myth), but I did daydream through most of my time in school. In the seventh grade, I failed several subjects and was given a "provisional pass" that slid me into the eighth grade. When I look back on this period of my life, I don't see any clear patterns. I did poorly in the seventh grade, but I made honor roll in the eighth grade. Then I started to scrape by again in the ninth. In the seventh grade, when I was failing academically, I was popular. Then, I went through several years of weak grades and few friends. I wasn't teased very often. I more was lost in a crowd—unacknowledged by other kids and hidden from teachers. In high school, lunch was a particularly difficult. I didn't have the confidence to walk up to kids, even ones I sort of knew, cafeteria tray in hand, the most vulnerable situation for high school

109

males, and sit down, so I often spent my lunch money in a vending machine outside the gym. I tried to blend into the background while I gulped down some Lance peanut butter crackers. One day, a gym teacher saw me eating crackers and gave me a hard time, mumbling something about "nutrition" and "muscles" and "manhood" and "what if there's a war?" I felt like saying, "Leave me alone. I'm just painfully shy." But I didn't.

After my crackers, I would drink some water from a fountain in the hall (this was before high schools were filled with soda machines), head to the library and look through magazines. I gravitated toward *Life* magazine because of the pictures. At the time, *Life* often had incredibly shocking photographs of lynchings in the deep South. Like most of the white kids living in completely white neighborhoods and attending almost completely white schools, I had accepted the racism of my community. It was through these photographs that my views began to change. About the same time, I read an interview with a guy named Rockwell, who was then the Grand Dragon of the Ku Klux Klan, in an issue of *Playboy*. (J.C. kept his collection hidden in his room. When he wasn't around, I sneaked in to look at pictures and occasionally read an article or interview. Yes, I actually read some of the articles.) Hugh Hefner had sent Alex Haley to interview Rockwell, and it was Rockwell's own words that managed to convince me that he and all other racists were ignorant. He talked about how bad it was that white teenagers had to listen to "nigger music" when they were making love in the back of their 1957 Chevy. I liked the Temptations and James Brown, so I didn't get it. Soon, I just didn't get racism period.

When adults gathered in our kitchen at night to smoke, drink coffee, and talk, their attitudes about race started to emerge from the fabric of their stories. I began to argue with them, and then some of the adults began to joke about how they couldn't talk about Negroes around George. It became a running gag at our house.

While I might have demonstrated some potential by reading interviews and articles in *Playboy*, this particular bent toward the printed word did not affect my schoolwork. In general, I was bored with school. My ninth grade English teacher spent two months on *My Fair Lady*. We read it out loud and listened to the music on a scratchy LP (that stands for Long Playing record) and watched her tear up. I don't remember her name. My sophomore history teacher reeled off facts from yellowed lecture notes in a monotone voice. I pulled straight Ds in his class. I don't remember his name. We'll just call him Mr. Whoseitsface. For six weeks, he was replaced by a student teacher, Mr. Fez, who was excited about the ideas of history. I made an A for that six weeks. Then Mr. Whoseitsface returned, and I started to pull Ds again. For the most part, the teachers left me alone. I never caused any trouble, so I wasn't viewed as an object of concern.

Even though my mother was a teacher and, by the time I hit high school, a guidance counselor, I don't think she knew how to turn me around. (Or maybe I wouldn't allow her to help. I often try to play a role in the education of my sons, but they are generally uninterested in what I know, and whenever I say, "I don't know," they rise in their chairs and their eyes widen, something like what NASCAR fans do, in unison, when cars collide on the track, tumble, and ignite.) My mother talked to me about going to college, and she made sure that I sat down each night to do homework. She went to PTA meetings and Open House events at my high school. She knew I was adrift and depressed, without purpose or friends. She just didn't know how to fix it.

Then I discovered surfing. When I was fourteen, I worked small construction jobs with our next door neighbor, Bill Price. He had a civil service job at the navy base during the days and picked up small construction jobs that he worked in the evenings and on weekends. When he laid bricks for an outdoor barbeque, I mixed mortar. When he finished someone's basement, I was an extra set of hands. By November of 1965 when I was fifteen, I had enough money to buy a used surfboard for $70 from Ben Smith's nephew. It was a Dexter, an off-brand. What surfers call a pop-out. In other words, a piece of shit. But it was a surfboard, and I had an identity, even though I would have to wait through a long winter to learn how to surf. Skip, the son of one of my mother's friends, someone I sort of knew, got a new Hobie for Christmas. Hobies were the Cadillacs of surfboards. At the time, anything that was good was the Cadillac of something.

Somehow, I believe our mothers suggested it, Skip and I started to surf together. Then, I had a friend. Skip already had his license and an old Ford Falcon, which definitely was not the Cadillac of cars. Skip's father, who started more tasks than he finished, had almost—but not quite—renovated the Falcon. He had done a little work on the engine, filled in the dents with putty, and painted it with bright orange primer, using a brush, so that brush strokes were all too apparent (in this sense, the Falcon was almost like a Van Gogh), and then he stopped. The car remained bright orange with brush strokes, but it ran well enough to get us to the beach. So, with Skip, my new friend, his Hobie, my Dexter, and our new identities as a surfers, we headed for the beach in his bright orange Falcon with the brush strokes almost every day in the summer, whether the surf was up or not.

The beach became our new home. When the weather was good, we were at the beach—all day. When the weatherman said a hurricane was rolling in, we headed for the beach, hoping for some bigger waves, as the tourists escaped in the other direction. If the surf was up and a thunderstorm broke the horizon, we said "what the hell" and stayed in the water. If the weather turned warm in January, we surfed for as long as we could tolerate the chilly Atlantic. Skip was my first friend who remained my friend and is still my friend. We can be away from each other for several years, get together, and pick up an old conversation in mid-sentence. So it was surfing and Skip's friendship that helped me to survive the last years of high school. I started to talk to my mother about how I wanted to be a beach bum when I grew up. And she developed a new worry: Would George ever support himself?

With Skip and surfing, life was better but my grades weren't. When I was a junior, I went to my counselor to discuss my senior schedule. I don't remember her name, but I remember her looks. Skinny with short dark hair and bad acne. She glanced at the schedule I had scratched out on a mimeographed form and asked why I wanted to take Spanish.

"My mother says I need it for college."

GEORGE H. JENSEN, JR.

"With your grades," she said, "you'll never get into college." She crossed Spanish off my schedule and added Ceramics. It seems like she would have at least had some respect for my gender and added a shop class instead, which might have prepared me for some sort of manual labor, but she had her mind set on Ceramics. I spent a portion of my last year in high school making ash trays and beer mugs—even though I didn't smoke or drink.

At some point after my meeting with the counselor, something inexplicable happened. I decided I wanted to become a reader. I don't think it had anything to do with my counselor saying that I wouldn't be accepted to college. She was not trying to challenge me; she considered me a lost cause. And I didn't blame her. Not then. Not now. Despite the finality of her judgment, for some peculiar reason, I simply decided to start reading. I went into a bookstore and bought a copy of Crane's *The Red Badge of Courage* and Plato's *The Republic*. I struggled with both books, though oddly Plato was easier for me to understand than Crane. And then I went on to other books. This change is still puzzling. I can offer explanations that might make sense to others, but they don't fully make sense to me.

About this time, my mother sent me to a remedial reading course, which might seem to explain my move toward reading, if only the course were remotely inspirational. For two hours, twice a week, for eight weeks, I snailed through boring passages on reading machines, articles about building bomb shelters or the dangers of Elvis Presley's gyrating hips. One machine flashed passages on a screen with a diagonal strip highlighted, which moved from left to right. I think it was supposed to teach me to read two or three lines at once. Another machine pushed a bar down the page of a book. It was supposed to increase my reading pace. I could never keep ahead of the bar. The only useful information I learned during the entire course was that it was okay to pace myself with my fingers as I read. (At this time, almost every elementary school teacher in the country wanted kids to read without their fingers and without moving their lips. The future of democracy depended on it.) But, by the end of the course, I was doing better on the objective tests. Maybe the course made me a little more confident about reading, but I can't imagine that plodding through passages from *Readers' Digest* on reading machines inspired me to read Crane and Plato.

What might have helped more was my journalism class, taught by Mr. Lally, a loud, barrel-chested guy who had a James Dean haircut. As the only journalism teacher at Princess Anne High School, he was the advisor for the school paper, and he signed his name in the masthead as W. Steven Lally, which all his students thought was hilarious. I would have called him pompous if I had known what that word meant. His way of handling inane high school behavior, usually from the boys, was to mimic them by saying, "I just want to be cool." I didn't like him at the time, but he probably had more influence on me than any of my high school teachers. In Journalism, he required us to write a newspaper article once a week through the entire year. Our articles were then peer critiqued in class, as Mr. Lally read sections aloud and asked for comments. I am certain that it was this course that prepared me for writing in college, and writing probably also helped my reading. One of my few memorable moments in high school even occurred in Mr. Lally's class. One week, we were assigned to write up an interview. We could either interview a real person or pretend that we had interviewed someone, then write it up as an article. I decided to write my piece as if I had interviewed Mr. Lally. The piece began:

> "I just want to be cool," said the stout W. Steven Lally as he expressed his most cherished desire in life.

Mr. Lally spent about thirty minutes of the next class period reading from my simulated interview with W. Steven Lally. Most teachers in my school would have sent me to Mr. Cox, the Assistant Principal, but he thought, much to his credit, that it was pretty damn funny. I respect him for having a sense of humor. Mr. Lally later published a collection of poems about Boone, North Carolina, his hometown. About six years after I graduated from high school, his MG Midget was hit by a huge Detroit family car, and he ended up paralyzed. He was gone from

Princess Anne High School before I was mature enough to realize he had helped me and before I had a chance to thank him.

Mr. Lally's class certainly had something to do with me becoming a reader, but I think something else must have also been at work, because my decision to become a reader was not so related to newly developed skills as it was to a new attitude. The only other explanation I can muster is that Patrick Raymond's mother died. I hung out with Patrick occasionally, but we never spent time together after school (unless, perhaps, we ran into each other at a football game), and I didn't even know his mother. However, once his mother died, his family was not normal, either. He was the first person I knew who did not have both a mother and a father. It was at this time that I felt less stigmatized and began to tell my simple story to others. So maybe this had some effect on my becoming a reader.

As I began to read, my grades improved toward the end of my junior year, but I still graduated from high school with a D+ average, in the bottom third of my class. On the SAT, I scored 370 Verbal and a 328 Math—the second time I took it. Remember, that one earns 200 points on each section for putting a name (any name) on the answer sheet. The booklet that accompanied my scores let me know that, given my verbal scores, I had a 7 percent chance of surviving my first year of college in "good standing." Based on my math score, I had a -1 percent chance. How can you have less than a zero percent chance of making it? Understandably, I didn't think that I would make it to college, so I started to become even more depressed than the average teenager. I began to spend a lot of time in my room listening to Bob Dylan and feeling sorry for myself. I even fantasized about joining the army and dying in Vietnam. At this time, my mother worried that I might attempt suicide, but she never spoke to me about it. Instead, she asked Elsie Tereskerz to step in. One evening when my mother, Elsie and I were sitting in the living room, I mentioned something about joining the army. Elsie said, "I know you think you don't have any future right now, and you think you are going to go to Vietnam and get killed, but that's just stupid." Elsie went on for several minutes. She told me exactly what I had been thinking, and then she snuffed my pretty little fantasy.

By some miracle, I was admitted to Old Dominion College for the Fall semester of 1968. Like a number of institutions at the time, Old Dominion wanted to grow. They admitted a large number of marginally qualified (or, in my case, entirely unqualified) students and then gave them two years to prove themselves, without any remedial courses, writing centers, or tutorials. At orientation, I sat in the middle of about a dozen other graduates of Princess Anne High School. President Webb said, "Look at the person on your right and the person on your left. In two years, they will not be here." In two years, six people to my left and six to my right had disappeared. One of the smartest guys from my high school took eighteen hours his first semester and was booted in January. To my surprise, I was on the honor roll.

As my prospects of finishing college and finding a career improved, my mother worried less about my grades and more about my friendship with Skip and whether or not we would both be swept away by the counter-culture. A number of my friends from Princess Anne High School, not just Skip, were too involved in protest rallies or drugs. I was on the fringe of it all.

I marched against the war in Vietnam, often at the local level and twice in Washington, D.C., but I never burned my draft card. My student deferment kept me safe until the lottery. Then, during a nationally televised event, as old men in white shirts and thin black ties pulled birth dates from a large drum to determine who would be drafted in what order. My birth date was drawn 346th, and I knew I would never be drafted. So I never needed to burn my draft card or migrate to Canada.

I grew my hair and wore bell bottoms, but I never drove a VW bus to San Francisco.

I drank a little, sometimes too much, but not often. When a joint came around, I took my hits, but I never bought my own pot. A friend once gave me a bag of pot because I had helped him with his term paper, but I threw it out of my car window on the drive home.

I watched news reports about Woodstock on television and later saw the film at the Beach Theater on 21st Street and Atlantic Avenue. Skip and I tried unsuccessfully to attend a musical festival in Myrtle Beach, South Carolina. We started to drive there in his Ford Falcon, still covered with bright orange primer, brush marks and all. About 11:00 pm, somewhere in North Carolina, we had a flat. When Skip was changing the tire, two lug bolts snapped. So, rather than risk driving on a wheel tenuously held by two lug bolts, we decided to hitchhike the rest of the way. At about 3:00 am, the police stopped us in Jackson, North Carolina, and searched our backpacks for drugs. We were clean, except for my allergy pills, which I had luckily packed in the pharmacy bottle. So even these good ole boy cops didn't suspect that the pills were uppers or downers or anything illegal. About 8:00 am, we made it to Myrtle Beach, the day the concert was scheduled to begin. While we were eating breakfast at the International House of Pancakes, Skip decided he missed his girlfriend, Susan. So we finished our pancakes and then headed back to Virginia Beach. We hitched until we found his car, and then drove the rest of the way, worrying that his right rear tire might decide to head east as the rest of the car headed north. That was as close as I came to anything like Woodstock.

I went through the era of "Free Love" pretty lonely and frustrated. I wish I had been more a part of things. At the very least, I should have been at Woodstock because I really get tired of listening to people say, "I was there." It's not worth the effort to interject, "I remember watching it on TV."

As my friends flunked out, faced the draft, moved to Canada, or drifted away, I spent most of my time in the library, working harder for my Bs and As than my classmates, who had paid attention in high school. By about 1971, I had seen enough of my friends strung out on alcohol and chemicals that I passed the joint to the next guy and settled into having a social beer or two. I slowly lost contact with every friend I had in high school, except Skip. By this time, J.C. was in the Air Force. So, my mother and I spent a lot of time watching *Masterpiece Theatre* and other PBS shows.

TALES OF MY FATHER

WHEN I WAS GROWING UP, FROM THE TIME MY FATHER LEFT UNTIL ABOUT six months after his death, my mother never voiced one tainted word toward him. In fact, the only thing she ever said about him, good or bad, was, "Your father is a good man. He just has a disease." She repeated this comment sincerely, without any detectable anger or bitterness, almost as a mantra, and it seemed to satisfy J.C. and me. We never asked for details. Now, after I have learned about Twelve Step programs, I know that she had to learn this from Al-Anon. In the 1950s, this message had not seeped into popular culture. Even though she never told me she was a member, she must have at least gone to some Al-Anon meetings. She used the program's language. And, after her death, in one of my trips through her papers, I even found an Al-Anon pamphlet, entitled *Just for Today*.

The pamphlet is from another age, a time when all members of Al-Anon were women and before feminism changed our consciousness. One passage reads: "Just for to-day I will be agreeable. I will look as well as I can, dress becomingly, talk low, act courteously, criticize not one bit, not find fault with anything, and not try to improve or regulate anybody but myself." The advice reads like a paraphrase of Bill W.'s "To the Wives" chapter of *Alcoholics Anonymous*, the Big Book. For some reason, Bill W. decided to write the "To the Wives" chapter, which understandably angered Lois, his wife. The chapter, which was supposed to have been written by wives for wives, was actually written by a lone recovering alcoholic who adopted the plural, feminine "we" to advise women about how to handle their alcoholic husbands. Almost homiletic, the chapter retains the preachy "you" removed from early drafts of other chapters: "The first principle of success is that you should never be angry. Even though your husband becomes unbearable and you have to leave him temporarily, you should, if you can, go without rancor. Patience and good temper are most necessary." Later, Bill W.'s feminine "we" offers this advice about relapses: "Cheerfully see him through more sprees." The chapter reads like an alcoholic's protracted fantasy. Strangely anachronistic, it recommends the adoption of almost all of the standard medieval feminine virtues: patience, constancy, cheerfulness, and silence. Inexplicably, no words about chastity. The third edition of *Alcoholics Anonymous* (1976) adds a footnote: "Written in 1939, when there were few women in A.A., this chapter assumes that the alcoholic in the home is likely to be the husband. But many of the suggestions given here may be adapted to help the person who lives with a woman alcoholic—whether she is still drinking or is recovering in A.A." The footnote misses the point entirely. The problem with the chapter is not that it was addressed to the wives or that it assumes, contrary to evidence available even in 1939, that all alcoholics are men; the real problem is that the advice was not even very helpful to the wives who read it in 1939. Still, Bill W.'s recommendations even seem to have found their way into Al-Anon literature, as seen in my mother's *Just For Today* pamphlet.

My mother was certainly ahead of the 1950s thinking in Al-Anon, at least, as judged by the *Just for Today* pamphlet and Bill W.'s "To the Wives" chapter. She came to a point where she didn't want to "cheerfully" see my father "through more sprees." Maybe, many of the women in 1950s Al-Anon meetings thought beyond the program's literature, and I would guess that my mother found some of her strength from being their friend.

Of course, I can't be certain that my mother ever attended meetings. My father could have picked the pamphlet up for her, when he was attending AA for six months. But I believe it was hers. She must have attended Al-Anon long enough to learn that alcoholism is a disease and she should not blame the alcoholic, the more enduring message of that program. She may have gone to Al-Anon longer. Long after my father left, she had a number of friends with husbands who were recovering alcoholics, and she even later dated a few members of AA. I never wondered about this when I was a boy (that is, when I was in my self-absorbed, watery daze), but she must have met these AA men through her friends in Al-Anon who had husbands in AA.

So, as I believe she learned in Al-Anon, she repeated, "Your father is a good man. He just has a disease." This and nothing more until after my father died. Just as it was important for me to hear only the "good man" and "disease" explanation as I was growing up, it was equally important for me to hear something about the effects of my father's drinking once he was gone.

I can't exactly place the conversation in time. It might have been a few weeks or months after my father died. At the end of the summer, I was visiting home from graduate school, and we had gone out for ice cream. She started talking, unconsciously, almost hypnotically. She said that he kept cleaning out the bank account. He threw a knife at her, barely missing her head. His drinking was bad when they lived in Hawaii. He had nightmares about the war. He hit her. When the family went to visit her parents in Lexington, he went on a binge and was arrested. His name was in the paper. She went to her old church that morning, wondering how many of her friends had read about her husband, pretending everything was okay, trying to believe they didn't know, didn't even imagine, what she was going through. Then she said, "I don't know why I told you all that." It may have come from deep within her, and she may have known, at some level, that this moment would not change *the father* so much but might make *the mother* more real. About this time, I stopped calling her "mom" and began calling her "Louise." We became more like friends. I needed to be told.

She spoke of my father only once more, in the summer of 1986. Donna and I had been visiting Virginia Beach. On the way back to Atlanta, we decided to drive through the Carolinas, and we asked my mother to come with us. Donna was then about five months pregnant with Jay, our first born. Two or three days into the trip, late at night, we reached Charleston. After a morning of sight-seeing, Donna wanted to take a nap, so I drove my mother to the navy base where my father was once stationed. I parked near the gate, and we walked up to the chain link fence. She looked in, pointed to a building in the distance, and said, "The hospital where you were born was right over there." Then she told me that she was under anesthesia and didn't remember my birth. She didn't even see me until the next day. My father was on a binge. A neighbor in navy housing kept my brother. A different neighbor drove my mother and her new son home from the hospital. My father was supposed to hire a nanny, but he forgot. She was alone for several days with her three year old and a newborn. I was thirty-six when I heard this story, about to become a parent myself, and it was only the second time that my mother spoke of my father's drinking. The story of the events surrounding my birth is all I remember being told of my early childhood. For my mother, the events of my childhood during these years were probably too hard to separate from my father's drinking. She didn't want to speak of my father's drinking, so she didn't speak of those years. When I was young, there was a magic in her silence. A ritual. A promise of protection. Now, I wish she had said more.

After my mother died, in one of my trips through her chest of documents and photographs, I found some hurriedly written notes. A list of all of my father's sins. The scribbled phrases, which covered three yellow legal sheets, front and back, were arranged under the names of cities (Honolulu, Charleston, Bainbridge, Lexington, Ft. Slocum, Norfolk), locations of my father's offences. Under "Honolulu," where they lived when my brother was an infant, before I was born, she wrote:

...checks. Write checks when no money in bank—impossible to keep joint acct. Chief covered up—Leave every holiday go to club

Went to see play Mr. Roberts in Norfolk about 6 people— drove on wrong side of road across grass divider—terrible and miracle we got home

SOME OF THE WORDS ARE THEIRS

Friend advised—Leave while there is still time

Butcher knife to cut dogs head off—chased dog over yard

There is a frantic pace to these notes, probably written during a few free minutes away from the kids, an attempt to place incomprehensible events in some sort of order, and even then mixing the sins of Norfolk with the sins of Honolulu.

Under "Charleston, S.C.," where I was born, from where we moved when I was only a few years old, before the time of my memories, she wrote:

Found on someone's back porch—put in jail & car taken
Wrecked car in back of housing dev.

Went to school in Carlisle, Pa & had wreck with car
knew few details but had to hire lawyer & had hard time getting cleared

Had flu before Georgie born—brought colored woman who never showed up again—left me all day sick—Got in with crowd in bars—in naval base vicinity. Said he lost money trying to hit it big—then stayed out all night

Then under "Ft. Slocum," where we lived when I was three or four years old, just as I was beginning to store some memories:

Leave car in town not know where it was—
American Legion

Prep for picnic, got knife—threw it out back door with kids playing—Threw knife—by my nose from living room to behind washer in kitchen.

GEORGE H. JENSEN, JR.

Worked in tavern drunk all the time—pass by home & go to club called to him—no answer

Arrived to find car wrecked no one to meet us showed up drinking & friend with car in same shape—House awful

went to neighbors house by mistake—burned arm by falling into stove.

There is more in her notes, and I am certain that the notes are scattered memories, incomplete and superficial. These are only the large sins. She didn't write about the things that happened every day: how little disappointments turned love into resentment, how even the good times were full of anxiety, how hope turned into despair . . .

The drama in my mother's notes is missing from my memories. Even though I never felt "normal" when I was growing up, I didn't experience the kind of traumatic events that cannot be forgotten or must be forgotten. Someone might say that maybe I am very good at suppressing the unthinkable, that there must have been traumatic events, maybe I saw my father trying to cut off the dog's head with a butcher's knife . . . Maybe. I don't remember scenes like this, and I don't think I ever witnessed them. My brother probably did.

NORMALCY

WHEN I WAS A CHILD, I THOUGHT THAT I LIVED IN THE ONLY ABNORMAL FAMILY in our neighborhood and everyone knew it. As I grew older, I started to think that my family was "abnormal" in superficial, public ways, not so much because of events—the kind of "sins" my mother cataloged in her hurriedly written notes—but in the overt absence of a man, something had to be explained that could never, in that age, be explained adequately. The only way that the abnormal manifested itself was as a vague mood, a sense that something was not right. I was angry, not about anything definite, just about something.

One of the ways that my family was more normal than most is that I did not have to wade through some myth of the perfect family before I could even begin to find the *what* and *how* and *why* of my past. In the gray light of 1950s sitcoms, my family was overtly different. In this sense, it was maybe more healthy than many of the mom and pop families hidden in the cookie cutter houses around ours, and certainly more safe. Even at a young age, even though my brother hit me, I knew that I was safer than the kids next door. Their father screamed at them for not cleaning up after a family cookout and beat them with a leather belt, hard, with anger, in open view, as the entire neighborhood watched behind partially drawn curtains. I knew that I was safer than the woman and her kids from down the street because their man went on binges. One night, maybe close to 9:00 o'clock, this woman knocked on the window of our family room and asked me to let her in. My mother was at her second job, and my brother was some other place, maybe his room. I was in pajamas and a robe, ready for bed, but I still walked to our back door and opened it. She said that she needed a place to stay until her husband calmed down. Her husband wouldn't hurt the children, she explained, but she knew that he would beat her. I was about ten, alone, and hardly knew what to do, so we watched television and made small talk. After my mother came home, I went to bed, but my mother sat with her for a while and talked. Maybe they even talked about Al-Anon and how alcoholism was a disease. Later, I assume that my mother also went to bed, leaving the woman alone in our family room. When the woman was sure her husband had passed out, she must have left our abnormal home to return to her normal home. Over the years, she often used our abnormal home to escape from her normal home.

Now, I wonder why she chose our home as her sanctuary. She must have known something of our family history. Even if she hadn't heard that my father was a drinker and had left, she could have seen that my family was different, that there was no man in the house, and she could have assumed that alcohol was involved. She must have thought that my mother, of all the neighbors, would understand and would remain silent. The woman's son, who was a little older than I, often picked on me, probably because he, like his mother, knew my family was different. And, after the first fight, he knew that I always led with two jabs, and, if he led with a right cross, then I was an easy mark. I could have told the boy that his father was a drunk and that his mother had to stay at our house because his father beat up women, but I didn't say anything.

So, in some ways, compared to what happened in other houses around us, my family was normal. Boringly so. In my mother's papers, most of the family letters that I found were from about 1971 to 1973. In 1971, my brother was stationed in Thailand during the Vietnam War. In 1972, I started graduate school at the University of South Carolina, my first year away from home. I found letters from my mother to me and letters from me to my mother. I found letters from my brother to my mother. Surprisingly, I even found some letters from me to my brother and from my brother to me. How these letters, both sides of the correspondence, ended up in the same place, I can't say. But I read through them, searching for the big events, expecting to unearth lost memories, tease out family secrets. It was all quite boring. I wrote to my mother about my classes and professors, papers I was writing, troubles with roommates, and films I had seen. Often, I reassured her that I was doing well, that I was happy. My first year in graduate school, I wrote:

> My roommate's going to Richmond this weekend so I think I'll work on a paper. He's been studying more lately so I haven't been having to go to the library as much.

> I don't seem to get bored on weekends anymore. I guess I more or less accepted that things are not going to be much different down here, socially I mean. I know some people in my classes now, not real friends, but they're someone to speak to, now and again.

My brother wrote to my mother about the security at his base, how he was becoming disillusioned with the war, waiting for a promotion, waiting to come home . . . waiting and waiting. In one letter, undated, J.C. reassured my mother that he was safe:

> The whole area is electronically monitored and we would know well in advance if anything were going to happen and if we knew they wouldn't have a chance. All the aircraft on this base are counter guerilla warfare planes, in contrast to big bomber bases, an attack on the base would be suicidal to anybody crazy enough to do it.

My mother wrote to me about people she had seen that week, our weekly phone conversations, and her worries that I was happy. On September 16, 1973, my second year in graduate school, after my brother was out of the Air Force, living at home, and attending Old Dominion, she wrote:

> I'm watching Smothers Brothers on Glen Campbell special. They are so funny—
>> Perry Mason was a disappointment but JC liked it!
>> Still haven't seen any of the Keiths.
>> JC did a movie review for Mace & Crown & if it's published I'll really send you a copy. He got a free ticket. I think name of it was "Walking Tall."
>> Glen Campbell & guy who always plays on his show did "Dueling Banjos." Really good.

It is all mundane. The letters were about a family staying in touch, writing about the minutia of their lives. My mother could not make our family "normal" in a conventional sense, but by this time she had made our lives routine. She had raised her boys, and they had become men.

Shortly after reading the letters, all of them, feeling disappointed that they said so little, I watched the sentencing hearing for the "hockey rage" trial, televised on one of the news networks. Thomas Junta, forty-seven years old, had been found guilty for beating Michael Costin, forty years old, to death after a hockey practice for ten year old boys. Junta thought, ironically, the practice was too rough, so he confronted Costin, who had supervised the practice. A fight broke out, which ended with Junta pounding Costin's head into the concrete floor that surrounded the hockey rink. As I watched the sentencing hearing, I was struck by Costin's four children. They stood in a line, with other relatives, and stepped into the witness box one at a time, to speak before the judge. Each asked that Junta be punished. Each spoke of the father who was their place of stone. Their mother was a heroin addict, so their father raised them by himself. He was their all. They missed him, they said, because he would no longer be there to wake them up in the morning, fix them breakfast, pack their lunches, drive them to the hockey rink, fix them dinner, or help with their

---

homework. One of the boys mentioned how his father often played hockey with him and his friends. He always played with the weaker team so the game would be fair, so everyone would have a good time. None of the children spoke of special events, like going to Disneyland, that might have happened only once. They all spoke of the ordinary, prosaic, repetitive ways that they and their father came together, each day and every day. My mother certainly held our family together in this way. She worked hard to support us, fixed meals, drove us to the movies, and gave us hugs. We had less than many of the kids around us, but we were clean and fed and decently clad. The little things are important.

A Lost Place

As time passed, my mother found a comfortable life with her sons, her many friends, and church. She went back to school and earned an M.S. Ed. in Guidance and Counseling, then she began to work as a junior high school guidance counselor. My sense is that she helped a lot of students during these years. About the time I was in high school, as she was cooking dinner one night, probably one of her special recipes, like Hamburger Chunks and Gravy over Mashed Potatoes (at least, that's what I called it), she told me about visiting a family after school. A boy in her school was in crisis, and she went to his house to talk to the parents. When she knocked on the door, the father answered. He told her, without asking her in, "He's not my son anymore. I don't claim him." My mother couldn't understand it. J.C. and I never caused her any serious problems. If we did, I know that she would have been beside us. She would always have claimed us.

In her papers, I found two legal sheets, which she seemed to have used to do something like journal writing. The two sheets, the two journal entries, were written toward the end of her first year as a counselor. The first passage summarizes her feelings about her new job:

> I've been sitting here tonight—thinking-something I do for too
> little of—of thoughts about my first year as a guidance counselor—
> I've loved it— When someone asks me, "How do you like your

new job?" That's just what I answer "I love it. I can't believe the year is nearly gone. Time just flies by when you enjoy your work so much." Now that wasn't good public relations, was it? What I really should have conveyed was my real feeling, "Today I believe I helped someone—to be happier, to enjoy life more, to try harder to adjust to a situation, to perk up and work more." Hopefully, I did. This is the opportunity I've always wanted—to have the time to really listen to children. They do so need to be listened to.

The second passage, which is unfinished, appears to be a recollection of an episode that happened at the beginning of the year:

> I'd been sitting in my office for perhaps a couple of weeks, changing schedules, handling a few problems and beginning to have a feeling of confidence, when in walked a lovely girl who said, "I'd like to make an appt. to talk with you." We sat together and she couldn't talk and I tried to think.

I assume that she had, in some way, helped this girl. Maybe my mother was planning to write an essay about this experience or maybe she wanted her sons to know their mother had turned out okay, to feel reassurance, joy, that she had eventually found her place as she knew they would eventually find theirs.

I am actually pleased that the last journal entry, if it could be called that, is unfinished. It allows me to use my imagination and fill in the rest of the story with more than one story, with the stories of all the kids she helped—the boy she helped stay in school, the girl who got pregnant, the boy who was being beaten by his father, the kid with glasses who was being picked on . . . In her papers, I found a newspaper clipping about an after school counseling program for troubled kids in middle school, which she had helped to design. Her master's thesis argued that we needed to identify middle school kids in crisis and provide them with counseling.

GEORGE H. JENSEN, JR.

Some of her colleagues counted the days until their retirement. My mother continued to work until she was past seventy. When she finally retired, her school had "Louise Jensen Day," a school wide assembly, and two dinners. I flew in for one; J.C. for the other. She was clearly respected and well loved.

Shortly after she retired, she sold her house and moved into an apartment complex. I spent a week with her sorting through her belongings. It was a struggle because she didn't want to throw anything away. She didn't even want to give her junk to the Salvation Army.

When I pulled an old waffle iron from the attic, one of her wedding gifts that had collected dust for decades, she asked, "Do we really have to get rid of this?"

I argued that it hadn't worked since 1959, it would be too expensive to fix, even if we could find someone old enough to know how to fix something so obsolete, she didn't even like waffles, she always ate cereal for breakfast, the technology of making waffles had changed, etc., etc. I eventually convinced her that the waffle iron needed to be donated to the needy, who probably wouldn't prove needy enough to take it.

And that is how it went. Item after item. For a week. If I teased her long enough, she would relent and allow me to add the prized possession to a pile on her carport. When the Salvation Army came with two men and a large truck, they wouldn't even take half of it. So, I had to haul most of her prized possessions to the city dump.

Even though she had lived a fairly routine life, she was daring in her retirement. She had many friends and rarely stayed home. She went on trips anywhere with anyone. She went to Europe twice, and she drove across the country with the Smiths; on that trip, they all went white water rafting down the Colorado River. She stayed active for a long while.

It was Tom, my cousin, and Sharon, then his wife, who first noticed that something was wrong. They had a daughter and son, and my mother often visited them, especially before she had grandchildren. She loved to watch Kelli and Brian while Tom and Sharon had a night out. Probably in the late 1980s, on one of these visits, she started to have periods of confusion and even hallucinations. The confusion was apparent enough to frighten the kids, who were then about five and eight. After Louise returned home, Sharon called me to share her concerns.

For a while, Judy, my mother's friend from church and a neighbor in her apartment complex, checked on her. On one of my trips to Virginia Beach, I arranged for an agency to send a woman during the day. I also talked to her financial advisor. She already had her entire estate planned. Her will was written, and all of her papers were in a single accordion file so that settling her affairs would be easy for J.C. and me. On the visit, she told me that she had recurring nightmares about men coming into her apartment. The dreams seemed real to her. On Sunday morning, as she was preparing to go to church, her mood changed abruptly and she accused me of trying to take her money. Just as quickly, her mood changed again. She began to cry and said, "I don't know what's happening to my life."

By 1990, her symptoms began to progress. In the spring, she was diagnosed with breast cancer and underwent a mastectomy. I flew in for the operation and stayed for about a week. Then J.C. flew in for a week. I flew out on Saturday morning, and J.C. flew in on Saturday afternoon. I don't remember why we missed each other so closely, but I do remember that she was upset that we did not see each other.

Her operation seemed to accelerate the Alzheimer's. In the summer, Judy put her on a plane in Norfolk so she could fly into Seattle and visit J.C. in Bremerton. J.C. went to the airport, but she wasn't on the plane. The details of what happened over the next few days are fuzzy. I remember J.C. calling me to say that she had missed her flight when she changed planes in Salt Lake City, that he had driven home, a long drive, and had to drive back to the airport later to pick her up. From how J.C. described it to me, it seemed like a small problem. Later, after J.C.'s death, I heard varying accounts of how long she had been missing. Some said five or six hours; others said over a day. All accounts agree that a man in the Salt Lake City airport found her. Judy, her friend, had put cousin Cindy's phone number in her purse, so this stranger called Cindy, who picked her up at the airport in Seattle. Later that day, J.C. drove to Cindy's and took her to his condo. During the visit, she went outside for a walk and became lost. After this, J.C. asked cousin Vicki to watch her during the day, every day, for the rest of the week. Then, he took her to the airport. Her flight home was uneventful.

In the fall, after Donna and I had moved to Missouri, Judy put her on a plane to visit my family. She was lucid most of the time, but she had episodes of real confusion. As when she had visited J.C., she left our house for a walk and became lost. During the trip, Donna and I realized that she needed more care. We decided to keep her in Missouri and move her into an assisted care apartment. The facility checked on residents several times a day and also provided meals and activities, but she had trouble finding the dining room. Donna bought several packages of gold stars and made a trail from her apartment to the dining room, but even this didn't help. The supervisor soon advised us to move her into the Alzheimer's wing.

I am grateful to Donna for handing most of the details. It was a big step, one that I was not ready to accept. Once my mother was transferred, however, she seemed relieved. When she entered the facility, the residents were having a sing-a-long, and she joined right in.

About a year after she moved near us, I began to worry about losing her. With Alzheimer's it is not death that parts loved ones, but the loss of memories. I could not have long talks with her anymore, so I began to feel that the relationship was dead even though my mother lived on. I knew that soon I would be a stranger. About this time I dreamt that I was in the front yard, digging a hole to plant an evergreen. My mother was inside the house watching the first Gulf War on CNN. She came to the door and said, "Come inside and watch." The dream wasn't about planting a tree. It was about digging my mother's grave. I had convinced myself she was already gone. The war was a symbol for the difficult times we were having, and the difficult times ahead of us. But my mother, in the dream, asked me to join her. She was saying we still had time together.

133

I discussed the dream with Donna, and we as a family decided to make the most of her last years. One of us went to see her every day, and she was able to spend a lot of time with her grandchildren. Jeff often talks about the time, when he was three or four years old, he ran to give grandma a hug and accidentally knocked her down. I would bring her ice cream or donuts, or we would all take her out to lunch. Donna even occasionally took her fishing. They would sit on a dock, sipping beer and talking, lines in the water. On one trip, my mother caught a huge flathead catfish, in the range of twenty-four inches. She was quite proud of it and made Donna pack it in a cooler so all her nurses could see it.

If I missed visiting her for even one day, she was nearly frantic, pacing up and down the hallways as if she were going somewhere, looking for me and wringing her hands. She was, she would say, worried about me, or she thought that I had abandoned her. When Donna went to visit, she sometimes said that I had just been there with my girlfriend. Donna would play along and ask questions about the imaginary girlfriend.

Toward the end, she had trouble eating and taking in fluids. She often became dehydrated, so the nurses would ask me if it was okay to give her fluids. Then, she rallied for a while. One day, the head nurse called me and said that she thought it was time to "let nature take its course." We talked, and I decided to stop the IV fluids. By this time, I was attending a number of open AA meetings. Later that day, I went to a meeting. The topic was "delaying decisions." As one person after another spoke about the importance of putting off decisions, I sat there, silent, hardly listening, thinking to myself, "I have just made one of the most important decisions of my life, and I have to come here and listen to this?" When it was my turn to speak, I introduced myself, as I customarily did to let everyone know I was a visitor, an outsider: "I'm George. I'm a friend of Ted's. I pass." But as my friends continued to speak, I started to realize that I hadn't made this decision quickly, that I had done everything that I could for my mother. Now, it was time to let go. Then the voices in the room became muted, muffled, as if distant, and the colors in the room turned pale and yellow, and I was at peace—centered and calm. People in twelve-step programs say that you will hear what you need to hear at meetings. At this meeting, I heard just the right message. I heard that I had waited long enough, that I had made the right decision. She died on February 19, 1994.

Shortly before she entered the nursing home, I published a composition textbook, which was dedicated to my mother. I wanted my students to know about her. Here is the dedication page:

> During the Great Depression, her mother and father made sacrifices to send her and her sister to college. Her family did not eat well and she had to borrow textbooks from her classmates, but she finished her degree. She then raised two sons by herself on her teacher's salary, working two jobs, earning a master's in education counseling, and making sacrifices to send the next generation of her family to college. In her last years as a counselor in junior high school, she saved money to send grandchildren to college. This textbook is part of her legacy.

135

When she read this, she said it wasn't true, but I could tell that she was pleased. I signed a copy of the page and framed it next to the proof of the textbook cover, then hung it on her wall in the nursing home. Her nurses and guests of her roommate often commented on it. Now, it hangs in my office. To this day, the dedication is the story that I tell my sons about their grandmother.

In 2002, I visited Virginia Beach for the first time in about eight years. I flew in to attend the funeral of Skip's mother. Back when we were surfing buddies, Skip's entire family adopted me; his siblings still introduce me as their brother. In college, after most of my friends from Princess Anne High School had flunked out of Old Dominion University and drifted away, I often spent time at Skip's house on Tyson Road, one street over and two blocks up from my childhood home. I drank a few beers with his father, mother, his sisters and brother, even if Skip was elsewhere. And now both Skip's parents and his sister Margie are gone.

On the day before the funeral, when I had some spare time, I drove by the house where I grew up, my father's quarter acre of America, the place where my mother kept us sheltered and fed. When the weather was bad, she often looked out of the picture window in our living room and said, "It's so good that we have a house where we can be warm and dry." She was speaking of the place that she created for J.C. and me. This was no small accomplishment.

The house seems smaller all the time. And now it is run down, missing shingles, screens hanging from windows, grass uncut, trash in the yard. All who were our neighbors have died or moved to nicer houses. This is not a street that will go through a period of deterioration followed by gentrification. The houses will not be bought up by young professionals and renovated. They are too small, too poorly constructed.

My mother's other place was Appalachia, and it has been some three decades since I walked through the town. Last summer, I was close. Jay, my older son, and I decided to go camping and fishing in the Smokies, which straddle the border of Tennessee and North Carolina, not far from the western end of Virginia. Before we camped, we spent the night in Kingsport, Tennessee. Cousin Doris drove from Appalachia to have dinner with us. I had not seen her for about twenty years, and she had never met Jay. I suggested that Jay and I might drive through Appalachia the next morning, but Doris said the town had changed. The coal mines had shut down, many houses were abandoned, and few businesses survived. The community of my mother's childhood had long passed. Uncle Billy had closed his hardware store in the 1980s. He had too many customers who bought tools or washing machines, said "charge it," and then disappeared. They didn't return on payday, cash in hand, to pay their bills.

I could sense that Doris felt bad about not inviting us to her house. After her mother died, she began collecting cats and dogs. She had, she said during dinner, thirty-three of them, and she also fed some stray animals that lived along the highway. I told her that I was allergic to cats, and she seemed relieved. After dinner, we said goodbye to Doris. In the morning, Jay and I headed toward the Smokies. My mother is gone, and her places have changed beyond recognition. Even Doris is gone. A few years after we had dinner with her, she was feeding a stray dog along side of the highway. She got in her car and began to make a U-turn to go home. She was hit by a truck and died instantly.

137

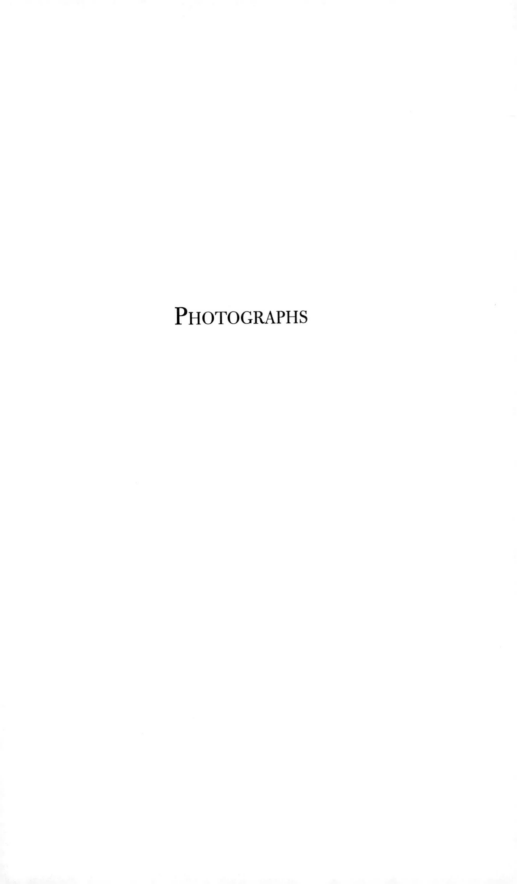

PHOTOGRAPHS

*My father and mother
early in their marriage.*

FOURTEENTH NAVAL DISTRICT
OFFICE OF COMMANDANT
Pearl Harbor, T. H.
Navy Number 128 (one two eight)
c/o Fleet Post Office
San Francisco, California

Firday -

Hi Darling -

Just got the good news that you are pratically on your
way.. believe me I need you and am so happy that everything
is pau or just about.

By now you no doubt have the dope on the furniture and
everything. I misssed yesterday - conference day and I was
really bushed at the end of the day which ended about 8p.m.
I went up to my room had a shower and just kinda laid down for
a few moments and woke up this morning at 830. Boy what a sleep.

I'm so damn excited this will probably sound very confusing.
But Baby I have waited so long for you and longed for you so
much - every day - that when I did get that word that you are on
the way I'll just be jumping from now on. Don't worry about
my time. Your little trundle bed will be made up and all ready
for you. I'm going to take thaday off and just baby you from
then on.

I broke a headline story today. Some civilian tugboat
captain on his way from Manzanillo Mexico to the philpinnes
lost his tow or dropped it rathwr to go into Palmyra Island to
re-fuel when he came back to pick up the tow she wasn't there.
(that last is done in mexican) Anyway he has been lookng for it
since 24 sept and no find. Finally he calls on the navy -m
victor in war and guardian in peace (Navy day) soooo we send out
planes to help find the little lost lambs. Three men aboard with
ten days food and water. I checked the pilot charts and thare
are two currents which give up to a 60 mile a day drift. One
is the equatorial current which goes west and the one above is
the counter equatorial current which goes east. Complicated
but good news as long as it isn'tna navy tug.

This will be short honey - I'm too excited to say anything
sensible and boy are you going to be met with full honors.
Photogs - pix in the papers - Maybe even Barbara Murray . I hope not.
But don't worry about the ship - she is a luxry liner and about the
best of the bunch that areon the run.... You will be very comfortabl
R.T. is thinking of the USS Randall - This is the General Randall.
You will be here on 20 Oct...... Bye now,

Love and Kisses,

George

My father wrote this letter to my mother when she and
J.C., barely-born, were about to join him in Hawaii.

COMMONWEALTH OF VIRGINIA

MACK I. SHANHOLTZ, M. D.
COMMISSIONER

DEPARTMENT OF HEALTH
RICHMOND 19

Division of Alcohol Studies and Rehabilitation
Box 174 - Medical College of Virginia Hospital
Richmond 19, Virginia

June 26, 1957

Mrs. George H. Jensen
1000 Cunningham Road
Norfolk, Virginia

Dear Mrs. Jensen:

Thank you for your letter of June 19, 1957, in regard to your husband's account with this Division. Mr. Jensen's account has been carefully checked and the correct amount due is $63.00. An itemized statement of account is listed below:

1/5/57 Hospitalization to 1/11/57	$102.00
Drugs ("Antabuse") on discharge	1.00
Psychological Tests during hospitalization	+20.00
Total Charges - - - - -	$123.00

Jan. 11, 1957 - On account	$50.00	
Feb. 19, 1957 "	+10.00	
Total Payments - - - -	$60.00	
Remainder on account -		-60.00
		$ 63.00

We have noted on our collection calendar that payment will be made on Mr. Jensen's account on July 1, 1957. We trust that we will hear from you by that date.

Yours very truly,

Roland G. Blandford
Accounts Supervisor

els

7/5/57 - 10⁰⁰ check

53

My mother told me that my dad sobered up for six months.
She never mentioned that he went into rehab.

During World War II, my mother (in the middle) served
in the Red Cross. It was a slower time.

My mother and her boys,
probably shortly
after we moved to
Virginia Beach.

When my mother looked at this picture, she said, "This is the man I should have married." I don't know his name or how his life turned out, but it looks like he had a great golf swing.

One of the many classes my mother taught in her long career.

I've been sitting here tonight - thinking - something I do far too little of - of some of the thoughts about my just year as a guidance counselor - I've loved it - When someone asks me, "How do you like your new job?" That is just what I answer "I love it". I can't believe the year is nearly gone. Time just flys by when you enjoy your work so much." Now that wasn't good public relations, was it? What I really should have conveyed was my real feeling. "Today I believe I helped someone - to be happier, to enjoy life more, to try harder to adjust to a situation, to perk up and work more, Hopefully, I did. This is the opportunity I've always wanted - to have the time to really listen to children. They do so need to be listened to.

Toward the end of her career, my mother reflected on her work as a counselor.

*My father
and me on the
parade field
of Ft. Slocum.
This is the time
and place of my
first memory.*

*My father and his sons.
J.C. is the dapper lad with
a bowtie and hat. I am
wearing a sailor suit.*

This is me at about age five. I think we were living in a trailer in Florida while my father was on a cruise.

I often forget that my brother, my whole family, had many moments of pure joy.

J.C. and me dressed as pirates for Halloween.

J.C. and me after a good day of fishing.

This must have been our last Christmas in naval housing, shortly before we moved to our first house in Virginia Beach.

My brother and I pretend to be cowboys in front of naval housing in Norfolk, Virginia.

We dressed up for a family portrait and could not get one good shot.

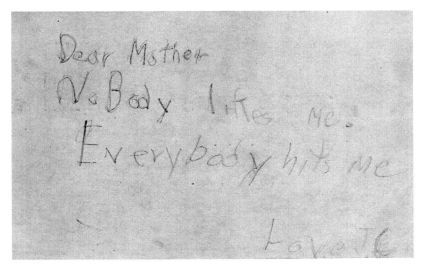

My brother wrote this postcard from camp, probably when he was about eight years old. He later had some of his best times camping when he was in the Boy Scouts.

Childhood Traumas — Book 1

Whenever my mother was late getting home, I used to sit in the living room waiting, not knowing if she would come home or if the police would come to tell us she had been killed in an auto accident. I guess it was the uncertainty of what was beyond that tempted me. I always figured that Aunt Betty Sue would take George and that he would eventually fit in with their family. I knew she wouldn't take me and I assumed that after the funeral the police would take me off somewhere. I don't think I really had a vision of where they would take me, I guess some vague vision of some type of Boys Town was in the back of my mind.

A page from the journal my brother began and never finished.

Bremerton Wash
17 April

Dear Jc & Georgie,

Daddy meant to write to you sooner
but he was in the hospital for a few
days. he had a real bad cold and now
I'm much better but pretty weak -

I'm staying with Grandma Jensen
for a few days. I don't know what I'll
do then - maybe go down to California
and try and get a ship. There is no
work here at all - your uncle Frosty
has not been able to sell any timber
for about three months and he
is looking for work -

I put in for a rigging job in
adak alaska but won't hear anything
for a week or so. I also put in
for a job with MStg but that is
not certain either. I hope to hear
something from them next week -

Grandma Jensen is going to send
you guys each a real buffalo horn
soon. Your Grandad bought them
from an indian years ago in
colorado and she has kept them all
this time. she will tell you all about
it when she sends them and you can
take them to school and show them
to you classes.

I don't know when daddy will
be back to see you but you can
believe he loves you very much and
your mother too - I miss you so much
but things may work out sometime

and we can be Together again.

I want you guys to do everything you can to help your mother and be very good to her - you are lucky you have such a wonderful mommy - don't forget that.

Ask your mother to send me Mr. Farris address as I want to write to him. And tell her to read a couple of articles in the Saturday Evening Post that came out the past several weeks.

Billy & Vicki are fine, Billy is still making models - he sent a drawing in to a TV station and won a model as a prize - boy was he excited. It was a drawing of a rocket ship - they give models of airplanes & ships as prizes -

I can't think of any more to say but I want to hear from you, what you are doing and what grades you get in school and how mommy is - will you write to me? Please try because I do miss you all so much.

all the love in the world
Daddy—

*J.C. and I grew up believing that our father
abandoned us without much regret.*

Sunday -

Dear JC & Georgie

Daddy has been so busy
looking for work he just
hasn't written you as much
as he would like to -

I'm sending you guys a
pack. e tomorrow - it has two
real buffalo horns in it that
your Grand-dad Jensen got
from a Sioux Indian many
years ago - this was back in
Nebraska. Also there is a
spoon which was one of
your great grand father wedding
gift that is over 100 years old -
I thot you might like to keep
it as a souvenir. And there
are some agates and a stone
that grandma Jensens daddy
found - oh yes and a cigarette
holder that was your great
grand fathers.

JC. - Grandma Jensen is
going to send you a watch

2

that was grandpa Jensen for
many years - I think she is
going to send it for your birthday
It is a pocket watch and
you will have to be very
careful with it. Maybe some
day you can give it to
your son -

the agates are some that
daddy picked up on the
beach when he was a boy
There are lots of them out here -

I guess daddy will go down
to California next week to
look for work - there is not
any jobs here - and Los Angeles
seems to be better -

I sure miss you guys - I hope
I can get back and see you
soon - I'll write you when
I get to Calif. Be good and
help your mother all you can -
                  lots of love
                  Daddy

Another letter from my father sent shortly after he left our family.

My father as sketched by a fellow seaman.

Pearl Harbor, December 7, 1941.

Once the Dewey *was underway, her crew would have sailed past the devastation on Battleship Row.*

Ships move off into Pacific.

WH CHIEF QUARTERS GANG
U.S.S DEWEY DD349

THIS IS TAKEN ON BOARD THE U.S.S. DEWEY
DD349 SOMETIME IN 1944.

FRONT ROW, LEFT TO RIGHT:
1. Jensen - Yeoman
2. Morella - Boilermaker
3. Kassel - Mach. Mate
4. Hill - Mach. Mate
5. Strong - Quartermaster
6. Osborne - Gunner' Mate
7. Fenno - Commissary
8. Bob Burdette - Store Keeper
9. Ross - Electrican
10. Yorden - Shipfitter
11. Tomlinson - Water Tender

Stephen Yorden sent me this photo of the chief crew on the Dewey. I keep this on the wall of my office.

Name **JENSEN, Geroge Henry**
(Name in full, surname to the left.)
No. **393 06 53** Rate **Y.1c** (A. A. / P. A.)

Date reported **1 September 1941**

Ship or Station **USS DEWEY**

From **SHQ 13th Naval District**

6 FEB 1942

Crossed the Equator. Lat.

Long. **169** ...

J. P. Canty
Lieutenant, U.S. Navy,

Served creditably in the following engagements:

12-7-41: Pearl Harbor.
2-20-42: Bougainville.
3-10-42: Salamoa.
5-8-42 : Coral Sea.
6-4-42 : Midway Island.
8-7-42 : Occupation of
Guadalcanal-Tulagi.

J. P. Canty
J. P. CANTY,
Lieutenant Commander, U.S.N.
Executive Officer.

Date transferred _____

To _____

Signature and rank of Commanding Officer.

Date received _____

Ship or Station

From

Signature and rank of Commanding Officer. 4—6111

Battles seen December 1941–August 1942.

Name JENSEN, George Henry
(Name in Full, Surname to the Left)

393 06 53   Rate CY(PA)
(Service No.)

Date Reported Aboard: 1 Sept. 1941

U.S.S. DEWEY (349)
(Present Ship or Station)

SHQ, 13 Naval District.
(Ship or Station Received From)

Served creditably in the following engagements:

8/9/42:   Defense of Guadalcanal.
8/23/42:   Battle of Eastern Solomns.
Aleutian Campaign. 1/1/43 to 9/4/43.
1/11/43:   Occupation of Amchitka.
5/11/43:   Occupation of Attu.
8/16/43:   Occupation of Gilbert Is.
           (Makin)
1/31/44:   Occupation of Kwajalein
           (Marshall Is.)
2/17/44 : Occupation of Eniwetok
           Atoll (Marshall Is.)
3/8/44:   Shore bombardment Milli Is.
3/30/44:   Attack on Palau, Yap, &
           Woleai Is.

Date Transferred 8 April 1944

To Com Nearest NavDist. West Coast.

F. W. BAMPTON, Lieut., U.S.N.
Signature and Rank of Commanding Officer.

Date Received Aboard:

(New Ship or Station)

(Last Ship or Station)

Signature and Rank of Commanding Officer.

ORIGINAL
FOR SERVICE RECORD

Battles seen August 1942–March 1944.

*Toward the end of his career in the navy, after World War II
had ended, my father worked as a journalist.
Through photos like this, I learned that my father must have
been a pretty funny guy.*

This photo of my father was probably taken toward the end of the war.

My father when he retired from the navy.

*My father's correspondent identification card,
issued toward the end of his career in the Navy.*

*My father's U.S. Merchant Mariner's ID, taken about twenty years
later. The look on his face haunts me.*

Donna reading to Jay and Jeffrey.

Relaxing with my boys before bedtime.

Jay and Jeffrey during a family trip to Florida.

The entire family during a school event.

An Only Child's Brother

CHILDHOOD STRATEGIES

I WAS AN ONLY CHILD WHO HAPPENED TO HAVE A BROTHER. A STRANGE statement, perhaps. But only to people who have not grown up in alcoholic families where children feel more stress and siblings develop strategies to make themselves feel more secure. If the siblings develop their strategies together, they can become like warriors who survived a firestorm by covering each other's back. If not, their strategies may work against each other, without them even realizing it. My brother and I developed our strategies in isolation.

One of my childhood strategies for survival was to hate my brother. Through childhood and adolescence, I defined myself as *not my brother*. In my eyes, he was mean, obsessed with food, a slob, inconsiderate, and crude. I was none of this. At least, that is what I told myself. I was able to convince myself that I was the "good kid."

Soon after our father left, when my brother was only ten, I felt like he ruled the entire house with his anger. His mood was inescapable. He often hit me, usually when our mother was working her night job, grading papers in the other room, or visiting a neighbor. If we passed in the hallway, he might punch me in the arm, or he might not. I always flinched. If I wanted to have my turn watching a television show, he was known to hit me and then turn the dial back to his show. Once, when I was in bed, my arms under the covers, he jumped on top of me, hit me two or three times, and then left. His rage surfaced quickly, without warning. And, just as quickly, it was over. Then, he acted as if nothing had happened, while my anger simmered for weeks.

As much as I could, I tried to avoid J.C., but it was hard to avoid my brother in such a small house. For a long time, I even had to wear his hand-me-downs, so I felt that he was around me, covering my skin, as if I were living in his world. And, since he was always larger, this meant that my clothes—his clothes, his world—didn't fit me. In one of the most vivid memories of childhood, I am about five years old, walking through the streets of Norfolk, trailing behind my father and brother, holding mom's hand with my left hand, pulling up my underwear—really my brother's underwear—with my right hand. The underwear slipped down, then I pulled it up, then it slipped down, and again I pulled it up. I was miserable.

When J.C. and I watched television together, we rarely spoke. He would drink sodas from glass bottles and then bend over and roll them under the couch. His room was cluttered with ice cream dishes, cereal bowls, and candy wrappers. At the dinner table, he ate fast, chomping away with his mouth open. I glanced at him occasionally, in disgust, wondering why Mom never told him to close his mouth while he chewed. (I am using "Mom" here instead of "my mother" or "Louise" because I don't think that J.C. ever started to call our mother "Louise," as I did, and when we spoke of her, we always said "Mom," as if we were both still boys.) After J.C. had his driver's license, he would come down to dinner, sit down, and look at what Mom had cooked. If he didn't like it, he would get up and drive himself to McDonald's, without saying a word. I don't ever remember Mom or me commenting on his departure. We just ate, as if this were a normal part of family life. We never said, "This is not like dinner time at the Cleavers' house."

This was the simple story that I constructed about my brother. At some point, I grew out of it. Not dramatically, as when I read my father's letters and saw a different man behind the role of father or the behavior of a drinker. But slowly, as we gained some distance from each other, as we both found our place in the world. As time passed, I learned to be proud of him. I talked about him to my friends. But we rarely talked about our relationship, what had happened between us during childhood and how we felt now. I assumed that he knew my attitudes had changed with my behaviors, but I know now that he believed our family was frozen in time. Now, I know that I should have said that *my* childhood embarrassment was part of being an insecure kid in a ruptured family. It was one of my ways of coping. I should have said I was sorry that my strategy hurt him and separated us. Maybe then he would have talked about his strategies.

When we were younger, an honest talk would have been difficult, especially since our private strategies worked against the other's benefits. In 1962, the year we celebrated Christmas with the Youngs in Appalachia, J.C. and I shared a double bed in the guest room. One night I woke up. J.C. was rubbing something on the wall.

I asked, "What are you doing?"

"Shut up," he said.

I went back to sleep. The next day, he asked if we could switch sides of the bed. Like a stupid, naive, younger brother, I said, "Okay." Another day passed before cousin Doris, who was already grown, found the dried snot on the wall.

"Who slept on this side?" she asked.

"George," J.C. said. Doris gave me a long lecture. Occasionally, I interrupted to say, "I didn't do it." I could hardly sound convincing.

About the same time, J.C. went through a phase of carving my name on the window sills around the house. Of course, Mom, when she was dusting, found my name memorialized in the woodwork. She asked me about it, and I told her I didn't do it. I think that she knew, somehow, that it was J.C.'s work, even before she talked to me. So, this time, I didn't get in trouble.

When I was still in my childhood underwater daze, these events puzzled me. I couldn't understand why J.C. would want to implicate me. At the time, I saw only how my brother harmed me. I never thought about his pain or how I might have added to it. Later, after his death, after much reflection, I began to realize how much he resented me and how much I deserved it. He seemed to believe that our house only had a limited amount of love. If I were the favorite, as he believed, then he would receive less love. If I were in trouble, then he would receive more. This was his part in our separation. My part was I reveled in being the golden child.

Food, I would guess, was one of my brother's strategies. He ate to dull the pain, but eating might also have been a means of protecting himself from rejection. As long as he was overweight, he could tell himself that others rejected him because they could only see how he looked. They didn't know the real person inside. This is just my conjecture. We never spoke about his weight, even though it was always a part of our family dynamics.

Mom worried about his weight obsessively. She constantly talked to him about dieting. She hid cookies from him, under dish towels in a drawer or behind pots and pans, but she told me about the hiding places. Maybe, she also worried that I was too skinny and, therefore, needed to eat cookies. When I was about ten, when J.C. was about thirteen, he saw me pulling cookies from a hiding place. Maybe, I even intentionally pulled the cookies out in front of him, so he could see that I knew where the cookies were hidden, so that he would know he was different. I wouldn't be surprised if I had a smirk on my face. He burst into anger and hit me several times. He yelled, "Why didn't you tell me we had cookies?" Even after J.C. was an adult, Mom apologized to others about his weight, or forewarned people who had not yet met him that he was "heavy."

She apparently felt it was her fault. After I was a teenager, maybe already in college, she told me that she didn't have enough milk to breastfeed J.C. He often cried from hunger and she couldn't console him. Once she switched to a bottle, she said that he ate ravenously. This was why, she believed, he ate so much. Her guilt probably exacerbated her concern about his weight.

I am not so sure that the events that separated my brother and me, when described as factual incidents, were unusual. Many siblings feel that one of them is the favorite. Many fight. Many are embarrassed to be seen with their brother or sister. And many feel that they were scarred by their childhood. From reading decades of freshman essays, I know that everyone carries pain from childhood, and the pain, no matter how slight or horrific, bears its own density. One student writes about being raped, and another writes about a rude gym teacher. They both feel scarred. It is senseless to tell someone that his or her pain doesn't amount to much. I also know that there are traumatic events—being diagnosed with cancer, a father having a heart attack, a mother dying in a car wreck, a grandmother's passing—that can bring families together, and there are seemingly more benign events—tension, perceptions, looks, words—that can make us feel like our pain is our own and that our childhood is unique and tragic. Because our father was an alcoholic, because he abandoned us, because our parents were separated in the age of perfect families, every problem seemed to gain its own momentum. The bad seemed larger than life, the good was too often overlooked.

When I was about ten or eleven, my family attended a cookout at the Smiths' house. The kids and a few of the adults were playing volleyball in the backyard. I did something, I don't remember what, to anger J.C., and he began to yell at me. He hit me on the arm and pushed me. This was a rare event because he rarely hit me in front of other people, even our mother, maybe especially our mother. A neighbor, a muscular young Marine who hoped to become a professional wrestler one day, a guy I considered to be a total idiot, a little boy in a big body pretending to be a man, pushed J.C. and yelled, "Lay off." J.C., who was only thirteen or fourteen, began to cry. He ran home and did not return. But I stayed. Not because I was having a good time, more because I was afraid. I certainly wasn't going home without Mom. I must have been moping because Karen Smith, who was a little older, asked me, "What's wrong?" I didn't know. I honestly didn't know. Then, Rebecca Smith, who was J.C.'s age, answered for me, "J.C.'s his brother." I was, in some ways, pleased that the Marine, the grown man who believed professional wrestling was real, had protected me. This was the only time that anyone told J.C. to stop hitting me. But I was also upset. I didn't like seeing my brother hurt. He was my brother, always. We held an unspoken world between us. I never said, "I'm sorry he embarrassed you." Not then. Not ever.

SOME OF THE WORDS ARE THEIRS

I don't think that I needed to interpret the event for J.C. He probably understood that the Marine was being a bully in his own way, that the situation could have been handled better, that maybe Mom should have stepped in, and that the Marine was a father figure. J.C. could have come to these insights on his own. But I could have helped him by giving him an opening to talk or by just letting him know that I felt bad about how he was treated. He probably thought that I enjoyed his embarrassment.

Certainly, our strategies for survival were at odds, but my brother and I were also very different. I was a naturally quiet kid who felt stigmatized by the absence of our father and so withdrew deeper into my own world. Even though I had a few friends, I spent much of my time sketching blueprints of houses with a drafting board, T square, and triangle that my father left behind. The designs fed elaborate fantasies about a normal family. My brother seemed to need friends more than I, but he often felt rejected, and I suspect, he was often teased about his weight. When he was in the eighth grade, he was an unpopular kid who had the guts to run for class president. He lost. I remember him taking other kinds of risks. When he was only about thirteen or so, he would walk about a mile to the highway and ride a bus into Norfolk to see a film, go to the Boys' Club, or study judo. I never had the courage to explore the world in this way. Yet, J.C. also spent much of his time in his room, sitting in his chair, reading bestsellers about hunting down Nazis, playing solitaire, listening to an odd assortment of music, sometimes The Beatles, but also Earl Scruggs, Tom Jones, Steve Lawrence and Eydie Gormé, and The Glenn Miller Orchestra. He usually had a bottle of aspirin beside him. He seemed to take a lot of aspirin. We were often in our house, in different rooms. For him, even though he enjoyed social situations more than I did, being alone was probably peaceful. Or uncomplicated. Without pain.

Even though I tend to forget it, J.C. and I did spend some time together and we did, on occasions, enjoy each other's company. He could be unusual in rather delightful ways. When I was about fifteen and he was about eighteen, we were out for a ride in Mom's VW Bug. J.C. was driving, and a middle-aged woman was tailgating us. J.C.

said, "Watch this." He slammed on the brakes. As the woman was about to hit us from behind, just as she was screaming "Oh, my Lord," throwing every pound of her weight onto her brake pedal, locking up her brakes, sliding, tires squealing, J.C. downshifted and floored it. When the woman recovered, she sped up and passed us. Her face was red and tight. She looked over at J.C. as if she wanted to kill him. He looked at her and smiled, his face speaking nothing but silly innocence, and shrugged his shoulders as if to say, "Gee, lady, I'm sorry. I thought I saw a squirrel crossing the road." Then, after the lady was well down the road, a smug smile grew on his face and stayed there for a long time. This is one of my favorite stories about him. I have told it to my sons so many times that they say, "Yeah, Dad, we know. He slammed on the brakes, then down-shifted and floored it. The lady got pissed. We know." I guess I want them to know that their uncle was funny and interesting, eccentric in a way that they might have enjoyed. In quiet moments, they tell me that they wish they had known him.

DIFFERENT PATHS

ONCE J.C. AND I WERE ADULTS, OUR PATHS RARELY CROSSED. HE WENT TO Old Dominion College (it was not yet a university) for two years, from fall 1965 through spring 1967, until the president of the growing college sent him a "Dear John" letter. Like a number of his friends, he had spent too much time in the billiards room at the student union, which the students called the "Vietnam Room." After this first try at college, J.C. worked at Pep Boys Auto Center for a few months, drove a truck delivering magazines, and then joined the Air Force. In 1968, the year I began college, just one year before the height of anti-Vietnam protests, the Air Force developed a program that enlisted overweight men and placed them in a longer boot camp, which included an extended regimen of diet and exercise. For most of the time that I was living at home and commuting to Old Dominion, J.C. was stationed in Las Vegas or Thailand. When he left the service, he lived at home and finished his degree at Old Dominion, which was by then a university. After his return, I was at home for just two months before heading to South Carolina for graduate school, just long enough to realize that the war had changed him, long enough to watch him paint the walls and ceiling of his room a dark blue, almost black, and the woodwork a glossy red enamel, long enough to watch him install a black light, hang psychedelic posters, and start a collection of heavy metal albums.

Almost as if I were already an old fart, I thought his new identity was silly and out of synch. For me the 1960s were already over: They ended when a friend of mine, who was addicted to heroin, killed himself by sitting in his idling car with the car windows open and the garage door closed. But for J.C., the 1960s were just beginning, in a desperate way, as if he were attempting to grasp a short window of opportunity. By the time I returned for Christmas, J.C. had already realized there was no magic in his redecorated room; he seemed to realize the black light and the psychedelic posters wouldn't give him back the years he had spent in the Air Force. He seemed to accept that he had totally missed the 1960s, so he settled down and studied hard. When he graduated with honors in 1974, he found a job in the civil service as a safety manager at one of the local navy bases. It was his job to make sure that OSHA safety standards were followed and that the work environment was safe. About every six months, the base had to pass a meticulous evaluation from a team of inspectors, and his performance was on the line. His job could be difficult and stressful, but he apparently did well. After about two years, he was transferred to Bremerton, Washington, near our father's relatives. We were never geographically close again.

In summer 1980, three years after I finished my PhD, the first year I worked in Chicago, Mom and I both visited J.C. in Bremerton. I'm sure he made an attempt to clean up his one-bedroom condo, but it was still grungy, and he had a table saw in his dining room. When I asked him why he bought the saw, he said, as if the question were absurd, "To cut boards."

"Don't you need a place to eat?" I asked.

"I eat in the living room. You can also lower the blade on the saw and eat there. It is a *table* saw, you know." If I had to guess, I would say that he probably cut wood on the saw two or three times. Then it just sat there. In the dining room. Covered by a waterproof tarp. Just in case it rained, I guess.

We all enjoyed the trip. I finally met Cousin Vicki, who was my age. As I was growing up, I had heard Vicki's name and seen a picture of her sitting at a piano, but that was about it. Throughout my childhood, she had been my mysterious cousin, one close to my age, who lived about as far away as she could and still be an American. We hit it off immediately. I had always wanted a sister, and, once I met Vicki, I felt like I had one. She even seemed to draw J.C. and me a bit closer. One afternoon, Vicki came over to J.C.'s condo with Shannon, her new baby. As Shannon took a nap, Vicki began to talk about her alcoholic father, our father's brother, and I began to talk about our alcoholic father. J.C. talked, also. He said a little about our father yelling and how he always felt he had to walk on egg shells. Mom just listened.

I hadn't seen Uncle Rusty, Aunt Jean, Cindy and Sharon for about twenty years, so it was like meeting them for the first time again. When J.C. and I were growing up, Cindy was always good about sending us gifts from Alaska, where her husband was working as a bush pilot. She also sent some pictures of Uncle Rusty, who worked for several decades as a logger in Alaska. In one picture, he was walking across logs that were jammed together in a river. I always believed that Uncle Rusty was larger than life, a Paul Bunyan type. I loved to tell my friends about him, even though I didn't have much more to say than, "My uncle's a logger in Alaska. He walks across the logs in the river and breaks up the log jams." When I first saw him on this trip, I realized that he was only about 5' 7", so, when we were both standing, I looked down on him. It was a shock to me because I had always thought he must be a huge man. During the trip, I kept staring at him because he looked so much like the pictures of my father. It almost felt like I was sitting with my father, talking to him. Rusty liked to talk about the Old Country, meaning Denmark, as if the Jensen family's embarking for American in the 1880s had happened when he was a kid, and the pioneers, the families who settled Vaughn, Washington, as if they came across the Oregon Trail a few years ago.

In addition to visiting all the Jensens, the three of us—Mom, J.C., and I—visited the Fish Market in Seattle, drove around the Olympic Peninsula, and took a ferry to Vancouver. I remember J.C. and me fighting only once, and that lasted only a few minutes. When it was over, Mom clapped her hands, almost like a little girl about to be fed ice cream, and said, "Oh good, everyone is getting along again." She

---

GEORGE H. JENSEN, JR.

probably wanted, more than anything, for J.C. and me to be friends. I certainly want that for my sons.

During down times in J.C.'s apartment, we watched television. J.C. liked the Weather Channel. At the time, I thought it was strange. If I'm going on a trip, I might watch the Weather Channel for about five or ten minutes. J.C. watched it regularly, sometimes for hours. I sat there, silent, perplexed, bored. Excruciatingly bored. Later, much later, I realized that it was his way of staying in touch with friends. As he watched the weather patterns move across the country, he thought about friends who might be caught in snowstorms or hailstorms, floods or tornadoes, droughts or heat waves. Whenever I talked to him on the phone, he always said something like, "I guess it's been pretty hot there."

When I was still living in Chicago and still single, J.C. flew through and had a three-hour layover. (He tended to plan visits with friends and family around layovers to or from conferences. This way the government paid for the plane ticket.) I met him at the airport for coffee, and we talked a bit about our father and our childhoods. I don't remember what we said, but I was surprised that he even brought up the topic of our father.

Shortly after this visit, I started having heart palpitations. After some tests, I was diagnosed with mitral valve prolapse, which is not a dangerous condition for most people. I was warned, however, that I should take antibiotics before having dental work or surgery. Mom had already been diagnosed with the same condition, so I called J.C. and said that, if he had palpitations, he might see a cardiologist. It is hard to read a person's reaction over the phone, but J.C. seemed to freeze up. I had the sense that he didn't want to discuss health issues. Not Mom's. Not mine. And certainly not his.

In 1983, my life began to change. In short order, I moved to Atlanta, met Donna, and asked her to marry me. When we began to plan our wedding, I asked J.C. to be one of my ushers. At Mom's suggestion. It should have occurred to me that the groom always asks his brother to be an usher, often best man, but it didn't. Maybe this was part of my distorted world view, but I thought that it was normal for brothers to be just brothers, not friends.

J.C. initially seemed pleased and said he would come. Then he called me later and backed out. He had an excuse ready: He would rather spend the money it would take to fly to Atlanta to buy us "a really nice present." Mom thought that he was embarrassed about his weight. I wondered if my marriage raised issues: Why wasn't the older brother already married? Why didn't he have a family? One of J.C.'s close friends, who understood how he used cynicism to protect himself, later told me that he might have thought, "They'll probably end up divorced in a year. I'd rather spend the money on a vacation."

Donna and I were married on December 2, 1984. J.C. sent us a nice espresso machine, and I would guess that he fretted about the gift. He was living near the city that spawned Starbuck's, and he loved latte. He knew I, also, had been a coffee lover since graduate school. It was a great present.

In 1987, shortly after Jay, our older son, was born, he visited us. (He arranged one of his layover visits on his return from a conference in Charleston.) He was thinner than he had been in a long time, so I asked him if he had lost some weight. He said that he had recently established a policy at the Supply Center that prevented people from smoking inside buildings. He was concerned about the dangers of secondhand smoke on workers, but he didn't anticipate the reactions from hardcore smokers. He even received death threats. Some of the more angry smokers pointed out that J.C.'s size wasn't doing much for his health. So, to maintain his credibility, he felt he had to lose weight.

Once we were in my home, he sat in our living room, looked around and said, "When are you going to clean your windows?" I wasn't insulted. I probably wouldn't even have remembered the comment, except that I thought it was odd. He was the guy who shoved empty soda bottles and ice cream dishes under the couch (or the old bed that served as a couch) in our family room in Aragona Village, and five minutes after he entered the house that Donna and I had recently bought, he started to criticize our cleaning. Surprisingly, it was the only odd moment during the entire trip.

For a few years, I had been doing research with John DiTiberio on how personality types can explain differences in writing processes. In our research, we used an instrument called the Myers-Briggs Type Indicator. When J.C. visited, I was in the process of drafting the first book that we would publish on the topic, so I asked if he wanted to take the instrument. He agreed. We spent about two hours talking about his results. He came out as Extraverted (outwardly oriented toward interacting with people), Intuitive (more likely to deal with general impressions, abstractions, the big picture), Feeling (more likely to base decisions on personal values or how the decision will affect others), and Judging (task oriented, quick to reach decisions, and good at meeting deadlines). I shared that I am Introverted (more oriented toward the inner world of reflection), Intuitive (like him), Thinking (more likely to value objectivity and base decisions on criteria or principles), and Judging (also like him). I told him that Mom, who had taken the instrument about a year before, was Introverted, Intuitive, Feeling, and Perceiving (more likely to be flexible and spontaneous, to delay decisions, maybe even have difficulty with reaching decisions). J.C. seemed most interested in what I said about Feeling types, maybe because this was one of the dimensions where we differed. He spent a lot of time talking about his need to protect people at work. He said that he often found himself sticking up for people who were scapegoated, and this, on occasions, caused problems for him with his superiors.

181

I recently reread some comments about J.C.'s type in Otto Kroeger and Janet Thuesen's *Type Talk*, a popular book on the Myers-Briggs Type Indicator. Kroeger and Thuesen explain that people of my brother's type are "pleasers, wanting strokes from adults," and they even consider "a negative stroke" to be better than "being ignored." They want to reduce "interpersonal conflict," but they are very sensitive and may become "bitter, even wounded." My type was described as the "most independent" of those identified by the Myers-Briggs, which may come across to others as aloofness. Mom's type was described as being a person who has a having deep emotional life that may not always find a means of expression. As parents, people of her type tend to be "easy-going and quick to meet a child's needs," but they might sometimes "be slow to give overt, positive strokes, not because they don't feel approval, but because they find it difficult to express." They are often respected for their "inner strength." Even though he was loved, J.C. might not have received as much nurturing or reassurance as he needed, either from me or our mother.

While J.C. was visiting my new family, we took a photograph of him holding Jay in his arms. (I later heard from some of his friends that he was proud of the photo. He often showed it to others and bragged about his nephew.) It was the only time he held Jay. He never held Jeff, our second son. During the trip, J.C. was also able to meet my in-laws, and I was pleased that they liked him. My father-in-law was particularly fond of J.C.'s loud laugh. Many found his laughter and humor infectious, but, behind his self-deprecating humor, I saw pain that many overlooked. I thought his laugh was too loud, forced and artificial. A friend of his told me that, whenever he talked about me, he would always add, "It's not fair that I got all the looks and brains." She always laughed, she said. To me, a joke like this hid all of his childhood fears that I was the favorite and that he was only tolerated. While I also loved his laughter, I felt it had an aftertaste. What I sometimes failed to see is that there was real joy in his humor, even if it did sometimes cover pain. I think he viewed every joke, every laugh, as a small victory.

J.C. always had a sharp wit. After he spent four years in the Air Force as a medic, his humor became darker. When he was stationed near Las Vegas, he once told me, the doctors, nurses, and medics all went to see the movie *M.A.S.H.* together. He spoke of how they all needed that dark humor to deal with the traumas they witnessed. I think humor was his therapy, his way to get things out without having to worry about how people would react to the content.

When I was doing research on AA, I found that one of the most striking features of oldtimers' talks is the humor, parody, and even self-parody. They poke fun at everything—their drinking self, their current self, their sponsor, even the program. Every idea and belief, no matter how sacred or cherished, is thrown in the air and tested against the standard of laughter. The talks of oldtimers are often filled with laughter from beginning to end. It is as if they are saying, "Laughter heals us and laughter brings us back to ourselves." Or, "It is through laughter that we first see ourselves as others see us." I think J.C. used humor in this way.

In 1989, I went to a conference in Seattle. The night before the conference began, J.C. took the ferry from Bremerton to meet me and some of my friends for dinner. It was a good evening, and my friends said that they enjoyed meeting him. On Saturday, after the close of the conference, I took the ferry to Bremerton to spend the night. He met me at the dock, and we had a leisurely lunch. He talked about watching Bradshaw's PBS series on family (the show that introduced the concept of the dysfunctional family to America when we were still bathing in Reagan's nostalgia for the good old days of the 1950s, a reality largely created by reruns of 1950s sit-coms) and how Bradshaw had helped him to understand our family. He also told me how he tended to be friends with women who needed him, how he dated women only until he slept with them. He talked about friends who saw therapists. He felt that they wallowed in the pain of their past. They talked about their problems and weren't happy; he just pushed it all aside and was happier than the people in therapy. Through lunch, I mostly listened. I wanted to say, "How could you treat women like that?" Or, "How can you ever be happy when you try to repress all the pain?" But I didn't. I just listened.

Then we visited his closest friends in Bremerton, Jim and Lauren. J.C. worked with Lauren at the Supply Center, and Jim worked in civil service on a different base. He spent most of his weekends at their house, and they often went camping together. Jim, who was tall and had the look of someone who was once an athlete, spoke with a lot of volume. He told me stories about how he and John (all of J.C.'s friend in Bremerton called him John) watched a PBS show about how to make a picnic table. They ordered the plans, bought wood, and spend an entire weekend learning the meaning of the axiom "Measure twice, cut once." They measured twice, cut once, tried to put the table together, cussed more than once, bought more boards, measured again, cut again, cussed again, but eventually ended up with a fairly functional picnic table that they used on rare occasions. The

183

entire time that Jim was telling stories, Lauren, who was thin, frail in comparison with Jim, sat at a table in the kitchen tying flies. I wanted to talk to Lauren about fly fishing, but it was hard to get away from Jim. For several hours, I sat on their couch and just listened.

It seemed important to J.C. that I meet his friends. After a few hours, J.C. and I left and spent the rest of the afternoon watching television in his condo, actually videotapes of his favorite shows and movies. Before the visit, as I later learned, he had told a friend, "I need to stock up on videos before George's visit." At the time, I didn't realize how uncomfortable he felt around me.

That evening, we went to Vicki's house for dinner. We watched a home video of Jay and Jeff, who were then one and two. At the time, I didn't imagine that J.C. probably watched with mixed emotions. He was, I know, proud of his nephews, but he may have also seen my family as an implicit judgment on his life. I had a wife; he cut relationships short. I had children; he joked that he didn't have any children that he knew about. I had a comfortable, suburban house; he owned a one-bedroom condo with a table saw in the dining area. It must have pained him when relatives told me that I had cute children or a nice family. I later heard, from one of his friends, that he often said, "George has a perfect life."

In the morning, he drove me to the airport. My flight was delayed, and I was surprised that he stayed for several hours and visited with me and my colleagues. I felt that we had grown closer during the trip. After I left, I later learned, he told a friend at work, "George and I have so much we need to talk about, but we just sat around my condo and watched videos."

A LETTER

SHORTLY AFTER DONNA AND I BEGAN DATING, AS WE WERE IN THE EARLY stages of learning about each other's family history, I gave her one of the versions of my simple story. I told her, "My father was an alcoholic. My parents were divorced when I was six. I never saw my father again." Unlike most people, she wanted to know more about how the separation affected me and how my father's drinking affected the family. When she asked me questions, I remember that I shrugged my shoulders a lot. Maybe I could have answered some of her questions, but I just didn't like talking about the past. I did, however, tell her that the one thing I knew about my childhood is that my mother loved me. Donna didn't ask me more questions until after we were married, and even then I didn't have very satisfying answers.

185

Once we started our own family, I set fairly simple goals as a father. Goal number one was to make sure that my kids knew I loved them. About 1992, when Jeff was four, he was feeling some competition with his older brother and he began to tell Donna and me, "You don't love me." It hit hard. Typical of many parents of our generation facing an episode of normal childhood development, Donna and I began to have long conversations about where we went wrong, how we could be more nurturing, or how we needed to be more strict. The answer, we brainstormed, was more bedtime stories, less sugar, more chores, another dog, on and on. During one of our talks, I mentioned to Donna that J.C. had said the same thing to our mother occasionally, so we decided that

I would write J.C. and ask for advice. In my letter, I told J.C. what was going on and that I didn't want Jeff to feel unloved. I wrote that I had remembered him saying something similar and asked if he could provide any insight that might help us to understand what Jeff was feeling and how we might be better parents. For four months, he didn't respond. I began to fear that I had raised the specter of the past, that I had split us further apart. Then a letter arrived. It is long, but I feel I must include it all because it is his memoir, in his words, in his voice:

186   Dear George,

I would be glad to help you with Jeff by sharing my feelings on childhood. Please feel free to share this with Donna. I'm not sure of the worth of what I will discuss since I was in a very different family situation than Jeff, but I will share with you what I understand about myself since I'm not sure what is relevant. One caveat, what I will discuss is not meant to be a criticism of Mom or anyone else. We all have our strengths and weaknesses, it's what makes us human, and I am not carrying any baggage on who did or didn't do what to me. It also might be that what Jeff is going through is natural for a four-year-old.

One of my concerns has always been that there is some kind of genetic element to all this. I don't have any scientific basis for this, it just seems that a number of people in the family, men mainly, have come from disparate backgrounds but ended up with remarkably similar personalities. I would typify it as an addictive personality (alcohol, drugs, food), a need to escape from something and problems with bonding to other people (love equals pain). I'm also not sure what type of family life Dad's generation had growing up, but all the rest of us could easily be explained as products of alcoholic or dysfunctional families.

I'm fairly sure I didn't understand much of what was going on while I was growing up. At Jeff's age, I was watching our father be carried home drunk by his buddies and went through Christmas at the Navy Chief's Club where Santa didn't show up because he got drunk. I don't recall any physical abuse but there were a lot of verbal fights between Mom and Dad and that was also emotionally draining. Childhood was somewhat of a surrealistic blur. He left when I was 9 or 10 and things got calmer but I don't think anybody ever explained things to me (like it wasn't my fault). I don't ever recall having a conversation between Mom and me where we discussed emotions or anything else. The only talking seemed to be me reassuring her that there was nothing wrong and my goal was to protect her feelings. I felt the family was very dissociated, we never seemed to discuss anything and hid our feelings from each other.

My own personal voyage of discovery didn't begin until I was 35. At that time I would have told you that our father's alcoholism did not have an effect on me, that I was an introvert and that I was shy. None of these perspectives was true, but it's what I believed until that point in my life. It shows how little I understood about what had happened and how my life had been affected. On July 4th of that year, I was sitting home alone, flipping through the channels and came across a program in which a 12 year old was explaining his feelings. They had to do with his alcoholic family and I realized that the alcoholism had affected me as well. I have read a lot on the subject since then and thought about it a lot. The books by John Bradshaw seem to make the most sense.

I seem to come up with new revelations or perhaps theories every couple of years. The most recent theory is that I ended up exactly like Dad even though it was the last thing I wanted to happen. I never understood why he left and never contacted us again until I saw the same tendencies in myself. I still don't know why getting close to people is so uncomfortable, but for me it's definitely better to be alone. Maybe it's just what

I am comfortable with and don't want to change, but there seems to be a strong urge not to bond with people, something beyond the fact that it's outside my comfort zone. Superficial friendships and relationships are okay, but when it gets close, it's time to leave.

My personality seems to be super extrovert/loner which makes me difficult to understand at times since I send conflicting signals. While my lifestyle seems better suited for a brooding misanthrope, I am rarely depressed and almost always upbeat. My theory on that is that I never had anyone to lean on emotionally and couldn't give into depression since it would finish me. My guess is that most of my personality was formed at a very early age and that it is primarily a function of the alcoholism. It would seem to be at that time that love began to equal pain. I always felt that I was on my own emotionally, even as a child, and figuring out things yourself is probably not a good way to grow up.

I always felt I was emotionally walking on eggshells at home and needed to have nothing go wrong for someone to love me. Having to be so careful of other people's emotions becomes too big of a job and eventually love isn't worth it. I don't think that love was conditional, but it always seemed that way. I also have a strong feeling of abandonment. No one ever explained why Dad left so I guess I never figured that out. I remember as a teenager worrying whenever Mom was late, fearing she had been in an accident or wouldn't be coming back for some reason. I used to sit in the living room waiting for her to return. If something had happened to her I always figured that our aunt would take you but I really couldn't figure out anyone who would take me. I had some vague vision of Boys Town out in the middle of Virginia somewhere. Wherever it was, I knew it wasn't going to be good.

So anyway, that's pretty much what I felt and what I understand. My advice for parents has always been to explain things to kids. Do it calmly, without a big production and end by telling them that your love is unconditional. Never use emotional blackmail.

Sorry this took so long to answer, but it wasn't easy to put on paper.

J.C.

The letter was written on a word processor, so he probably revised it repeatedly over the four months between the time I sent my letter and the time he sent his. Maybe he even debated with himself about whether or not he should mail it. As soon as he put it in the mailbox, I wouldn't be surprised if he wished he could reach in and take it back. He probably wondered, in the time between mailing his letter and my response, how I would react.

How did I react? I was surprised and pleased that he had been so open with me.

As I read the letter, over and over, I began to see how similar our lives were. We both felt abandoned. Like me, J.C. thought that he had been spared growing up in an alcoholic family and only discovered much later in life, actually at the exact age I had the same insight, that alcoholism was ingrained in our family.

But I was also struck by how differently we each saw our childhoods, and how different the realities were that we experienced in the same family and the same house. I don't remember the "Christmas parties at the Chief's Club" or "verbal fights between Mom and Dad," but I had always suspected that J.C. had witnessed more of our father's drinking. I was particularly touched by J.C.'s fear that our mother might never come home and that no one would take care of him. I don't ever remember feeling that, except briefly, when I listened to Rita tell about how her daughter, who was raising two boys on her own, was killed in a car accident, and I was almost grown by then.

SOME OF THE WORDS ARE THEIRS

From reading his letter, it is clear that J.C.'s childhood was filled with fears and pain, and that he never found an outlet for these emotions, except in anger. In *Real Boys*, William Pollack argues that boys have difficulty understanding and expressing their emotions: "Even when questioned directly about difficult situations—a divorce, a death, an alcoholic parent, academic troubles—the boy may deny he's feeling unhappy." If a mother asks a boy if he has had his feelings hurt or if he is depressed or afraid, the boy will say, "I'm fine." Anger, he says, "is one of the main ways boys indirectly express other feelings like grief, disappointment, and hopelessness." Pollack says that parents need to guess what boys are feeling and then say something like, "I would think you blame yourself for the divorce." Or, "I believe that it must hurt you that your father never writes." When J.C. lashed out at me, it was the only way he had to deal with an anger that masked so many other emotions. Pollack's book attracted a lot of attention when it was published in 1998. When J.C. and I were growing up in the 1950s and 1960s, boys who cried or talked about their feelings were ridiculed by their friends, coaches, and fathers.

This might seem like an odd observation, but I was struck that J.C. called our father "Dad." I'm sure I called him "Daddy" or "Dad" at a young age, maybe even for a few years after he left, but then I started calling him "my father." For me, "Dad" seemed too personal, too involved. By the time I was about eight, probably about the time that I asked my mother, "Is Daddy ever coming back?" he became "my father" in the sense of being "my biological father," some distant person who had not raised me. So, in some sense, J.C. seemed to remain closer to him. J.C. even felt that he had, in some ways, become like our father. He wrote, "I never understood why he left and never contacted us again until I saw the same tendencies in myself." I think J.C. meant that he understood that our father felt that "love equals pain," and he had to leave and never contact us because it was too painful. J.C. saw the same pattern in his own life, as he wrote, "a strong urge not to bond with other people."

I learned a great deal from J.C.'s letter, but what puzzled me most was his view of our mom. Like him, I felt the need to protect her (though I assumed only I felt this, I didn't think that he experienced the same feeling), but I don't ever remember walking on "eggshells," and I never doubted that she loved me, unconditionally. I tried to take on J.C.'s view of our mother, to see her through his words, but I can't find *his* mother in *my* memories, at least, not with any consistently.

As hard as I looked, I only came up with one memory. When I was only seven or eight, I remember asking Mom to watch a Saturday morning cartoon with me. She was cleaning the house, with that hurried, driven look that usually consumed her face; she apologetically said she didn't have time just then, but maybe later. I don't remember asking again. Later, years later, after I was grown, she told me that she remembered the incident and that she regretted that she didn't stop her housework to spend some time with me. Yet, even when I was seven or eight, I don't think the event bothered me that much. I remember thinking something like, "Okay. She's busy." And, as I grew older, we did spend time together listening to my records or talking. We had long conversations about politics, her trips, my hobbies. Mostly, we liked to try to figure people out, get past their persona, make hunches about what was going on inside, what they were really thinking and feeling. Through the years, I felt closer and closer to her. We moved past being just mother and son, and also became something like friends.

In the span of one of our discussions about our family, although I can't remember whether it was at the airport in Chicago in 1982 or during lunch in Bremerton in 1989, J.C. said something about Mom not being "a strong woman." This didn't shock me, even though friends and relatives thought that she was one of the strongest women they had ever known. They, from outside the family, saw a woman who raised two boys on her own, seemingly without difficulty, because she never spoke of her fears or hardships. J.C. and I saw this side of her, but we also saw moments when she was overwhelmed, in tears, when she repeated, "I don't know what I'm going to do." To young boys who had been abandoned by their father, who relied on her for survival, such episodes, even if they were infrequent, made us feel like we needed to take care of her. I believe that such episodes only happened for a short period after our father left, but they must have had a more dramatic effect on J.C.

We all, to some degree, moved past the aftershocks of my father's departure. And I believe that J.C. moved past his childhood image of our mother, probably during the years he came back home to finish college, after serving in the Air Force. He and Mom lived in the same house again for three years, without me. I suspect that they became much closer during this period, without me there to triangulate the family. I can see a closeness in his letters to Mom after this period. On September 4, 1984, shortly before Donna and I were married, he wrote to Mom:

> I haven't really been doing much of anything, mostly just staying by myself. I have gone out some with a friend of Kathleen's but she is as crazy as Kathleen and has a drinking problem so I am not really that interested. Anyway she doesn't really let people get close to her (except Kathleen), so there's not much to offer. I guess you're not supposed to get serious with anyone crazier than yourself anyway and while I have my problems too, she's definitely worse.

I read an intimacy here. J.C. refers to a former girlfriend (Kathleen) and dating her friend (who has a drinking problem), how they are both crazy, how these women didn't have anything to offer him, and how he has problems of his own. And this doesn't seem to be the first time that J.C. spoke or wrote to Mom about these girlfriends, which indicates a degree of intimacy that I didn't really have with her. If the letter did not begin "Dear Mom," I would assume that J.C. was writing one of his closest friends. In his 1992 letter to me, when he was attempting to explain how he saw our family, he wrote: "I don't ever recall having a conversation between Mom and me where we discussed emotions or anything else." But this letter seems to indicate otherwise. While I might have had a "back formation" about our mother (reading later experiences into earlier ones), J.C. seemed to have had more of a "front formation" (reading earlier experiences into later ones). He seems to have read the relationship he had with Mom in the first years after our father left into decades of a relationship that clearly changed and developed. Emotionally, he seemed to remember his relationship with Mom as he experienced it in the later 1950s, when she was often frazzled and overwhelmed by the prospect of raising two boys on her own. I remember our mother as she existed in certain key memories; J.C. does the same with other memories. Neither of us seem to fully grasp the history of our mother or the ways that she changed. We had both fixed her in time, but in different times.

Even when I was seven or eight, I understood our family differently than my brother. I never thought that Mom didn't love me or she didn't have time for me. As I often tell people, "I'm just not that sensitive." By this, I don't mean that I am incapable of caring about others; I mean more that I rarely have my feelings hurt. Sometimes people apologize for having insulted me a day or week ago, and I have to admit to them that I didn't even realize I was being insulted. J.C. was much more sensitive.

When I was about eleven and J.C. about fourteen, we were playing golf in the backyard with wiffle balls. J.C. was finishing his back swing just as Tiger, our cat, decided to pounce on the ball. In full swing, J.C.'s club caught Tiger on the side of the head. Tiger flipped three or four feet in the air, several times, then was still. I was stunned. J.C. ran in the house, yelling, "Mom! Mom!" We all thought Tiger was dying, but we wrapped him in a blanket and took him to the vet. The vet said that we just needed to wait and see, but he was probably thinking, "This cat's a goner." When we arrived home, I took Tiger to my room. For weeks, I fed him water or milk with an eye dropper, cleaned up his vomit, and watched him struggle to stand, then fall. J.C. couldn't even look at him. As soon as Tiger could walk fairly well, he disappeared. That was one resilient and smart cat.

To others, I might have appeared to be the sensitive one. After all, I cared enough to nurse the sick cat. But J.C., I think, was far more shaken by the entire affair than I. Because he was more sensitive, the dynamics of our family—when we were in crisis, in the years leading up to our father's departure and the years that followed—probably affected him more deeply.

As I would find out later, many of my brother's friends deeply loved him, but the relationships were often conflicted. Because he was so sensitive, he seemed to be unconsciously drawn into transference and counter-transference. As he became close to people, in some subtle way, something was triggered and he began to act like their fathers or brothers or ex-husbands. One woman he supervised had a father who always argued with her. J.C. quibbled with her over insignificant details. Another had a father who followed a pattern of ignoring her whenever he was angry. With this woman, J.C. went through the same pattern: he would become angry with her and then ignore her. I wonder if he triggered something in our mom that then triggered something in J.C. When I was younger, I reacted to J.C. as if he were the alcoholic father. It took me a long time to realize that he played this role before me, and it took me even longer to realize that the role was as much my creation as it was his. In an odd sort of way, I must have needed to be around an alcoholic father. I really wish I figured this out earlier.

194

When I received the 1992 letter from J.C., I was a forty-two-year-old abandoned child, trying to deal with mid-life issues. I was beginning to see my family of origin in a different light. My mother, whom I had once idealized as the martyr who sacrificed so much to raise her children, I now saw as someone who didn't know how to deal with her own pain, at least initially, in the early years after my father left. She had to work to recover from years of living with an active alcoholic, and she did, with time. My father, who I once felt deserted his children, I now saw as someone also isolated by pain. My brother, who I once felt victimized me, I now saw as another victim, probably the most victimized in our family. Only after reading his 1992 letter did I realize that his take on our family, in some significant ways, was different than mine, and I knew I must respect his view, not try to explain it away. We each had our own reality, and I have come to feel that I need to listen to *his* story.

Just listen.

The Death of a Family

As soon I received J.C.'s letter, I wrote to thank him. It seems like this exchange should have opened a series of correspondence, but it didn't. At the time, Mom was being worn away by Alzheimer's. That is the only way I know how to explain it, as a process of erosion. Slow and inevitable. Most people pretended that it wasn't even happening. Even J.C. After Donna and I moved Mom to Springfield, he never came to visit. And we talked less often. My memory may not be accurate, but I remember calling him a few times during the first year or so that Mom was in a nursing home. I don't remember him calling me. Right or wrong, I felt that I was busy taking care of our mother, fathering my children, being a husband, and holding down a job. My life was complicated. He was less busy, I thought. Let him call me. So I stopped calling. This is more of the alcoholic family logic that made perfect sense to me at the time and, now, years later, after the damage was done, seems so obviously petty, self-absorbed, and stupid.

Now, I wonder if J.C. was waiting for me to call him. He may have even dreaded my calls because he knew, at some point, I would have to call to say, "Mom is dead." I don't think he realized how difficult my life was during this period, and I must take responsibility for not telling him, for not finding some way to bring him into the care of our mother. But, when I did talk to him, he kept saying, "I'll let you decide." So I decided. Without him.

As Mom's condition worsened, I called him a few times to say that she might die soon, maybe within a few days. Then, she would rally, come back a bit, but he never called me back to see if she was still dying or if she was better. And I applied the same logic. If he wants to know how she's doing, he can call me. It all had an odd logic to it, which is typical of how I tend to deal with a crisis. I see the problem and move to a solution. If people are willing to help, then fine. If not, then fine. I can handle it by myself.

Donna didn't understand why I wasn't angry at J.C. My reaction was simple. I suspected he was having trouble even thinking about our mother's deterioration, probably because he had so many unresolved issues about our family, as his letter had helped me to understand. I was sure that he admired our mom for raising the two of us on her own, and I was sure that he considered her to be the one person he could always turn to, if he really needed help, but I don't think that he ever felt a sense of security around her. His feelings toward her were conflicted. I felt that I understood what he was going through, but I didn't talk to him about it. I was too overwhelmed. I just let him be.

When I called to tell J.C. that our mother had died, he was shaken, but he didn't cry. I remember him saying, "You've already lived with this loss a long time." I told him, "Yes. A long time. It's been hard." I could hardly voice the words. I really appreciated his acknowledging that it had been hard to care for our mother, especially toward the end. We spoke a few more times about whether or not we should have a formal service, how to handle her remains, settling the estate, and he always said, "I'll let you handle it." Because Mom had no friends in Missouri, I eventually decided to have a private service and spread her cremated remains across a peaceful stretch of river. He decided he wouldn't come.

Unlike many conflicted families, we never exchanged one harsh word over settling the estate. I arranged to have Mom's annuity and life insurance split between the two of us. When I called J.C. to tell him that I would be sending him a check for his part of the assets in Mom's bank account, he told me to keep it. I should have it, he said, because I took care of her. I said, "This is your money. Mom would want you to have it." I sent him an itemized account of the bills that I paid, the remaining assets, and a check. He never questioned any of it. I am certain that Mom would be pleased that we settled the estate so amicably.

On one of my trips through her papers, I found a clipping from a "Dear Abby" column. The letter to Abby was from a man whose family had fought over his mother's estate. Abby responds that this would have been the last thing his mother wanted. Mom had clipped the piece so that she could show it to J.C. and me. Typical of so many of her clippings, it ended up in the bottom of a drawer, lost in a clutter of documents.

Jim, J.C.'s friend in Bremerton, later told me that J.C. never recovered from our mother's death. Darcy, a loyal friend who was one of J.C.'s assistants at the Supply Center, one of the women he confided in, told me that J.C. said, "That's the last straw." He may have already been sick himself.

In the months that followed, we began to talk more often. It was like an invisible wall had come down. Maybe, with only the two of us left, we felt a need to be closer. Maybe, with our mother gone, the structure of the family changed. We could step out of our roles. All I know for certain is that something was different.

At Christmas, I called to invite him—beg him—to visit us. We had a long talk. He had sent the boys some camping equipment, sleeping bags, canteens, and packs. One of his friends later told me that he "studied" finding the right gifts for Jay and Jeff. I could tell that a great deal of time had gone into selecting these presents. They came from the heart. Camping was always important to him. He had some of his best times in the Boy Scouts, and he still camped with a group of friends whenever the weather was good.

We talked about his coming to Missouri so we could camp with the boys. I wanted to see him, and I wanted him to know my family. He actually spoke as if he might come. Then he mentioned that he had been having trouble with an ulcer, but he had not been to the doctor.

About three weeks later, Jim called to say J.C. was dead. He didn't know the cause yet. He said that J.C. had been sick. Everyone around him knew it. When friends expressed concern, he would explode. Darcy, his co-worker, later told me that "towards the end he got so cutting and sarcastic." She wrote to me: "Often times, I would blow him off or ignore him but it wasn't because I didn't care—he just began treating me like my Dad did." She eventually talked to him to try to "recapture the closeness" they once had, but he talked in "circles." All of his friends felt shut out. No one knew how to help. Jim kept saying to him, "I need to call George and let him know you're sick." Each time, J.C. became angry and told him to mind his own business.

Lauren, Jim's wife, had talked to J.C. on Friday night. No one heard from him over the three-day weekend, the Martin Luther King holiday. When he didn't show up for work on Tuesday, Lauren and another friend went to his apartment. They found him lying on the bathroom floor.

That was what was happening in Bremerton. In Missouri, I had a vague sense that something was wrong. For about two weeks before his death, the film of Norman Maclean's *A River Runs Through It* was playing almost every day on a cable station. I had seen it before, when it first came out, and then read the book and had identified with the story. I was, like Norman Maclean, a fly fisher and a college professor. I had always found the story moving, but I first experienced it as a father. As I watched the two brothers, Norman and Paul, I thought of my sons and wondered if one of them would become an alcoholic. I wanted my sons to be close, and I feared that they would drift apart, have trouble talking about what really mattered.

In the weeks leading up to J.C.'s death, I watched the film from a different perspective. Every time it was on, I watched, thought of my brother, and cried, which in itself was unusual, because I rarely cry as I watch movies. I am certain that I was watching the film on the day that he died, maybe at the very moment of his death. The coroner fixed his death date as Saturday, January 14, 1995. I was watching the film that Saturday night. I don't believe this was a coincidence.

Shortly after Jim called to tell me about J.C.'s death, I had a vague recollection of a passage from *A River Runs Through It* that might say what I wanted said at his funeral, but I couldn't find my copy. I went to a bookstore, pulled the book from the shelf, opened it to the ending and read:

> Now nearly all those I loved and did not understand when I was young are dead, but I still reach out to them.
>
> Of course, now I am too old to be much of a fisherman, and now of course I usually fish the big waters alone, although some friends think I shouldn't. Like many fly fishermen in western Montana where the summer days are almost Arctic in length, I often do not start fishing until the cool of the evening. Then in the Arctic half-light of the canyon, all existence fades to a being with my soul and memories and the sounds of the Big Blackfoot River and a four-county rhythm and the hope that a fish will rise.
>
> Eventually, all things merge into one, and a river runs through it. The river was cut by the world's great flood and runs over rocks from the basement of time. On some of the rocks are timeless raindrops. Under the rocks are the words, and some of the words are theirs.
>
> I am haunted by waters.

I stood hidden between the bookshelves of a crowded store, trying to stifle sobs for a long while. I thought of an old family picture. My brother and I climbing the bank of a lake, my brother holding a stringer full of fish, and grinning, a grin that was asking for love and acceptance and seemed, for a moment, to find it. More often than I tend to remember, his face sang.

Donna said that she would handle everything, and I let her. She made plane reservations, called a funeral home, and arranged for a minister. We were ready to fly to Seattle the next morning when fourteen inches of snow hit Springfield, closing the airport. So we pointed my four-wheel drive Toyota economy car to the desolate highway, headed west, and eventually made a connection at a small airport in Joplin. We didn't arrive at the hotel in Bremerton until about 3:00 am, the morning of the funeral.

SOME OF THE WORDS ARE THEIRS

It was a day of contrasts. Cousin Vicki had arranged some appointments for us. We first went to the coroner's office. The coroner told us that J.C.'s body was wedged between his toilet and the bath tub. They had a difficult time getting him out. The autopsy showed that he had colon cancer. His intestines had perforated, and he died in a matter of minutes, maybe seconds. His heart was huge. If he didn't die of cancer, he would have probably had a heart attack within a few years.

Then we visited a lawyer to talk about settling the estate. J.C. had died without a will. He once told me that the inheritance laws in the state of Washington were very clear, so he didn't need one, but I think he couldn't contemplate his own death. With the lawyer, we talked briefly about what kind of assets I thought J.C. might have, what kind of papers we needed to look for as we sorted through belongings in his condo, and the process—all the complicated details—of settling an estate.

Finally, we went by his one-bedroom condominium. There was a yellow "Police Line" banner across the door and a sign that warned against entering the premises because it was a potential crime scene. The door was unlocked, so we went in. I was expecting a mess. J.C. had never been neat, but I was still shocked. As we walked in, the odor of urine hit us. Jim later told us that he and Lauren had, a few months earlier, taken J.C.'s cat and had it put to sleep. It was old and urinating on the carpet. They said that J.C. knew the cat needed to be put down, but he couldn't face it, so they took care of it.

Then we walked in and followed little paths through junk, boxes, clothes and trash to his bedroom, bathroom, and living room. His kitchen was waist high in garbage. Not trash—garbage. His toilet did not work. He had been using a bucket of water to flush it.

I could see the routine of his last days. Buy a frozen dinner on the way home from work. Microwave it. Eat it with a plastic fork. Throw the trash into the corner of the kitchen. Pick up some clothes off the floor. Stick them in the washer. Take Imodium for the diarrhea. Advil for the pain. Watch a little television. Go to bed early. Try to sleep

GEORGE H. JENSEN, JR.

through the night. Wake up the next morning and try to get through another day of work.

Under the corner of his couch, which had been pushed aside so that the coroner could wheel his body out on a gurney, Vicki found a notebook. She read a few lines and then handed it to me. Apparently, J.C. was trying to do something like a fourth step, "a searching and fearless moral inventory." He began it when he was forty, seven years earlier, as he was probably dealing with mid-life issues, so it was written before we talked in Bremerton, before he wrote me the long letter about how he saw our family. In the journal, he wrote four short entries, each on a separate page. Maybe that was all he could face. This is more of his memoir, his voice, his words. I started to read the first entry:

Family

Why should it be so painful to be around my family? It shouldn't be so but it is and seems to get worse. I guess the problem is that we just never talked about anything. My father's alcoholism and subsequent abandonment of the family scarred me. I didn't realize how much until I was about 35. I've tried to make changes since then but it seems futile. Mom was a sweetheart, but not an emotionally strong woman. I felt like I walked on eggshells my entire childhood trying to keep from hurting her. As I entered adulthood, the chore of pretending everything was OK seemed to get harder & harder to deal with. In the end, all I wanted to do was escape and seek solace. The relationship with my brother has not been close. The dissociated family we had become took its toll on that relationship. I guess I should have sat down with him to try & work things out, but like my mother, I was always afraid of what they would say. While I'm probably wrong, I assumed the talk would have let loose 40 years worth of venom towards me. I assumed they tolerated more than loved me and that the love that was there was because I was family more than loveable.

I read down until he mentioned me and I could read no more. I couldn't face it on that day. I didn't imagine that he thought I still hated him. This was the story of our relationship. We would come close to opening up to one another and then pull back. The family seemed held together by withholding.

The three of us left to dress for the funeral. I didn't know what to expect. I had heard that he had friends, but, after walking through his condo, reading a page of his journal, I found it hard to believe that he had many. Or that he was really close to anyone. When we arrived at the funeral home, I went into the office to write a check, talk about the cremation, and give last minute instructions to the minister. She was a buxom, bleach blonde, probably in her early fifties with an ample coating of makeup. She looked a little like Tammy Faye Bakker, the wife of televangelist Jim Bakker. This was her first funeral, she said, and she wanted to get it right. I showed her the passage from *A River Runs Through It* and gave her the broad details of J.C.'s life. She kept asking me to go through it all, one more time. She wanted more details, anecdotes, hints into J.C.'s character, and I just didn't know what to say.

When I came out of the office, the chapel was already full. I asked the funeral director to start escorting his friends into the family room. Soon it was full. Then the director began to move people to a large room downstairs, where they could watch on closed circuit television. Soon it was full. When every room was full, an additional forty or fifty friends waited outside to pay their respects.

I don't remember many details about the funeral. The minister was clearly nervous and repeatedly said that John liked camping. Yes, John. All of J.C.'s friends called him John. She struggled to find something to say, and it was probably the only bit of our conversation that she remembered. When she said that she was going to read a passage from *A River Runs Through It*, Lauren, who was sitting near me, said, "Oh God." I later learned that J.C., I mean John, loved the film and watched it repeatedly. He had first seen it with Lauren and Jim, so the next Christmas he bought Lauren a fly tying kit. She began to fish and spent most of her weekends tying flies.

The minister stumbled through the passage. She misread "I still reach out to them" as "I do not reach out to them." Later, Lauren said that J.C. was probably watching the minister during the funeral and having a good laugh. I don't doubt it.

At the funeral and during the week after, I began to realize how much others were affected by John's death. I was told that the Supply Center where he worked "shut down" when word came that he was dead. People stopped working, talked in small groups, or went to their offices to cry. On the day of the funeral, the Captain closed all of the offices. At the memorial service, a man told me that John had helped him through a divorce, a woman said he had coached her softball team, another woman said that he had been the one person she could confide in and had bought a plane ticket for her sister to visit. Story after story. A few weeks after the funeral, the Captain at the Supply Center hired a grief counselor for John's friends. About forty people attended the session to talk about my brother.

Even after I returned home, people wrote long letters to say that they were sorry they could not attend the funeral. They were too distraught, they couldn't face it. I felt like they were all talking about someone I had never known. Not the moody, angry J.C., the brother I loved, the brother I had once resented. They were talking about someone else—not J.C. but John. Someone I had only glimpses of during our childhood. Someone I saw more of during our brief encounters as adults. Someone I liked and someone I was proud to call my brother. I didn't even know what to call him anymore. Sometimes I called him J.C., almost as a reflex. The next moment, he was John.

My brother's given name was John Charles. *John* was from our paternal grandfather; *Charles* from our maternal grandfather. Our parents didn't want to show favoritism, so they called him J.C. That was how I always knew him. *John* was my brother's conscious creation. He started to call himself John when he entered the Air Force, when he gained some separation from the family and started to construct an identity that was his own, the person he thought he could be or should be. Later, when he returned to college, he wrote for the school newspaper and signed his music and film reviews with John Jensen.

SOME OF THE WORDS ARE THEIRS

I realized that some of his friends started to call him John, but I never knew that the name change signaled a change in identity, that *John* was so important to him. After his death, for about a year, I tried to refer to him as John, but then I realized he had never asked me to call him John, and I don't think he wanted me to. He wanted to keep J.C. and John separate. So he remained J.C. for me, unless I was speaking to one of his friends in Bremerton.

J.C. was the wounded boy I knew as a brother when I was a wounded boy. John was the adult whose work won the national Meritorious Civilian Award—only a handful are given each year—and who had more devoted friends than anyone I know. I felt that I knew J.C. better than even his closest friends. I knew most of what he hid— and perhaps this is part of what kept us distant—and I knew what it must have cost him to keep this pain submerged and contained in the small rooms of his condo. Before his death, I caught only glimpses of John. I came to know John later. I tell my sons stories about John.

One of these stories I heard at his funeral. The characters are John and Sandy, who was an inspector of safety at Supply Centers. So, she evaluated John's work at the Supply Center in Bremerton, which never set too well with him. They both had to take a Radiation Safety Officers' course, which demanded some complicated mathematics to determine safe distances from radiation, proper shielding for employees, the half-life of contaminated materials, and safe limits of exposure to radiation. All of the participants were struggling with the math, but John noticed that the teacher of the workshop had a particular brand of calculator. On his lunch hour, John bought one just like it and asked the teacher to show him how to use it. From then on, he was the star of the workshop, much to the chagrin of his arch rival. He didn't tell her about the calculator advantage until after the workshop was finished. For years, whenever Sandy visited Bremerton to evaluate John's work, he brought the calculator with him to every meeting and placed it on the table, in full view. Whenever the woman said something critical about his work, he tapped the calculator with his forefinger. There was certainly a rivalry at work here, but, as far as

I can tell, it was never vicious or hurtful. It was playful. John liked to mess with people.

When Donna and I went to John's office to pick up his belongings, Darcy, his assistant, was there. She was the one who told me the story about John's calculator, so I gave it to her. In return, I asked only that she pull it out the next time Sandy was at the shipyard in Bremerton for an inspection.

We also spoke to Rachel, whom John supervised and one of the many women in whom he confided. She told me that my brother was upset that he and I never talked. He told her, after my stay with him in Bremerton in 1989, that we had just watched television, without talking, when there was so much that needed to be said. She was referring to the very trip when I felt that John and I had such a good talk over lunch. Rachel kept saying, "People just have to learn to talk to each other." I had the sense that she blamed me for not opening up to John, that she thought I had failed my brother. Then she said that there were "things" she needed to tell me. She would write me or call me. She never did.

Whenever I talked to John's friends, I had some sense that many of them felt like they needed to defend him, like I would think badly of him, like I wouldn't understand. They said, "There are things you need to know." Or, "When you see his apartment, remember he was sick. He was very sick." Or, "John was glad that you two were starting to speak again." There seemed to be an entire history behind each of these comments that they knew but I didn't. I also felt like some of them resented me, like they felt I was a bad brother, I was never willing to talk about our family, or I gloated about being the favorite son.

A few months after John's death, Darcy wrote me. Among other things, she talked about how difficult work had become. She had been John's assistant, and, typical of a bureaucracy's reaction to a death, she was soon faced with doing her job and John's, without a raise and without a promotion:

Rachel and I miss John. We are short our boss & mentor, we have been forced to take on John's duties & everything we touch has John written all over it. Little yellow sticky notes that he gave us–or programs that he wrote, & other numerous things. Some days it's really hard. Last Wednesday I missed him so bad. It was a feeling I've never had before, a gut feeling. I put a picture of John in my calendar & pull it out & ask his advice.

He was very good at his job, and he had many friends. He was deeply loved. And anyone who knew him also knew full well he was complicated.

Many Lives

As I talked to John's friends after his death, I came to understand how compartmentalized he kept his life. We all, certainly, have many personae. We are different people in different situations. The demanding boss at work might become the nurturing parent at home. It seems to me, though, that my brother's personae were more separated, maybe even more consciously constructed than with most people. It is certainly not easy to make sense of his multiple roles and the contradictions within those roles. It seems to me that he consciously worked to keep these personae separate because he believed that his entire self, if fully known, would be rejected. I also think that what he wanted more than anything was to have all his identities known and accepted—and loved— by someone, even if only one person.

Long after he had become John to most people, he referred to himself as J.C. around me or other relatives. This was one kind of compartmentalization. His life also had a clear geography. When he was at home in his condo, I suspect he rarely spoke to neighbors. I also think he rarely had visitors. He kept his condo as his sanctuary, a place where he could be alone and safe. He once told me that he was a "withdrawn extravert." Being with people was his greatest joy. But, when being with others caused too much pain, he needed a retreat. In his condo, he watched videos and read bestsellers, also books about genetics. He thought that genetics might explain his addiction to food. While his condo was a sanctuary, I assume that it was there that he had the most difficulty controlling his depression. Despite what he said and what his friends said, I believe that he was often depressed. He met most of his friends and dates on their territory.

When J.C. moved to Bremerton, he visited our relatives fairly frequently. (He was always J.C. around the Jensens.) Then, as he made friends, he only attended family gatherings on Thanksgiving and Christmas. He never brought a date or a friend (this would, in *Star Trek* terms, be something like mixing matter and anti-matter), and he seldom talked of work or his friends. For a while, Vicki made him a cake for his birthday (at the time, she worked in a bakery and had learned to decorate cakes that were like works of art); every year, she asked him to come over for a birthday dinner. She said that he would sit at the dinner table and look at his watch every few minutes. Later, he started to make excuses: he was going camping, he had an inspection next week, he was going to take a drive to Oregon with a friend. When I talked to relatives in Seattle or Bremerton, they said they rarely saw J.C., but they heard, from second or third hand sources, in what was a fairly small community, that he had a lot of friends. After his funeral, Vicki hosted a wake at her house. Several of John's friends told her that they didn't know he had relatives in the area. When he moved to Bremerton, we had an uncle, aunt, three first cousins, six second cousins, and two cousins-in-law, all within a few miles of his condo.

At the Supply Center, he was typically in good spirits. Everyone who worked with him talked about how much they loved his sense of humor, and he spent time and energy on maintaining relationships. When he arrived at work in the morning, he would pour a cup of coffee, grab a donut, and make rounds. He walked through the entire Supply Center, touching base with everyone who was not in a meeting. Only then would he settle into his job. After work, he went out for drinks with friends (or a particular friend in crisis) and, every few months, he sponsored a keg party. Despite his socializing (or maybe partly because of it), John was very good at his job, but his closest friends at work told me that he expected to fail at everything. He talked about how failures were "no big deal" and that failures were necessary for personal growth. This attitude gave him enormous courage, and he often took chances. His work was described to me as being brilliant, and some of his plans for cleaning up toxic spills or reducing injuries were later implemented nationally. He was also courageous about defending his staff and anyone who was being scapegoated. On occasions, people at work saw John's darker side when they became the object of his biting sarcasm. I don't think he ever intended to show this side at work. Most typically, they saw his humor.

He had close male friends, though I suspect not as close or as numerous as his female friends. He drank with these men, loaned them money, and watched television with them at their house. When he began to receive an annuity as part of our mother's estate, he bought a canoe and asked Jim to keep it for him. This was his way of giving the canoe to Jim without coming across as too sensitive. He never stepped foot in the thing, and he never intended to. He avoided any situation where his weight might become an issue, which is probably one of the reasons that he didn't fly in to visit Mom or me. Sitting in a canoe would certainly have been one of those situations. I don't think that he ever opened up to his male friends, unless they were in crisis. Several men told me that John had helped them through a difficult divorce or a trying time at work. When the crisis was over, he remained friends with these men, but the closeness seems to have been short lived. And, with these men, John listened, but he only seemed to share bits of his own history. He was probably on guard around men. In one of the four entries in his journal, he wrote: "I don't care much for men, probably because of the pain my father caused. I've had a few male friends but don't seek their company. Doug, my roommate in the service; Kirk, who I worked with; and Jim, who I met through my friend Lauren, are the only ones I've spent much time with."

He opened up to his female friends, especially those who were going through divorces, trapped in difficult marriages, or had lingering issues with their fathers. John became the one man that many women could confide in when they felt that all men were scum or when they needed a man to step up and rescue them. Unlike with his male friends, he also confided in them, saying that his father had abandoned him, his mother had never really accepted him, that both his father and mother favored his brother, that his brother was perfect and had a perfect life, that his brother had received all of the attention, that he felt uncomfortable being around his brother. When Donna and I moved our mom to Missouri, he told one of his female friends that she had once again chosen his brother over him, which makes me think that John didn't completely believe everything that he said around his female friends. I don't think that he really wanted to care for our mom when she was suffering from Alzheimer's. After the funeral, Jim told me that he often spoke about how he was grateful that Donna and I had taken care of her. And I don't think that he believed I had a perfect life. He knew that Donna and I both suffered from Crohn's disease, and that the disease had a dramatic effect on our lives, especially on Donna's. But he understood that these confessions made women feel safe. Then they confessed to him. These relationships were probably his longest and most satisfying, and, with these friends, he found some of the acceptance and security he never found with our mother or me. As he was rescuing them, they were nurturing him.

The women he dated formed another compartment. On my visit to Bremerton in 1989, he told me that he romanced women he wanted to date. He sent them cards and flowers. He wrote them long letters. Then, once he slept with them, he fled. I don't think that his approach to romance was as cynical as he made it sound. When he was explaining this pattern to me over lunch, he was casting it in the most unfavorable light he could. He was, to some degree, testing me. He wanted to see if I would judge him, if he could make me reject him. I think that he recognized a pattern, but, beyond or in spite of this all too conscious recognition, I believe he always began a romantic relationship hoping that it would work. He believed, each time, that it might be different with this woman. Then the relationship progressed, he and the woman became closer, and he began to feel too vulnerable. I don't think he fled from the woman as soon as they slept together. I don't think sex had anything to do with it. My guess is that he could handle the emerging intimacy for a while. Only when his fear of rejection became too intense did he flee. It was, I believe, painful for him each time a relationship ended, but he could handle the pain of a failed relationship better than the vulnerability of a deepening relationship.

In all of the compartments of J.C.'s life or John's lives, he showed bits of himself. But never all of himself. After his death, a few of his friends almost seemed angry at me because, they felt, I didn't know J.C. as well as they knew John. Some of them seemed to believe that I didn't even attempt to know him. When I talked about this to one of his friends, she said, "If you didn't know the real John, it is your loss." I'm not so sure that any of us knew the real John, a person that was the entire man in all of his complexities, because he was always on guard. I think my brother, more than anything else, wanted people, even if only a few close friends, to know him completely and accept him, but he feared that if he said all, really opened up, he could not be loved. Even in his closest relationships, he seems to have always protected himself by remaining cynical. He didn't think anyone was truly happy. He didn't believe in God. He didn't think life was meaningful. And his cynicism seemed to grow toward the end of his life. After our mother died, he told some friends that he had nothing to live for.

Even though John said he didn't have anything to live for, even though he didn't have any children, he had life insurance. When we were going through his papers, I was surprised at how many of his regular monthly checks were written to insurance companies. In his final days, he seems to have debated over whether or not to list me as a beneficiary. We found multiple copies of one beneficiary form, partially completed. My name was listed on some versions, then crossed out. Other people's names were listed, then crossed out. He probably knew he was dying, and he struggled over whether he should leave me anything. One of his friends said that he thought I had everything. Actually, Donna and I were, at the time, struggling financially. We always had a lot of medical bills, and Donna's health kept her from working for long stretches. We were trying to manage an entire family's expenses on a professor's salary, and it was not easy.

He eventually decided to split his money between two of his female friends and me. When he left the money to me, he was probably thinking about Jay and Jeff. We used some of the money to add to Jay's college fund, which our mother had started, and some to establish a fund for Jeff. I am sure that this would have given him much pleasure. One of the women he left money to was a close friend. She was religious. After his funeral, she wrote me that she and John often argued about the existence of God. I suspect that this woman was able to break through John's cynicism. The other woman was feeling trapped in a difficult marriage and he wanted her to have the option of leaving her husband. This woman, at first, wanted to refuse the money. Then, Donna was able to talk to her and explain why John wanted her to have it. She accepted the money and eventually left her husband. In my brother's last days, he thought to save a woman who was seeking the courage to end a marriage. With this act, I am sure he was thinking of our mother.

After the funeral, Donna and I spent another week in Bremerton, starting the process of settling the estate, shipping home a few boxes of his possessions, giving some things away, arranging for others to be sold, and cleaning his condo. From his small, one-bedroom condo, we carried out enough trash bags to fill six or seven Dumpsters. Donna, Vicki, John (Vicki's husband), and I worked all day long for about five days, wearing rubber gloves, often nauseated. We cried, but we also laughed. I was going through his bookshelf and found three or four books on home decorating. Considering the state of his condo, it was wonderfully ironic. In a storage area, we came across a box of thirty or so X-rated videos, which, we later learned, he was keeping for a married friend. We laughed as we read the titles aloud to each other. I wish I could remember some of them, but I can say that the videos were not of the urbane, sophisticated porn ilk, which might be suitable for couples and a romantic evening at a bed and breakfast. It was more like the guys-night-out-and-a-sixpack porn.

I handled my brother's death much differently than my mother's. When my mother died, I hardly cried at all. Maybe because I had been grieving for years, and I felt that there weren't any loose ends. It was her time. When my brother died, I relied on others, mostly Donna. I allowed myself to cry. I was sad because I lost my brother before we were, I sincerely believe, close to becoming much closer, just as we could fully share the pain that kept us apart.

The sense of loss was deep. As I came to know my brother's friends, I came to know more of him, sides of his personality that he had never shown me. Many of his friends were wracked with guilt. They felt they should have done more to push him into seeing a doctor. They felt like they had let him down. He apparently wanted them to mind their own business. One of his closest friends told me that he didn't want to live. His mother had died. He had been moved into a new position at work, which he hated. He was in pain.

As I heard these stories, I kept thinking of a scene from *A River Runs Through It*. Norman's wife had convinced Norman and Paul to take Neil, her pompous yet incompetent brother, fishing. Paul was reluctant. He knew that Neil would show up with angleworms in a Hill's Brothers' coffee can. Under pressure from Norman, Paul relents. As narrated in the book, the outing, which began with all of Norman's in-laws piled onto a flat-bed truck, ends disastrously. Neil has a hangover. Old Rawhide, a prostitute that Neil met the night before, shows up. They drink, make love, and fall asleep, naked. By the time that Norman and Paul find them, they are both sunburned. Norman, who knows he is in deep trouble, asks Paul, "How do you help a son of a bitch like that?" Paul responds, "You can't. But maybe all he wants to know is that someone wanted to help." I'm not trying to compare Neil or Paul or anyone else to my brother. I just think that Paul's message is true. Even if we aren't helped, we want to know that someone wanted to help.

I'm not sure that I ever helped my brother, but I do think I tried—maybe only a few times, maybe not enough. After I went through the Family Program at Hazelden to start dealing with my own anger, I told him about my experiences there. I said that he would get a lot out of it. He said he might "check it out." When I wrote to him to ask for advice about my son or when I asked him to visit my family in Missouri, I hope he saw this as a statement of love. And others also wanted to help, like his friends, who begged him to see a doctor. I hope he knew that "someone wanted to help."

It is difficult to know when you are being honest with yourself, and I might be deluding myself when I say, "I tried." But I think I did. And I think J.C. tried. And John tried. We just didn't know how to break through the walls. The walls were assumptions. I assumed that I knew how he felt, and he assumed that he knew how I felt. We needed to say, "This is what I thought you felt. Is that accurate?"

It is hard for most of us to find a way to slide this kind of comment into the flow of conversation. When I asked for his advice, he opened up. When I listened without judging, he spoke. I wish I had done more. What I most regret is that I didn't imagine the depth and range of my brother's pain.

I am glad that we were growing closer before his death. I feel like we grew even closer at his funeral, but I certainly have many regrets. I wish that I had said that I was proud of him. For some reason, I didn't realize he needed to hear this from me. I wish that I had spent a day with him at work, so I could have seen him in the life he created for himself away from our family. I wish I had spent more time with him when he was around his friends. We should have talked more about the pain of our childhood and celebrated our survival.

Our relationship, I believe, didn't end when he died. When I am going through tough times, I ask for help from him, our mom and, more recently, even from our father. About a year after he died, in the manner of twelve-step programs, I made amends to him. I wrote him a letter and said everything that needed to be said and then I burned it. I do believe, that writing, whether it is a letter or a memoir, can be a way of making amends, even with the dead. I hope that my brother is pleased that I am attempting to understand him, all of him, in my all-too-frail and human attempt to move toward something like absolute love.

The day before we left Bremerton for home, I went with Jim and Lauren to spread John's ashes. We took a long drive to a park where he loved to camp, walked out onto a dock, and poured his cremated remains across water that flows west, as I had done with our mother's remains less than a year before, across different water that flows south. It doesn't matter where the ashes were spread, or the direction of the current, because all waters merge into one.

I don't know that I am haunted by waters, like Norman Maclean, but I am drawn to them. When I am in a river with a rod in my hand, I come home to myself and those who have loved me. I hear words that should have been spoken.

SEARCHING FOR THE FATHER

NOTES ON GRADUATE SCHOOL

ONE DAY, I WAS LIVING AT HOME AND COMMUTING TO OLD DOMINION University, comfortable in my world. Then, the next day, it seems, I was in graduate school at the University of South Carolina, and everything had changed. Even the classrooms at South Carolina—at first glance, like any classroom in the country—seemed engulfed in a strange orangish light. My eyes couldn't quite focus. I blinked a lot. I floated. Didn't really walk. But floated. I was twenty-two, living away from home for the first time, and without a real friend, but it seemed like something else was going on. I felt strange, but I didn't have a clue why.

So I'm not at all sure how to write about this phase of my life. My mother, if she were telling the tale, would probably give it a "heroic overcoming all odds and ending triumphant" twist. My fellow graduate students—who sat with me in the same classrooms with the orangish glow, trying in our own ways to impress professors (World War II vets and not easily awed), who struggled with me to figure out academic politics—would probably spin the events toward farce. If I were relating the tale when I was still in the middle of it, I would gravitate toward the surreal.

Yes, surreal. As I was attempting to adjust to the rigors of a demanding graduate program, I noticed that my classmates kept disappearing. Smart people. They were in class one day, and then they were gone. When I asked about them, I might hear: "Dropped out." Or, "Couldn't take it." Or, "Said it wasn't worth it." More typically, I heard, "Don't know."

Or, "I've got my own problems." It was like these smart and capable classmates decided to give up on graduate school and get a real job in the dark of night; then, without waiting for the sun to rise, they packed all of their belongings into their VW Bug and disappeared on some country road. If a rumor had circulated that these people had be abducted by aliens, I would have believed it.

I remember three things about my first year in graduate school: (1) people kept disappearing, (2) my bicycle was stolen, and (3) my routine. I woke every morning at 7:00, except on the weekends, when I might sleep in until about 7:30. I showered, went to the cafeteria for breakfast (two eggs, over-easy; sausage; grits; biscuits; coffee, black), then I headed for the library. If things were going well, I was there about six minutes before 8:00, waiting with about a dozen other graduate students for the doors to open. I studied until lunch. After lunch at The Big Bird, a greasy spoon across from my dorm, I attended class. I ate dinner in the student union and then studied until the library closed. (There were rumors about graduate students who feel asleep at a desk deep in the stacks and woke only after the library doors were locked. They would have to slip out through one of the windows on the ground floor. For some reason, it never happened to me.) Then I went home, watched Carson's monologue, and studied until about 2:00. That was pretty much it, with a few variations. Some afternoons, I went to the gym and worked out. If I was tired at night, I went to the student union theater to watch an art film. Oh, I remember one other thing—I survived. That's the "heroic overcoming all odds and ending in triumph" part of the story Mom would have told.

After my first year in graduate school, I returned to Virginia Beach for the summer. It would be my last extended stay at home, and it was certainly a good break from my studies and the confusion of a foreign culture. A few days after my arrival, I began to work for my old surfing buddy Skip, who had landed a contract to do exterior cornice work on apartment buildings. By this time, we had both given up on being professional surfers or nonprofessional beach bums.

Before my first day on the job, Skip said, and actually believed, he would pick me up at 7:00 am. But I knew Skip. I woke up at 6:30, took

GEORGE H. JENSEN, JR.

my time eating a bowl of Cheerios, and then went back to sleep on the couch in the living room. Skip arrived at about 9:15. On the way to the construction site, he stopped at the 7-Eleven and bought two beers so he could make it to lunch, when he drank a few more beers and ate nothing. As the summer progressed, Skip was around less and less and I sort of fell into running his work crew. Most evenings, I spent time with Skip and Terri, his live-in girlfriend. Sometimes, we hung out at the house they were renting, which probably should have been condemned years before.

The entire summer, which came as the wake of 1960s rippled into the 1970s, was strange. The Vietnam War was still winding down, but no one bothered to protest against it. Some guys were cutting their hair and settling into professional jobs. Others, who had once played at being counter-culture, were now sliding into poverty. And people who experimented a little too seriously with drugs were now addicts.

Toward the end of the summer, Skip was arrested for selling dope to an undercover cop, who happened to be dating his sister. The cop appears to have been one of the most ineffective narcs in history of law enforcement. After a year undercover, he became so desperate to crack into the drug world, sporting his neatly pressed chinos and a military haircut, that he tried to make contacts through everyone he knew, including his girlfriend, which eventually led him to Skip and Skip to the long (in this case) preppie arm of the law. Skip hired a lawyer who showed up for the court date in a wrinkled suit and interviewed witnesses about thirty minutes before the trial started, scrawling notes on a yellow legal pad. I watched and thought, "At least he is using a legal pad instead of cocktail napkins, so maybe he has some idea of what he is doing." Largely because of his mother's testimony, which impressed the judge, Skip received probation, but with one condition: Terri had to move out. Then a series of transformations almost as surreal as my first year in graduate school. Skip and Terri decided to get married. I was Skip's best man. And Skip started attending AA meetings. By the grace of God, now over thirty years later, he is still sober.

In August, I returned to South Carolina to finish my MA course work and submit my thesis, a collection of poems, under the direction of

James Dickey. And this is where the story is most farcical. Dickey, a big man, somewhere between 6' 2" and 6' 6", around 240 to 270 pounds (I'm not really sure how big he was, and I don't really care enough to research it), was already attracting national attention. He had received the National Book Award for *Buckdancer's Choice*, and *Deliverance*, a bestseller, was being made into a film. As an undergraduate, I read Dickey's poetry and had even written a paper on the blood imagery in his work, so I came to the relationship with high expectations, which may have set me up for a bad experience. I was looking for more than constructive feedback; I wanted approval and validation. Dickey, however, was more interested in large quantities of bourbon, multiple affairs, mostly with his students, and mass media fame, more or less in that order. It was a relationship doomed from the start.

Soon, I learned that I would have to force Dickey to meet with me by waiting down the hall from his office. Every Tuesday and Thursday, the days he taught, I sat on a bench across from the elevator, starting about half an hour before his last class ended until about an hour after it ended. Sometimes, he didn't come back to his office. If he did appear, he would emerge from the elevator with his research assistant, who functioned more as a secretary. She was a tall doctoral student in creative writing with straggly dark hair and frumpy garb. The department head probably selected her to work with Dickey because she was not the kind of female he would attempt to seduce. (But what do I know? He probably hit on even her.) Every time the pair emerged from the elevator, I flagged Dickey down, introduced myself (he never remembered my name or face from any previous encounters), and asked him when we could meet. It was always next week. Sometimes, he had a good excuse. For three weeks, he was preparing to leave for an appearance on *The Today Show*. Each time he offered this excuse, he reminded me about his upcoming appearance on *The Today Show* and made me promise to watch. Then, for over a month, he was practically blind and could not read. He had allowed an artist to make a "life mask" of his face, but the artist had left the plastic compound on too long, burning his cornea. "Blinded by vanity," I thought to myself.

After weeks of pestering, he finally asked me back to his office. He read a few poems from my collection, which I titled *The Woods Shall Answer*. The poems were mostly about my family. For the volume, I used an epigraph from Captain Howard Baine's *Virginia's First Fleet*:

> The seaman's code maintains that once survivors are counted and numbered well, their comfort outweighs the captain's, their course precedes the ship's, unless they abandoned a ship not lost.

He read "An Unknown Cousin," which is about a cousin I never knew, Doris's brother, Uncle Billy and Aunt Anna's son. All I knew about him was that he once worked in the coal mines in Appalachia, his wife left him, and he died young:

> Remaining through the night,
> the blackened crust runs unbroken
> along the quick, a stigma
> to break the touch;
> my wife afraid the contamination
> might enter, turns away
> and leaves.
> Intertwined in the mine paths, workers
> shoulder their brothers as
> they fall, falter and carry on
> till the clearance horn sounds,
> but even here
> the weather penetrates,
> soaks through the earth
> and drips from the mountainsides
> to show our patience weak;
> the canary halts
> and is secretly replaced at dawn.

SOME OF THE WORDS ARE THEIRS

Dickey reread the lines "the weather penetrates, / soaks through the earth / and drips from the mountainsides" several times. He said, "Those lines are as good as any I have ever read from a student." This is what I had wanted to hear, but, by this time, I was skeptical about Dickey's character and wondered if I should believe him. He went on to say something about how poems have to be narratives and that a poem should "always try to tell a story." Then he put my collection on a shelf and said, "I want to live with these poems for a while." "Sure," I wanted to say.

I gave him a few weeks off and then revived the ritual, waiting in my spot, across from the elevator. After considerable pestering, he spent another fifteen minutes with me. He pulled my poetry from the shelf, wiped the dust away with his hand, sneezed, and read a few more poems. Then he agreed to sign my title page so I could graduate in December.

But it was not over. I prepared a title page and again began to wait in my spot. When I next caught him, weeks later, he was more drunk than usual. I watched him, reeking of bourbon, slurring his words, bounce from wall to wall as I followed him back to his office. He asked me about the title of the thesis. Shouldn't it read *The Woods Will Answer*? I told him that the title came from a Milton poem. He said "oh" and signed the title page.

"Free," I almost screamed. I ran down the stairs, leaping two or three steps at a time, and twisted my ankle. I walked around campus for a while, wondering if I need to have my ankle checked, thinking I needed to eat something, but just walking, a little dazed. I threw up. Then I threw up again. I need to get this man out of my system, I thought.

In December 1973, I took my MA comprehensive exams. I felt good about my essays. During the three or four months I spent preparing, I had memorized a lot of poetry, including every line of *The Waste Land*, so I was able to include extensive quotes and demonstrate my ability to pull off a New Critical close reading. This, because I was shooting for a high pass, which would grant candidacy to the PhD program. Unfortunately, it was Dickey's job, as my advisor, to read the exam. Week after week, spilling into January of 1974, I waited for the results. After I complained to the Director of Graduate Studies, he sent a memorandum to Dickey, and Dickey checked off his evaluation on the departmental form. I passed, but not with distinction. When the Director of Graduate Studies gave me the results, he saw that I was surprised. He handed me the form. At the top, Dickey had checked a box by the word "Pass." Down one line was another box and beside it the words: "High Pass, Admission to Ph.D. Program." This was before most English departments taught technical writing. Now, the form would have benefited from document design; the "High Pass" would have been above the "Pass."

225

I know what happened. My exam was placed in Dickey's mailbox. His RA picked up his mail and placed my exam on Dickey's desk, where it sat for weeks. Once the Director of Graduate Studies sent Dickey the memorandum, he might have pulled the exam out and glanced at it, but I doubt it. I don't think he read one line of my exam, and I don't think he even read the departmental form carefully. He glanced at it, assumed that the top box indicated the highest honor and checked it. I don't think that he would have given me anything but what he thought was the highest honor. In fact, he was known for giving nothing but As in all of his classes because giving students the highest grade was the safe way to protect himself from appeals. If a student filed an appeal, he would have to justify his evaluation, and it was well known among graduate students that he rarely read comprehensive exams, theses, dissertations, or even course papers. The course papers, which required comments, were read by his graduate assistant; for the other tasks, he simply signed off. So, I do think he intended to give me a High Pass, but I couldn't prove it. I could hardly ask him if he had checked the wrong box, or if he had even read my exam.

Throughout the spring semester of 1974, I was in limbo. I took additional classes hoping to gain admission to the PhD program on the merits of my course work and earn an assistantship. As a backup plan, I looked for a teaching job. So I had to approach Dickey once more, this time to ask for a letter of recommendation. As much as I dreaded asking Dickey for anything, I could hardly apply for jobs without a letter from the director of my thesis. After the usual amount of pestering, a confidential letter appeared in my file at the placement center, and I began to send about fifty or sixty application letters to colleges and universities. About a dozen department heads asked for my credentials, which indicated that I made it past the first cut, probably because Dickey's name was on my resume. Each time, I sent off my file from the placement center, which included a letter from Dickey. Then I heard nothing. Several years later, after I had finished my PhD, I went to the placement center with new letters of recommendation. The clerk asked me if I wanted the old letters to remain in my file. "I'm not sure," I said. She opened a manila folder and handed me several letters, among them was Dickey's letter, all three sentences of it, written by his research assistant, who had signed Dickey's name and added her initials. I threw it in the trash.

As I was in the transition between being an MA student and a PhD candidate, I started to hear more and more rumors about the political undercurrents of the department. For some reason, departments of English tend to be even more political than departments of History, Anthropology, or Philosophy. At this time, across the country, South Carolina was often said to be an "asylum." (My fellow graduate students and I began to hear comments like this once we began to interview for jobs at the annual Modern Language Association convention.) During the decade before I entered the program, Robert James (in this case, I supply a fictitious name) was Department Head, and he was able to recruit a superior group of scholars—almost overnight—by being entrepreneurial and dictatorial in ways that had not yet been seen at most colleges and universities. When he hired one prominent scholar, he walked into a departmental meeting and asked, "How many of you want to hire him?" Two or three professors raised their hands. "How many are opposed?" The rest of the professors cast their votes. Then he said, "Okay, I guess that settles it. We'll hire him." When a number of professors jumped to their feet and pointed out that the majority was clearly against the hire, James said, "That's not how I counted." When he was interviewing another distinguished scholar, he handed the man an envelope. He said, "In that envelope is my last and final offer." The scholar opened the envelope to find a blank piece of paper. He was confused and embarrassed, assuming James had made a mistake. He finally said, "There's nothing on the paper." James replied, "That's right. That's my first and final offer." In other words, write your own ticket. When the editorship of *Journal of American Literature* changed, he tried to buy the prestigious journal. He called up Duke University Press and asked, "How much do you want for it?" The director of Duke University Press, a southern gentleman unused to carpetbaggers like James, was flabbergasted and insulted. These kinds of rumors were rampant.

James's administrative style, his gunslinger attitude, was not the way academic life worked at the time. CEOs of *Fortune* 500 companies might have wheeled and dealed this brashly, but not the head of the Department of English at a southern university. Yet, using these tactics, he built a department that was ranked among the best in the nation by the time I enrolled, eclipsing many departments at Ivy League institutions. The disadvantage, which I assume he did not anticipate (or care about), was that the faculty split into factions, and then the factions split into factions. Soon single professors formed their own factions, and many of the faculty were not on speaking terms. Part of being a graduate student at South Carolina (at least, during this era, I hear things are much different now) was learning to be loyal to a professor who would direct your dissertation and mentor you through your first publications, but not so blindly loyal that you were perceived as someone's foot soldier—that is, easy prey.

I don't want to overdramatize. To the department's credit, graduate students were rarely harmed as professors fought over a research assistant, which happened without the wisdom of Solomon and without rationality prevailing in the end. I did hear a rumor about one hapless graduate student who sat through the oral defense of his dissertation as committee members squared off against each other, hurling veiled insults across the table. The graduate student sat there, bewildered, wondering why no one was asking him questions about his dissertation. This kind of thing apparently happened at the time, but only occasionally. I was only once caught in departmental politics.

SOME OF THE WORDS ARE THEIRS

Halfway through the spring semester of my second year, I lucked into a Research Assistantship, which meant, by fiat, that I was in danger of being perceived as haven chosen sides (an awkward turn of phrase, but accurate). Joseph Katz had just fired two of his research assistants on the Frank Norris edition because they were spending more time drinking coffee than working. During the previous semester, I had taken Katz's course in bibliography and textual criticism, so I was given the job collating texts, the tedious task of comparing different editions of Norris's novels, line by line, letter by letter, noting each variant. Because of his recent experience with research assistants, Katz kept a close eye on my work and was soon bragging to his colleagues about my speed and accuracy. So, after almost two years of graduate studies, I felt like I was finally on the inside.

During the same semester, however, I was also taking a Faulkner seminar with James B. Meriwether, whom many considered to be the leading Faulkner scholar in the world. Students from the Sorbonne and other prestigious universities traveled to Columbia, South Carolina, to study with him, and even leading Faulkner critics spent sabbaticals at South Carolina to draw from Meriwether's expertise and decades of research notes. In 1974, Cleanth Brooks, for example, spent an entire semester working out of an office across the hall from Meriwether. His Faulkner seminar had four basic requirements: (1) read everything Faulkner wrote, (2) read everything written about Faulkner, (3) give a fifteen minute oral report, timed to the second, and (4) write a damn good paper. For our oral reports, we were required to write our text then read it, in the style of a presentation at the Modern Language Association convention. As we began, we had to turn on a large red timer. The timer was designed to aid photographers as they processed film, but Professor Meriwether used it for his seminars because it had a large face, it was accurate, and it ticked loud enough to be a distraction. He double-checked us with a stopwatch. I guess he was concerned that we might pad a few seconds to our time as we reached over to turn off the clock. As we were reading our text and eyeing the big red clock, Meriwether noted our shortcomings on a legal pad with his squeaky felt-tipped pen. The squeaking of the pen was even more distracting than the ticking of the clock. When I gave my presentation, I came up three seconds short. Meriwether spent the next five minutes of class railing about how I had wasted three seconds of precious time, peppering his comments with a number of remarks about my moral character and dubious potential to perform graduate-level work. His course was a little like being in intellectual boot camp.

Most of us were petrified of the short, skinny man. One student, Lucy Stewart, who was caught in some kind of transition between being a hippie and a New Age spiritual vegetarian, was the only one who had the courage to even entertain the notion that Meriwether was a pompous ass. Before she delivered her oral report, she carefully scripted her talk, marking how much time should have passed at each key interval. On D-Day, she came into the seminar room with a gargantuan glass of water. Like a sloth, she turned on the big red clock and began to read her report at an even pace. Whenever she moved a little ahead of her scripted schedule, she casually took a drink of water. Then she was back on schedule. At one point, I think that she drank water for close to forty-five seconds, in measured and audible gulps. She finished at fifteen minutes, exactly. Not a second wasted. Tales of Lucy Stewart soon spread through graduate student offices and, from that point on, orbs of light seemed to dart from her forehead.

During the semester, since I had given up Dickey and everything to do with poetry, I asked Professor Meriwether to be my advisor. He tentatively agreed, providing I prove myself in the Faulkner seminar. I tried to impress him by writing an ambitious paper about Eugene O'Neill's influence on Faulkner, but the project was too big. I had also been having trouble with my roommate, Jim Martin. He was lumbering, affable guy in September, but, by April, I saw him as being a little too much like the protagonist of Frank Norris's *McTeague*. As long as McTeague's needs were met, he was generous and well loved. When he wasn't getting enough food, alcohol, or sex, the beast within him emerged. By April, I was seeing Jim's beast.

At the time, I was barely functioning on five hours of sleep, and Jim kept bringing his girlfriend into the room for romance. One night, at about 3:00 am, I had enough. I told him that I needed sleep and asked him to remove his girlfriend. He erupted. In a second, he was on top of me with his hands around my throat, screaming, "Why don't you fight back?" If he had taken his hands from my neck, I could have explained that I survived my childhood by being passive. That would have been an honest answer, and my passivity probably got me through this situation as well. Eventually, he backed off. I quickly dressed, walked into the streets of Columbia and checked into a hotel. A few days later, I moved into an apartment with a couple of friends. All this turmoil was in the background of my efforts to impress Professor Meriwether. Despite working about thirty-five hours a week on the seminar, I wrote a weak paper and received a C for the course. When I had my end-of-the-semester conference with Meriwether, he asked me, "Do you want to revise this?"

"Will I be able to raise my grade?" I asked.

His face turned a light shade of red (I suspect from anger, certainly not from embarrassment), his eyes squinted, and his entire body tightened. "No."

Like a sap, I told him that I would work on it over the summer.

I guess that he thought I should want to revise it, show it to him, just to purify myself. He then asked me to drop his grade sheets off at the Department of English, including the grade sheet with my C for the seminar. I felt like I was carrying the ax to my own beheading.

I never revised that paper, and I almost didn't make it to the fall semester. Katz's enemies in the department, who were then numerous, used my C in Professor Meriwether's seminar to try to eliminate one of Katz's research assistants (viz., me), which meant I would no longer be able to afford to work on a PhD. Katz won this fight, and I stayed in graduate school. The next year, for some reason, I was admitted to the PhD program.

Joe Katz proved to be an exceptionally supportive mentor. He issued me a contract to work on a bibliography of Arthur Miller's work, which became my first book, and he loaned me some manuscripts of Joseph Heller's *We Bombed in New Haven*, part of his personal collection, so that I could write an article on the textual history of the play, which became my first article. He also agreed to direct my dissertation on Eugene O'Neill, an edition of the letters exchanged between O'Neill and the Theatre Guild. Unfortunately, he was going through a difficult divorce as I began to write. He wasn't very accessible during the final stages of my work. Being pretty independent, I was able to complete the dissertation without much guidance, but I needed help pushing it through committee. By some miracle, John MacNicholas, a young Assistant Professor, one of the members of my committee, stepped forward and became my acting director. I will be eternally grateful to both Katz and MacNicholas for their confidence in my ability. In its final form, my dissertation was 930 pages long. My fellow graduate students called it "The Cube." In bound form, it almost was a cube: 11½" by 8½" by 10".

231

I should have been proud of this accomplishment, but I wasn't. I didn't even attend my graduation. Many of my friends felt the same way when they walked out of their oral defense. It was one part emotional letdown, one part loss of purpose, one part culmination of years of intense criticism, and one part crappy job market.

In December 1977, I officially graduated. According to data collected by the Modern Language Association, it was the worst year for finding a job with a PhD in English for the entire twentieth century, and I had trouble finding professors to write letters of recommendation. During his divorce, Katz had shut down for about eighteen months. Some of the scholars who had submitted manuscripts to his journal or one of the series of scholarly books he edited became progressively more angry as their work collected dust, so the extremely positive letter from Katz did not carry as much weight as it might have two years earlier. After receiving my C in Professor Meriwether's Faulkner seminar, I took his course on Southwest Humor. Even the "major" authors in the tradition of Southwest Humor, like Joel Chandler Harris or August Longstreet, were fairly minor and would not have warranted a graduate seminar, except their style of telling tall tales (usually about killing bears or whacking people with fence rails) influenced Twain and Faulkner. (Katz had an interesting description of what he considered to be the archetypal Southwest Humor tale: *A pregnant lady is walking down the street. A drunk redneck with no teeth kicks the pregnant woman in the stomach. The redneck spits tobacco juice and says, "Well, whata ya know, I just kilt a b'ar." Then everyone laughs like hell.*) Through a great deal of hard work, I earned an A from Meriwether who believed that most students deserve Bs and the few lost waifs who shouldn't have presumed to take his course deserve Cs, but only a few anointed ones ever deserve As. So, I thought he would write me a good letter. If he couldn't, I thought he would at least be tough-minded (a trait he much admired) and tell me that he couldn't bring himself to say much of anything positive. He agreed to write the letter and sent it confidentially to the placement center. I later discovered through a friend, who was on a hiring committee at another university, that his letter was lukewarm. He wrote that I was "less mature than most students." The statement might seem innocuous enough, and all that I think he meant by it was that I was shy and socially awkward. However, in an extremely tight job market, when over five hundred qualified PhDs applied for a single job, it was the kiss of death. When I heard that Professor Meriwether thought I was immature, I thought back to the time I saw him kick a chair across the room because a librarian had failed to put a book on reserve, as he had requested. It's all relative, I guess.

Even with Meriwether's ambivalent letter, I was a finalist for a few good jobs, but graduates with stronger letters were hired. For a year, I taught at South Carolina as a Teaching Associate, a position they invented so that they could hire unemployed PhDs to teach a twelve-hour load of freshman composition for $9,000. Even in 1977 dollars, this was a horrible salary, but I was pleased to have any kind of job. After this position expired (it was only awarded for a year), I spent a year teaching part-time for even less money. Each year, I applied for eighty to ninety jobs.

232

A Family

AFTER YEARS OF APPLYING FOR JOBS AND INTERVIEWING AT MLA, I WAS finally hired as the coordinator of a reading and writing center at the University of Illinois-Medical Center, my first job out of graduate school. Life in Chicago was good, for a while. From my first day in town, I loved the city. I still consider Chicago to be my spiritual hometown. Then problems started to develop with my boss. He and I had frequent arguments. After about three years of bickering, work became intolerable, and I reluctantly began to search for other jobs.

In August 1983, I began my first tenure-track position teaching developmental writing courses at Georgia State University. In March 1984, a pretty young woman with brown hair and green eyes and a great smile, whom I had seen around the campus, walked into an elevator moments after I did. We smiled. I asked, "Would you like to have coffee sometime?" She said, "Yes." We set a time to meet, then made some awkward introductions. "I'm George." "I'm Donna." All this, with another professor, probably in his fifties, standing in the corner, a bit embarrassed.

Over coffee, I asked Donna to dinner. A few nights later, we went to a Thai restaurant. During our getting-to-know-each-other conversation, Donna mentioned that she had Crohn's disease. She said that it was a gastrointestinal disease where one's own immune system attacks the intestines. She probably felt that she had to warn me early in the evening that she was sick, so, if I was going to be one of those guys who runs, I would run before she allowed herself to become vulnerable. When she talked about Crohn's, I remember thinking that I had some of those symptoms.

We began to spend most of our free time together and were engaged within a couple of months. At this point, we had some conversations about what kind of life we wanted to share. I told her that I didn't know if I wanted kids. I said it was the environment. The ozone layer was thinning. Life on earth could not last more than another generation or two. How could we bring a kid into this mess? I was certainly concerned about the environment, but I was more concerned about what it would mean to become a father.

Between the time that we met and the time we were engaged, Donna had an operation. Between the time we were engaged and the time we were married, she had another. Every few months, I had to take her to the emergency room. One of her doctors (she had many) told me, "You know that Donna has been very sick for a long time."

About a year and a half later, Donna told me that she was pregnant. Even though we had already talked about the ozone layer, she was probably surprised by the dull look of panic on my face. With some time, I adjusted to the idea of having a child; still, I secretly hoped for a girl. I thought somehow, someway, I could figure out how to father a girl. I couldn't fathom how I would ever learn to father a boy.

On December 19, 1986, after about nineteen hours of labor, Jay was born. Moments after the birth, the nurse handed me my son, wrapped in a blanket. I held him a long time. He stared at me, without blinking, a puzzled look on his face. He seemed to ask, "Who the hell is this guy?" Later, I went to the waiting room and told my in-laws that we had a boy, and that he had a nose just like Mae, Donna's mother. I could hardly speak.

About seven months after Jay was born, we learned that Donna was pregnant again. About the same time, I began to feel sick. I was losing weight and had abdominal pain; I soon turned the shade of a chemotherapy patient. Through a series of tests that spanned six or seven months, my doctor thought I might have liver cancer or other

234

liver diseases, none of which held a very positive prognosis. I was worried about dying before I could raise my children, but, eventually, the doctor decided I, like Donna, had Crohn's disease. I would have to manage the disease, but I could live a fairly normal life.

Throughout the pregnancy, Donna talked about how Jeff kicked more often than Jay did, and how he kicked harder. When the nurse handed him to me, swaddled in a hospital blanket, he arched his back and squirmed. He could not be still. I learned to watch him as he slept, because that was the only time he slowed down enough for me to get a good look at him. By the time he was about nine months old, he slept with "Bobo," a stuffed bear, dressed in a nightshirt and a sleeping cap with a cotton-ball tip. As he drifted off to sleep, Jeff would suck on his pacifier and rub the ball of cotton on Bobo's hat against his nose.

Even though we had a comfortable life in Atlanta, I knew, for the sake of my career, I had to move from the basic writing program at Georgia State to an English department. After several years of looking, I was offered a position at Purdue University-Calumet, a small regional campus of the Purdue system with about 7,000 students. It was not a great job, but English departments were reluctant to hire someone who taught in a basic writing program. I liked the head of the department at Purdue-Calumet, so I accepted the position with the understanding that it would be easier to move from this English department to a better job. Donna understood but was not thrilled. This meant that she would have to move away from her parents and relatives.

In September, we moved to Hammond, Indiana, near steel mills. When I arrived on campus, I was surprised that some of my colleagues would not speak to me. I later found out that the head of the department hired me against many of their wishes. It was pretty much all bad. The department. The town. The environment. Especially the environment.

The air often smelled of sulfur. From time to time, gray ash fell from the sky. The first time it happened, in late September, we thought it was snowing. We dressed the kids in winter coats and took them outside. Then I caught a few flakes in my hand and saw that the flakes

235

were ash. Needless to say, we rushed the kids back inside. One of my students wrote an essay about the high rate of a rare cancer in her family. As she researched the topic, she found out that her house was built on a slag heap, the toxic soil that remains after iron ore has been extracted. Another student told me, "I don't care about saving the whales. I'll never see one."

Still I enjoyed my teaching. I will never forget four male students in my Composition II class. For the first half of the semester, they did only the minimal work to earn Cs. Then, when I began to break the class into small groups so that they could collaborate on a research paper, the four slackers decided that they wanted to work together. I had a long talk with them and issued a challenge. I said that I had real concerns about them working together. They had only slid by. I had doubts that they would support each other. They were a little shocked by my honesty, but they told me they would work hard. And they did. They even chose a topic close to my heart: The depletion of the ozone layer. I was never more proud of any group of students. They all turned in well-written and thoroughly researched papers. I gave them all As, even though they, to the man, made the same odd mistake. When they read about CFCs, the chemical released from spray cans that destroys ozone, they thought the text said something about VCRs. They all, to the man, wrote in their papers that VCRs were destroying the planet. When I questioned them about this, they all, to the man, defended their research. They were damn proud of their work and confident in their findings, so I let it go. I sometimes wonder if they, to the man, continue to argue with their families about the dangers of using VCRs. They were probably thrilled, to the man, when DVDs came out and they could start watching movies at home, without harming the ozone layer.

If I had any idea of staying at Purdue-Calumet, a singular event convinced me to re-enter the job market. And the singular event had all of the elements of a tale in the tradition of Southwest Humor: A pregnant woman, senseless violence (in this case, the weapon was words), and some form of anti-social behavior. Early in the fall, the head of the department, who was pregnant, missed a departmental

236

---

meeting. One of the linguists, who despised the head, seized the opportunity to attack her by questioning her decision to hire the new "rhetorician." He spent forty-five minutes of the meeting explaining why the department should not have hired the "rhetorician," that this person might have been promised a lighter teaching load and a higher salary than the rest of the department, that the department did not need a "rhetorician," blah, blah, blah. Because three writing teachers were hired that year, it took me about thirty minutes to figure out that he was talking about me. I wasn't angry or hurt. Instead, I made a quick decision to find another job. That weekend, I sent out seventy-eight job letters. It is amazing how mature and rational I could be at work.

In February 1990, I interviewed for a job in Kentucky. After I read a paper for the faculty, the poet-in-residence introduced himself and asked me what it was like to work with James Dickey. I tried to be honest, yet politic, and said that I didn't have a great deal of contact with him. The poet seemed surprised. He then said he was at a creative writing conference and several of Dickey's students came seeking jobs. They all had long eloquent letters written by Dickey, their mentor. When I later read Christopher Dickey's *Summer of Deliverance*, a memoir about his father, I learned that Dickey did, for a while, sober up toward the end of his life, and I surmised that these long, supportive letters he wrote for his students probably came during this period of sobriety. But this poet-in-residence wanted me to sing Dickey's praises, and I didn't have anything to say.

"When I was working with Dickey, he was drinking a great deal," I said.

The poet's face changed. He said, "Many of us writers have a problem with that."

I didn't say anything about the three-line letter of recommendation Dickey's Research Assistant had written for me, or how she had signed his name and added her initials.

Almost everyone who reads my resume asks about Dickey. I have thought about removing his name, but some name has to occupy the slot of "advisor" for my MA thesis. I could substitute the name of another professor at South Carolina, but that could cause worse problems. If one of the faculty where I was hoping to be hired knew that person, a phone call would do me in. I have also considered inventing a poet, say Frederick Durst. No one would ask about him. If they did, I could develop an elaborate story: "He is a minor poet, very eccentric, writes only in Portuguese, you know. He's big, very big, in Brazil." I might get away with a lie like this, but the risk is too great. Search committees are usually rigorous about verifying every detail in a candidate's vita. If they called South Carolina and asked to speak to Durst, they would find that he had never taught there. Nowadays, I would have to create an entire identity for Durst on the Internet to support such the lie.

As much as I wanted Dickey erased from my life, it seems like I just could not be done with the man. For years, I found it difficult to read any of his poetry. When Christopher Dickey's *Summer of Deliverance* first appeared in 1998, I didn't even look at it. Donna, however, saw a review and said she wanted to read it. I bought her a hardback copy for Christmas, but she couldn't finish it. "Too gruesome," she said. That spring, we sold the hardback copy at a garage sale for $1.25.

In 2002, when I was teaching at Missouri State, after I began to research my own family history, almost thirty years after I finished working with Dickey, I checked a copy out from the university library and forced myself to read it. I found that the poet's life was a mess, an incessant string of alcoholic episodes and failed relationships. James Dickey felt neglected by his father, and he responded by neglecting his sons. In the family tradition, Christopher Dickey confesses that he, too, neglected his son. Generation after generation. This is one of the most intriguing aspects of alcoholic families: Why do we complain about the sins of the alcoholic father and then become like him? In J.C.'s 1992 letter to me, he wrote of our father: "I never understood why he left and never contacted us again until I saw the same tendencies in myself."

One passage of the book describes the early years of Dickey's second marriage to Deborah Dodson, one of his students. Christopher Dickey writes of his father in 1976: "[I]n mid-October, he told his

---

GEORGE H. JENSEN, JR.

class that my mother was in the hospital and dying, and after that class he asked Deborah to marry him." These events occurred when I was in graduate school, writing my dissertation. Of Dickey's early relationship with Deborah, Christopher writes:

> Debbie was in love. Debbie wanted a happy marriage, a happy family. But she would come back to the house in the afternoons those first couple of years thinking she would tell Jim something funny that had happened to her, just tell him about her day, and she would find him sitting in the living room looking at the lake silently weeping, and nothing that she could say or do seemed to make a difference. The more she failed to be all that she was expected to be, the more she became the child that is all she really knew how to be—the bad, beloved child who demands that her trespasses be forgiven so she can go out and trespass again. She became, without ever wanting or meaning to, my father's penance.

Reading this passage about the father surrogate that I had hated was a bit like reading the letters about my real father. I saw more of the man and felt less resentment.

I didn't get the job in Kentucky, but probably not because of my comments about Dickey. I think that other comments did me in, probably a few statements that were construed as being unflattering to Marxist critics. I am certainly appreciative of Marx's genius, and I am fairly unappreciative of how some scholars use his theory. I don't think that even Marx would want his theory, especially his critique of capitalism, to become a new ideology, especially when this new ideology attacks the notion of individual agency. I tell my students, "If you want to use Marx's theory, then use it in a way that accounts for the possibility of Marx, an individual, developing a theory that breaks with the best thought of his times." I also believe that Marx's theory, which analyzes the connection between historical contexts and ideas, has to be placed in its own historical context. I made some comments like this during my interview, and I think some of the Marxists in the department inferred that I was unenlightened or, even worse, naive.

A few months after blowing the interview in Kentucky, I interviewed for a job in Missouri. The faculty actually seemed more interested in talking about my research than chatting about James Dickey. They even made an offer. When I discussed the offer with Donna, she said, "I don't care where it is. Take it. I want out of here." She had enough of gray ash falling like snow in early October.

240

MID-LIFE

I HAD ALWAYS WANTED TO LEARN TO FLY FISH, EVEN AS A BOY OF EIGHT OR nine, as I watched the blurred images of the art on our black and white television. The broadcast, which came on every Sunday afternoon, was *The American Sportsman*, hosted by Kurt Gowdy. In my synthesized single memory of the show, I see a lone man standing in the middle of a stream that cut back and forth across a meadow in Wyoming or Montana, and a fly line looping back upon itself, slowly on a four-count rhythm. Oddly, I remember it all in color, the evergreens, the tall grass, the crystalline water, the bright orange fly line. I held to this image, and I wanted to learn, even though I was growing up in Virginia Beach, where fishing meant dropping a hook and worm from a pier or wading into the ocean and throwing a line between the breakers, even though I had never even seen a trout or held a fly rod.

241

I was fascinated by the entire range of the sport as I had pieced it together from sporting shows, commercials, and a few photographs in magazines. I remember watching a man tie flies on a television commercial. I remember hearing about someone in Norfolk who made fly rods from bamboo. I remember seeing a picture, perhaps in *National Geographic*, of someone casting thirty feet of line through still air. I imagined what happened as the line landed just ahead of a trout, the fish taking the fly, running, the whirl of line being pulled from a reel, a jump, the angler working the trout toward a net, landing it, gently removing the hook and carefully releasing it. And later, I read Hemingway's Nick Adams stories. A young man fishing alone, landing large trout, knowing what to do. It all seemed to fit me, or at least the person I wanted to become. But I never lived near trout streams. I never had time to learn. I never had anyone to teach me.

In 1990, we moved to Missouri, near trout streams, so I bought myself a fly rod, thigh-high waders, a plastic fly box, a handful of flies, and a cool hat. I drove through country roads, my gear in the back of my 1985 Cavalier, and whenever the road crossed a stream, I pulled over and tried to catch fish. Tried. Tried and failed. At every spot, I worked my way through my thin collection of flies, one at a time, in a random order, without any rationale. My flies came in two categories: dry and wet. If it floated when I hurled it upon the waters, it was a dry fly. If it sunk, it was a wet fly. I picked flies from my fly box like a dog lover buys dog food: If it looked like it would taste good to me, then I tried to convince trout to eat it. After about twenty minutes of beating the water with my first fly, I would bite it off the tippit (the thin monofilament at the end of the leader), stick it on my T-shirt, and then select a new fly that looked good enough to eat. The flies on my T-shirt were my record of failure, and soon every T-shirt I owned was filled with holes. Even though I didn't know it, I had apprenticed myself to myself to learn a sport that is part of an elaborate oral tradition. The how-to of fly fishing is usually passed from father to son, and I was trying to get it from reading books and watching videos, often with comic results.

My line was caught in trees. I didn't catch trout, only a few bluegills, which will hit just about anything. (When Jeff was about eight, he actually caught a bluegill with a bare hook. No bait. Just a bare hook. So catching a bluegill with a fly rod was no great accomplishment.) When I cast, I couldn't get the timing down. I cast rapidly and the fly line cracked like a whip, snapping the fly from my tippit in midair. I threw trailing loops, my fly line collapsing back on itself. My leader ended up in elaborate wind knots that even a patient man could not untie. And I was far from patient. Every time I came home from fishing, or attempting to fish, Donna and the boys would ask, "Did you catch anything?" Nothing. My new neighbors, most of whom were born from a long bloodline of sportsmen, watched me drive out full of hope and return home dejected. They began to wonder what was wrong with me.

Something was wrong. Something beyond my struggles as an angler. Fishing was just the metaphor. I was becoming more angry. I was forty, and I realized that much of my anger might have something to do with mid-life issues, but something else was going on. And it kept going on for years. I tried to figure it out, and Donna tried to figure it out.

Around October of 1992, Donna and I attended a local fly fishing club. It was Donna's idea. She thought that I might pick up enough tips to catch a few fish, and then I would be less angry, but the meeting didn't help. We listened for almost an hour as the members of the club attempted to plan a group picnic and fishing outing. They argued over who would bring the mustard and who would bring the bread and what kind of bread that person should bring—white, wheat, or rye, sliced or unsliced, store-bought or homemade. Later, I realized that this must be exactly the way they wanted to spend their time with each other: being together without exactly relating.

This club finally resolved the considerable and desperate issues relating to the picnic and then one of the members gave a talk about fly fishing for white bass. He gave no evidence of ever having spoken in public. He rambled on, talking past his friends, unaware that everyone was bored and ready to go home. Finally, he said, "I guess that's all I have to say." Someone in the back shouted, "Then sit down and shut up, dammit!" They were all members of a club, but they should have never met in the same room.

Donna and I never attended another meeting. Maybe it was a little too much like our marriage at the time. We argued about everything, and the source of our problems was not at all apparent. We even found it difficult to fish together. Donna, who fished with bait and always caught her limit, kept advising me to put a worm on my fly. I kept telling her, "I would rather fish my way and fail."

SOME OF THE WORDS ARE THEIRS

By the next year, I began to blame my usual failures as an angler on the local streams. The Ozarks are known for tail-water fishing, the trout habitat created by the cold water flowing from the bottom of a man-made lake into a stream, as with the White River area below Bull Shoals Lake in Arkansas, or into another lake, as when Table Rock Lake empties into Lake Taneycomo. These were not real trout streams, I told myself. These were manufactured streams with stocked fish, which were more accustomed to being fed than to feeding, more likely to strike at corn or trout balls launched from spinning rods than natural organisms or flies. Some anglers are successful by fishing a few feet from the pipe that dumps baby trout from the hatchery into the lake. Others are successful fishing with simple round, light brown fly, made with spun deer hair, a close imitation of the food pellets that the fish were fed in the hatchery. I told myself that I was a purist. I was more serious than these guys. Of course, they caught fish and I didn't.

I really believed that, if only I could fish in real trout streams like the streams in Wyoming, Montana, or Idaho, I would do better. I began planning trips that never materialized. Something always came up. My mother was in the early stages of Alzheimer's. Her breast cancer recurred, and she needed radiology. Or we were broke. Or I had to teach. Something always interfered with the trip.

Until I just decided to go, alone, to fish in Wyoming, certainly, but also to drive through Nebraska and Colorado, the land of my father's family. Grandma Musa's family had run a hotel in Brule, Nebraska. Grandpa Henry and his family had emigrated from Denmark in the 1880s and settled on a farm in Colorado, just across the state line. They met in the area and married before heading to Vaughn, Washington, where my father was born. I was particularly interested in learning more about my grandfather, who was a cowboy. When I was still a boy, Grandma Musa sent J.C. and me a pair of buffalo horns in an ornate, golden box, shortly after our father left the family. During the single visit Grandma Musa was able to take across the country to Virginia Beach, she told us that our Grandpa Henry had traded blankets for the horns with "real Indians" and then made a coat rack out of them. For me, this story and others stood in the place of a father.

GEORGE H. JENSEN, JR.

As I was growing up and coming of age, I did have more than stories. A number of men had an impact on my development. Ben Smith had taught me about home repairs. As he helped out our family by fixing a clogged drain pipe or a broken window, I handed him tools and he explained how to do the job, the right way. When I was in the Boy Scouts, Dave Southard took our entire pack camping, fishing, and hiking. When I was about fifteen, Uncle R.T. told me that he loved me. This is the only time I heard those words from a father figure. When I was in college, Dr. Conrad Festa, who would later become my advisor, told me I was smart. This was the first time I heard those words from a teacher. Mostly, however, I used stories and images to replace my father, like the stories about Grandpa Henry the cowboy or images I constructed from photographs about Uncle Rusty the logger. For a long time, this worked. I had no reason to think it wouldn't work for the rest of my life. Then that mid-life stuff started.

For years I had been putting off the tasks of mid-life transition, trying to keep the transition from becoming a crisis because my life was too stressed, too hectic, too chaotic. Systematically and routinely, I had been writing articles and books, advancing my career as a college professor, as I was taking care of my mother, raising young children, and not paying enough attention to my wife, my marriage, or myself. I joked that "I didn't have a life." It wasn't a joke. Somehow, in the spring of my forty-second year, I made the commitment to go on my trip, and I knew from the start, before I even left my driveway, that it was a psychological journey. I didn't know what I would find out there, but I knew I needed to find something.

Although I usually plan trips fairly thoroughly, I spent the remaining few weeks of the semester throwing some clothes and equipment into a pile in my closet. I bought some flies and freeze-dried food, borrowed a tent and backpack, but I didn't even bother to set the tent up to make sure it was in one piece. The process was thoroughly haphazard—a mirror image of my mental state.

The Land of My Father

By the end of the spring semester, my pile of clothes, camping equipment, and freeze-dried food had reached critical mass. I packed it all into my Cavalier, which I half expected to die on the highway, and took off, driving north on Highway 13. On the first day, I drove half way to Wyoming and stopped at a hotel somewhere in Nebraska. I don't remember where, because Nebraska is pretty much the same from one end to the other. Before I went to sleep, I read an article about the history of the area (in the hotel's local guide) that said that the Indian wars were over by the 1880s, the time when my father's family settled there. I had imagined, when Grandpa Henry traded blankets for buffalo horns, the area was still the frontier, the Indians were dangerous, my father's family had come to America and gone straight to the edge of civilization. Now, less than a day into my trip, I was already being forced to rethink family history.

In the morning, I quickly ate an orange, threw my luggage in the car and continued to drive due west. I exited Highway 80 at Brule, Nebraska, the town where my grandmother's family owned a hotel called the Polly House in the 1890s, but all I could find was a handful of abandoned buildings, none of which looked like a hotel. I went down the road about another twenty miles to find a restaurant and there called my cousin once-removed, Lloyd Petersen, whom I had never met. Over the phone, Lloyd said that he remembered my grandfather, his uncle, and that he would meet me for breakfast the next morning. With a little time to kill in a sleepy town, I checked into a motel that had seen better days and then visited the town's graveyard. There I found a number of Jensen family graves, including that of Peter, my great-grandfather.

I had heard of Peter, who sold his farm and bought the family over from Denmark to keep his four sons from being drafted into the Prussian Army. When his wife died on the voyage, he reportedly offered the captain $5,000 to turn back toward shore so he could bury her on land. The captain refused. Peter died, at ninety-four, after he broke his hip. He had jumped from a moving train because he was afraid he was going to miss his stop. This was all part of the lore of my father's family, stories my Grandmother Musa had told me. But the part of the lore that I remembered most, what I cherished, were the stories my Grandma Musa told about Henry, her husband. She told me that he traded with Indians, that he knew Bill Cody, that he had even poked his shotgun in the chest of Wyatt Earp's drunk deputy and run him out of town.

The next morning, I met Lloyd for breakfast. We talked and ate; he said "hello there" to all his friends as they came in or left and introduced me as his "long lost cousin." Later, he showed me the Jensen family farm and, as we were driving, told me stories about Peter, how he had designed a drainage ditch, which evened out the water table and improved crop production, how he was a homeopath, and how he built a small house that he dragged down to the Platte River each summer, where it was cooler, and then back up near the barn and farmhouse in the winter, where it was safe from high water. When I mentioned the stories my Grandma Musa had told me about Wyatt Earp's deputy and Bill Cody, he seemed a little surprised or confused. Politely, he said, "It could be."

I was hoping to hear more stories about Henry, but instead I realized that the stories I had cherished as a boy were probably tall tales. Lloyd had grown up in the area, a few miles from the family farm, and had not heard any of the stories that Grandma Musa told J.C. and me. I began to wonder if I had a rather average grandfather, if maybe my grandmother was a nice lady who wanted to give a heroic myth to a boy without a father. She must have known that I needed it, as I needed the buffalo horns in a golden box, which she sent me shortly after my father left. The horns were real, a wonderful family artifact. The golden box was one of those Whitman's Sampler boxes, decorated in gold paper for the Christmas season.

As I began to witness the myth of my cowboy grandfather die, I began to see the need of moving beyond the hero myth of young adulthood, the myth of the strong warrior who saves a victim from some villain or monster. Although I began to realize that I must let go of the cowboy hero, I wasn't certain what would take its place. As Daniel J. Levinson, author of *The Seasons of a Man's Life*, writes, the archetype of middle age "is still poorly evolved." I could think of archetypes of youth, such as Ulysses, and archetypes of old age, such as Mentor, but I could not think of any relating to middle age. Except, perhaps, the historical model of Paul Gauguin, the businessman, husband and father who chucks it all to move to Tahiti and become a painter. Part of mid-life transition, Levinson says, is "becoming one's own man," moving beyond the restrictions of social conventions, parental expectations, cultural notions of success, to develop a life pattern that he will find meaningful and that will make him happy. But most of us don't tend to see Gauguin's example as heroic. He is the man who acted irresponsibly. While we might admire—even desire— the freedom of this lifestyle, it is hard not to think of the wife and children he left behind. There must be some middle ground.

That afternoon, I said goodbye to Lloyd and drove on into Wyoming, to the Wind River near Shoshoni, where I stopped at a convenience store to buy a fishing license. On the wall hung a yellowed poster, an advertisement for a fishing guide. I stared at it, without really reading it, for a few minutes, thinking that I should probably hire a guide. My how-to book on fishing in Wyoming said that the Wind River had good fishing, but that the good spots were hard to find and hard to access—unless floating the river with a guide. I thought about it hard, but couldn't bring myself to make the call. Something in me rebelled against the notion of a guide. Even staring at the guide's picture in the center of the poster made me feel uncomfortable. He

---

looked too old, too overweight, too ready to smile. Maybe too fatherly. I tried to fish the Wind River, by myself, with no luck.

Once I reached Yellowstone Park, I hiked into the Yellowstone trail, which runs along the Yellowstone River, and camped by myself. I could have easily died. The first thing I noticed on the trail were the bones, entire skeletons of large animals, picked clean over the winter by scavengers. I said to myself, "I have entered the food chain." Quickly, but a little too late, I realized that I didn't have the knowledge or the equipment to take this on. I lost the trail, so I camped for the night on a hillside near a tree that had been struck by lightning (not exactly a smart location, but I guess I was thinking lightning would not strike the same burned-out tree a second time, but this is really more a matter of statistical probability, not a law of physics, and, with my luck, I starting thinking, I would be like the statistician who was afraid of flying because he figured out the probability that there will be a bomb on a plane, which he thought was too high a risk, until he figured out the probability that there will be two bombs on a plane, which was much lower, so he started to fly again but he always carried a bomb in his bag, because then he would be in the two bomb statistical range, so he felt safer, but his own bomb, the one in his bag, went off in mid-flight), worrying about a bear attack (of course, I didn't have a camp stove, so I didn't cook any food, my dinner was dried something, I'm not sure what, exactly, so I shouldn't, I thought, have the smell of food on my clothes, and I even changed clothes before crawling into my mummy-style sleeping bag, which is a vulnerable place, especially if a bear were trying to tear into my tent), worrying about hypothermia (I had a down sleeping bag, but wet down does not insulate, and my tent with a broken pole was pitched on a hillside, at about a thirty-degree angle, so, if it rained, I thought, but long after I pitched the tent, as well as it could be pitched with a broken pole, water would come down the hillside in tidal waves, saturate the bottom of the tent, then saturate my down sleeping bag, then, as night progressed and the temperature dropped, I would slowly slip into a cold death), and not sleeping (not surprisingly, for all of the above reasons, after all, I had a lot to think about that night). At first light (slightly before 5:00 am), I

249

said to hell with it. I crawling out of my mummy-style down sleeping bag and hiked out. I didn't even try to fish. I just wanted out of there.

Once back to my car, I bumbled my way south to the town of Green River, fighting to stay awake at the wheel, and checked into a Super 8, which was run by Indians (not Native Americans) or Pakistanis or some other recent immigrants (or, at least, not your typical Wyomingites), which I only mention because I was starting to feel like I didn't even know where I was anymore. The map said Green River, Wyoming, but it could have just as easily been Raleigh, North Carolina or Austin, Texas. The room was . . . well, it felt a little like camping but without a pleasant smell or vista. In the morning I woke at six, ate some dry cereal, checked out of the motel and headed for Blue Rim Road, which ran parallel to the Green River and looked promising on the map.

I found the river but I couldn't find a spot to fish—no pools, no gravel bars, no seams in the current, no vegetation, no logs or rocks, just even flowing water. So I kept driving along Blue Rim Road, which wasn't much of a road, loose gravel with potholes. I took detours onto dirt roads that cut through dirt fields to the river. At each place, I sized up the river, assumed, without even wetting a line, that I would catch no fish there, and then moved on. On one of these side roads, I found myself driving down a thirty-percent gradient filled with deep potholes. As soon as I started down, I knew I would have trouble getting back up, so I stopped and tried to back out. My wheels spun as I slid further down the hill. I started to have flashbacks to Yellowstone. I thought, "I'm going to die out here. Vultures will pick my bones clean. I'll have to leave my car here. Walk out. I'll expire on the march. It will be hyperthermia this time, not hypothermia, like in Yellowstone. They'll find me on the barren landscape. Or my bones. And a few scraps of clothing that they'll use to make the identification." I'm not saying that I actually believed this irrationalia (definition: a feast of irrational thoughts), but my vacation/adventure persona was starting to hit bottom. I was at the I-just-want-to-go-home-take-a-bath-and-sleep-in-a-comfortable-bed-with-clean-sheets stage. After a few minutes, long minutes, of sitting on the steep incline with both feet on the brake pedal, I decided that it would be easier to go ahead, turn around, and come out headfirst. About half way of moving headfirst up the hill, my wheels started to spin, so I let the car roll back down the hill.

My fears grew. I was probably thirty miles from another human being. What the hell, I thought, was I doing on this kind of road with an old Cavalier? All I wanted to do was get on the main road and head back home. I was sick of the entire trip. I was ready to quit fishing— or trying to find a place to fish—a few days ago, but I was afraid to return from my grand trip out west with no stories to tell. I was feeling incompetent and useless. Once again the fatherless son.

I can't tell how long I sat before I shifted the car into second gear and started up the hill again. The wheels spun a few time, but the car pulled through, and I was soon on level ground and heading back toward town. To hell with the fishing, I thought. I'm heading home.

As I began driving toward Laramie, where I planned to spend the night, I thought about something a female friend had recently said, which didn't make sense at the time. She had said that she felt I was, deep down inside, a very insecure person. When I was much younger, still in school, I would have agreed with her, but now I believed I was confident, very confident. I could speak in front of a few hundred people without notes, go into a classroom unprepared, wing it, and still lead a productive discussion, and I knew I could publish just about anything I wrote. I was very confident indeed.

Then driving East on Highway 40, I realized that I was confident about work, and it was to work that I fled whenever the rest of my life was falling apart. This was why I was able to continue to publish when my mid-life issues hit. Work was a place of security, a place where I was able to feel in control. I was, however, obsessed with competence. If I couldn't do something well, I didn't want to do it at all, and that was why I was ready to give up on fishing. I had an epiphany, which is a rare event for me. I realized that I needed to learn to enjoy fishing without catching fish, and this became my new metaphor. Enjoy the process; hang the results.

Later I would come to enjoy a day of fishing when I worked on only one fish, trying different flies and varying techniques, pausing and thinking of new strategies, even waiting a half-hour or so for the fish to forget I was out there. This would become my favorite way to fish, even when I failed to land that one fish I worked to catch for hours. Later but not now. Now I wanted to catch a big one so I could distinguish myself, so I could be competent, so I could be known as the kind of fly fisher who could go into any stream and select just the right fly and skillfully work it, and each fishing trip would fulfill my fantasy, I would imagine the fish I would catch and then I would catch it. I would be a technician who knew everything about fly fishing. And I probably wouldn't enjoy it at all. And fly fishing would be just another extension of work.

I began to realize an important part of fly fishing that would eventually help me to relax into it: The sport is larger than any one fisherman. The fly fishers that I really respected were the ones who had fished for twenty or thirty years and still said, "I will never master this art. I am continually learning. And there will always be fish I cannot catch." They are the ones who say that fly fishing is not about catching fish. This is something that doesn't make sense to beginners; you just have to grow your way into understanding it.

And then I thought of my childhood.

I thought of that seven year old who was abandoned by his father, whose mother struggled to raise two boys on her own, whose brother released anger and fear by hitting him. I thought of the child who had no childhood. I was forced to become an adult too soon, which means that I never really became an adult. I just learned to play the role well, so well that I lost myself in the role, forgot about the lost child who never learned to play, who was never allowed to grow up.

How could I not be insecure? I was an adult who trusted no one, who rigidly held to the few arenas of success that I had built with hard work, who could handle tragedy without blinking an eye but who did not know how to relax and have fun.

HEADING HOME

BY LATE IN THE AFTERNOON, MY CAR WAS POINTED EAST, AND I WAS HEADING
home, without having caught one fish. By the time I was driving through
Cheyenne, I was already tired and decided to stop for the night. This
time in a Motel 6 that offered free movies, which sounded good until I
saw their offerings. Too tired to read and bored with television and the
free, crappy movies, I decided to catch *Cliffhanger*, the new Sylvester
Stallone action flick. When I arrived at the movie theater, I was thirty
minutes early, so I drove around, wasting time, sight seeing in a small
town without sights, until I passed a community baseball field. Several
adult, hardball games were in progress.

It was an odd experience. As I watched these grown men play a boys'
game, uniformed and cleated, I found myself focusing on the culture of
the game, what happens in the dugout, between innings, after a play. I
saw the men congratulate each other when they did well, and outwardly
console the bungler after a strike out, dropped ball, or wild throw. I
say outwardly because "that's okay" or "good try" was clearly a mixed
message. The phrase seemed to mean something along the lines of "you
really screwed up but we will still grudgingly allow you to continue
playing on our team." The message was not lost on the bungler. When
his teammates said "that's okay" or "good try" as they patted him on
the shoulder, the player who screwed up hung his head in shame. Every
man on the field seemed to be a little boy trying to impress his father,

and the team collectively played the role of the stern father who, while appearing to forgive, accepts nothing short of perfection. The images were overwhelming.

A father came out of the dugout to tell his two boys to play catch over there, away from the action of the game, adding, "And don't throw like a sissy."

An outfielder made a beautiful catch over his shoulder, back to the ball, and a member of the opposition taunted him, "What are ya doing, slow-stepping it, trying to make it look good."

A batter struck out and threw his bat against the fence.

The Stallone movie was more of the same.

In the opening scene, Sylvester Stallone climbs up a sheer rock face to save a man and a woman stranded at the summit. He rigs a belay between the summit and a helicopter sitting on a second, larger summit about forty feet away. The man, Stallone's best friend, crosses safely. But the buckle of the woman's harness fractures halfway across. She begins to slip. Stallone quickly rigs himself to the line and pulls near the girl, just as she loses her grip. Inverted, he grabs her arm, strains to hold on. But we watch their hands slide apart. She falls hundreds of feet to her death.

We might say that Stallone was playing the male role by attempting to be the hero who saves the stranded climbers. But he really only begins to play the male role once he has failed, once he begins to brood, punish himself for not being able to hang upside down from a rope and pull a grown woman to safety with one hand. In other words, he punishes himself for having normal human limitations.

After the woman slips to her death, he leaves his job, even leaves the area for six months. When he returns only to collect his things (one has to wonder how he did without his "things" for six months), his former live-in girlfriend tells him that he did all he could, that it was not his fault. But he mopes more, whining about how he should have done something, how if only he were quicker, if only he were stronger, if only . . .

And we soon learn that his friend, his now ex-best-friend, blames him. As the ex-best-friend chastises Stallone for making the wrong decision, Stallone shifts from blaming himself to defending himself. He says, "I did all I could." Then he blames his friend, "You should have never brought her up on this mountain. She was not a good climber." Blame and counter-blame.

It is interesting that the script writers, someone else and Stallone, chose to have the broken buckle precipitate the woman's fall, because the buckles of climbing harnesses simply do not break. A more likely scenario might have been that Stallone would not have properly anchored the belay, or that Stallone would have improperly fastened the woman into her harness. But such a scenario would have given Stallone reason to blame himself; then, he might have had some justification for feeling guilty. But a fractured buckle, the event that is never supposed to happen, could not possibly be his fault. Stallone, a man's man, an actor who has made a fortune playing the quintessential hero, mopes like a little child when he was not responsible for the woman being on the mountain, when he was not responsible for the buckle breaking, and when he was not responsible for the woman panicking. The cards are against him. There is no way to win. But he must play the role and accept the guilt.

After the movie was over, I remained in my seat and watched the credits. I read lists of drivers, twenty or more, caterers, master chefs, grips, stunt men, consultants, camera crews, and scattered among these, Mr. Stallone's personal staff. I read the name of Mr. Stallone's hair dresser, Mr. Stallone's makeup artist, Mr. Stallone's trainers, Mr. Stallone's assistants, Mr. Stallone's double, and Mr. Stallone's costumer. I wasn't certain what the costumer actually did all day because Mr. Stallone spent most of the movie with his shirt off. When he was more fully clothed, he climbed up sheets of ice wearing only a torn T-shirt. So I imagine that Mr. Stallone's costumer might approach him and say, "Mr. Stallone, here's your T-shirt. I made sure all the rips are in the right places. Can I help you slip in on?" This was a full-time job. Mr. Stallone, our man's man, was being pampered like a three year old baby by his entourage.

This is the contradiction of the male role: He must be so competent as to accept responsibility for any harm to women or children, whether

255

by his own doing or an act of nature, he must show himself to be competent at all times in the eyes of other men, and he secretly wants to be mothered like a helpless child.

And it seems to have been this way since the beginning of western civilization. Achilles, the hero of Homer's *Iliad*, spends most of the epic pouting in his tent. Why? Because Agamemnon pulled rank and demanded that Achilles give him one of the women that he captured to be his sex slave, leaving Achilles, I guess, with only a dozen or so captured Trojan slave women to cater to his needs. It is only the death of Patroklos, Achilles's best friend, that draws him back to the battle, and then he seeks vengeance against Hector, a warrior who did what warriors do, and what Achilles himself does—kill the enemy. But to Achilles, Hector deserves no mercy. After Achilles wounds his enemy in the neck, Hector gasps, "Do not let the dogs feed on me." Achilles, who, of course, feels responsible for Patroklos's death while simultaneously blaming the death on Hector, answers: "You'll have no bed of death" because "dogs and birds will have you, every scrap." Real men agonize over what is not their fault, damn others for what is their fault, and pout. It's an odd combination.

All of this might seem like a detour on my search to find the father, but, with the help of the baseball players, Sylvester Stallone, and Achilles, I began to realize that I had spent most of my life thinking that all of my problems were related to the disappearance of my father. My typical line of thinking followed a basic pattern: If I had a father, I would have been a better athlete, I would have known how to defend myself, I would have done better at school, I would have known how to hunt and fish, I would have felt more comfortable with women, etc., etc. Then, at the end of my trip, feeling like a failure, I started to realize that some boys with fathers are not good athletes, do not know how to defend themselves, do not do well in school, do not know how to hunt or fish, are not comfortable with women, etc., etc. And, it was only as I watched grown men deride each other on the baseball diamond and Sylvester Stallone wallow in his manhood that I realized having a father wouldn't have solved all my problems. In fact, if my father had stayed around, even if he were sober, I might have developed a whole different set of issues to work through. I am not saying I would not have been better off with a sober, caring father, but I started to realize that I couldn't continue to point to the absence of my father as if it were catastrophic. All boys have to work past their father to become men.

A few small changes happened during my trip. One was that I started asking advice at fly shops. I learned to go into the shop, ask about spots where I might find fish, and ask, "What flies are working?" This sounds like a simple step, but, for me, it was a sea change. It was a simple move beyond trying to be so self-sufficient. About a year after I returned from my trip, Donna also helped me mature, largely because she was tired of my failures as an angler. For my birthday, she hired a guide to take me for a float on the North Fork of the White River. Chad, the guide, who was twenty-something, ran a local fly fishing shop, so I already knew him a bit. He took me to the North Fork of the White River. Chad was about twenty years younger than I, and it turned out that he was even an English major in the department where I taught. We had a fine day. I caught seven rainbows and one brown, which fought for about four or five minutes. I could give a list of things I learned from Chad, things his dad taught him, like how to fish with nymphs on a dead drift, how to find spots where trout should be, and what kinds of flies tend to work on the North Fork, but mostly what I learned is what he wasn't even trying to teach. It was a rhythm. Or maybe patience. After going out with Chad, I didn't hurry fishing. And I started to catch fish pretty consistently.

FINDING MY FATHER

OVER THE NEXT YEAR, DESPITE ALL THE INSIGHTS I GATHERED FROM MY TRIP, I still felt anger that seemed to come from nowhere. One day I was buying milk at the local Gas-N-Sip. The entire weight of my life must have hung on my face, because the woman behind the counter said, "Cheer up." Or something like that.

I snapped back, "I didn't come in here to entertain you." She took a few steps back, as if she had been slapped.

At the time, I was attempting to be a good father by spending a lot of time with my sons. I was determined to be a good father, but I was too angry, too often. Whenever Jay and Jeff threw a ball off the house, they would start to count backwards, "Five, four, three, two, one . . . " Just as they hit "one," I would swing the front door open and start to yell. I was far too predictable.

One morning, after Donna was already at work, I was getting the kids ready for school. They were whining about getting up. They wouldn't get dressed. I lost it and threw an alarm clock across the room. I sat on the stairs and started to cry. The kids ran to me, screaming, saying they were sorry. This was not what I wanted. This is not the kind of father I hoped I would be.

It was about this time that I attended the Family Program at Hazelden, which started the search for my father and began the process of dealing with my vague, free-floating anger. It was only a start.

In March 1994, I took Jay, who was seven years old at the time, to a national Tae Kwon Do tournament in Little Rock. He was already a black belt, so his competition was tough. After a few rounds, he was eliminated from the sparring. When performing his kata, he seemed to do well but did not win a trophy. He was upset. He grabbed his bag and started to walk off. I walked after him, playing at the role of the good father, trying to get him to talk about his feelings so I could console him. He started to cry. He turned to me and said, "You made me cry!" I was trying to be a sensitive father, not the kind of father who would call his kid a "baby" for crying, but I didn't have a clue about how to relate to my sons. Jay and I went back to the hotel room and spent the rest of the day watching movies.

I should have known to leave him alone, give him time to work through his emotions before talking, but I wanted to be a good father. I wanted to say a few wise words to him that would make everything better, and I wanted him to say, "Thanks, Dad. Thanks for helping me through this difficult moment in life." Part of my dream of being a good father was helping my kids in sports and being the wise one who lifts them out of their hurt and frustration with a few well-phrased aphorisms. Eventually, after I had read my father's letters, I started to realize that my dream of fatherhood was a shabby compensation for my fatherless childhood, that I would never quite feel comfortable with my own fatherhood until I came to know my father. Even though it took me years to move in this direction, I decided to start searching for my father. My real father. Not some substitution.

Earlier in my life, I convinced myself that my father was no longer in my life. Even though I attended conferences in New Orleans in 1981, 1986, and 1987, I never visited my father's grave. On these trips, the thought passed through my mind, briefly, more than once, that this is where my father spent his last days, this is where he is buried, but I never seriously thought about doing something, trying to locate his grave, or where he lived, or someone who might have known him. When I walked the streets of the French Quarter, I wondered, a few times, what my father's life was like there. But I wouldn't say that any of these thoughts occupied much of my time. These visits were before

I began to read his letters, before I began to work through my mother's papers, before I began to write about my family. As I came to know my father better, as I came to care, I wanted to visit his grave. I wanted to leave stones. This is the Jewish custom of letting the world know that the living care for the dead.

In the summer of 2002, Donna and I began to plan a trip to New Orleans. Donna searched on the Internet and found that my father was buried in Port Hudson National Cemetery in Baton Rouge Parish, plot D 2068 G. On August 1, 2002, while I was loading the car for our trip to New Orleans, Jeff went to our backyard and picked four stones from our rock garden. For the past twelve years, I had picked up stones on my travels and taken them to our garden. I picked up stones from Wyoming, Montana, Colorado, California, and streams from across Missouri. It seemed appropriate that some of these stones should be left at my father's grave.

As we are approaching Port Hudson National Cemetery, Jeff asked, "When your father left, were you angry at him?"

I tried to explain that, for a long time, I wanted him to come back. I prayed for his return. Then I gave up. I decided he didn't care about me, so I stopped caring about him. I don't remember, I said, feeling angry at my father. I certainly had a general feeling of anger in me a lot of the time, but it didn't seem to be directed toward my father.

Jeff said, "I think I would be angry."

"I think my brother was real angry," I said "And hurt, deeply hurt. I dealt with it by shutting down. I told myself, 'He didn't care so I don't have to care.'"

We arrived at the cemetery at 4:50 p.m., ten minutes before it was scheduled to close. We found section D quickly, but we could not find any plots numbers below 2300. For a while, we walked around in circles, trying to figure out the system, hoping to find the 2300 range of grave sites. When we were close to giving up, I was at the middle of the first row of headstones at the beginning of section D, and I decided to start a plot by plot search. I turned to look at the nearest headstone and found my father's grave. It was almost like I was guided there. The plot number was actually 2368, and the headstone read "U.S. Army" instead of "U.S. Navy." For a moment, I wondered if this was really my father's grave, but it had to be. We had checked all of the national cemeteries in Louisiana on the Internet, and this was the only George H. Jensen in any of them. Also, the birth date and death date were correct. This had to be his grave.

We said a prayer and left stones from our garden.

On the trip into New Orleans, Donna asked me if we should contact the cemetery and tell the administrator to correct the headstone. I told her that the headstone reads "U.S. Army" because my father was buried without any relatives or friends in attendance. I didn't care then. I didn't feel that I had a right to ask for the headstone to be corrected because I care now.

I was still wondering about the AA card in my father's wallet and what it might mean about my father's last days. Once we were in New Orleans, I decided to call the local AA office to see if they might know some way of contacting some oldtimers who might have known my father, if he were indeed in AA in his last years. The man working the phones gave me two names. I called them, but neither was in the program in the early 1970s. I didn't feel comfortable crashing a meeting, so I decided to send the AA office some fliers when I returned home. They might be willing to distribute the fliers to meetings. I knew from the beginning, this would be a long shot. I never received any reply to my inquiries.

Later in the day, I walked to 523 St. Phillips Street, to the address that my father listed as his residence on his Merchant Marine license in 1968. The narrow building, a few streets east of Jackson Square, was rather typical of the French Quarter. Three stories. Wrought iron balconies. A gate that leads to a courtyard filled with plants. Inside the courtyard, a stairway that leads to more balconies and the doors of each apartment.

As I peered through the gate, I could see a note: "Trash is collected on Mondays." It was signed by the manager.

On one side of the building was a tourist gift shop, which specialized in crystals and jewelry. I asked the man behind the counter if he knew anything about the apartments next door. He said, "Not really." On the other side of building was a sex shop. I walked in. The manager smiled and said, "Hi." The shop was filled with black leather, three foot dildos (yes, the dildos were about a yard long), and man-on-man videos. I just left.

Later, from our hotel room, I found the manager's name, James Thompson, in the phone book and called. James said that he was the owner and manager, but he had only owned it for about three years. I began to explain that my father had lived there in 1968, that we had been separated since 1957, and that I was trying to find people who knew him.

He asked, "What was your father's name?"

"George Jensen."

"My parents owned the building before I did. I remember a George Jensen. I was a kid then. I remember that everyone called him the Commander."

We talked for about twenty minutes. James said that my father often worked as a merchant marine and was a member of the Seafarer's Union. He shipped out for six months at a time. The building at 523 St. Phillips was a boarding house, and James's parents rented rooms for about $30 to $50 a week. The Commander lived there when he wasn't at sea. For a while he also lived on Rampart Street. Unlike many of the seamen in the French Quarter at the time, he shipped out often. He would stay in town until his money was gone, and then ship out again. He could always find a berth. James's parents had also owned a bar at 519½ St. Phillips, where the sex shop was now. He said that the Commander often drank there.

When I explained that my mother asked my father to leave because he drank too much, James said that my father was often at the bar, but he never saw him drunk. He was always well dressed and clean, unlike many who lived in the Quarter. James's father often said that you could tell that my father was an officer because he was always polite. James added that my father wasn't married and he never saw him with women. He was often with a friend, who wore glasses, but James could not remember his name. He added, "They were just friends."

Once again, I had to rethink my father's story. If, by some odd stroke of luck, I found someone who knew my father, I expected to hear that his drinking was even worse than when he was living with us, that he would have been depressed, out-of-work, barely getting by financially, without friends, or that he had stopped drinking and was a member of AA. I half expected one of these two extremes, but not a story somewhere from the middle, a story about an alcoholic father who still drank but did not get drunk.

In the months that followed, Donna and I often talked about James's view of my father in New Orleans. We struggled to interpret it. Would my father seem more polite, clean, and controlled in his drinking in the French Quarter, which has always has its share of indigent and chronic drinkers? How did James's age affect his memories of my father? He was younger, and he probably didn't see what happened in his parents' bar late at night. My father could have still have gone on binges in other parts of the city or other cities. Maybe my father was more of what is sometimes called a "pressure drinker," someone who appears to be an alcoholic for several years after returning from a war, when going through a difficult divorce or when dealing with the loss of a loved one.

I had to remind myself that, even after my conversation with James, I know so little of his life in New Orleans. I would like to think that he found some peace in his last years, that, however much he was drinking, he felt normal in the French Quarter, that he had friends, that he was able to work, that he even felt respected when the regulars in the bar at 519½ St. Phillips called him the Commander. I suspect that he still wished his life had turned out differently. I wonder if my father even thought we had abandoned him.

After we returned home, I wrote James to thank him for speaking to me. I enclosed a few stamped-self-addressed-envelopes, so he could write me if other memories came to him. On August 23rd, he wrote to say that my father was "very quiet, spoke in a soft voice, was very knowledgeable on matters, liked to get into long discussions." My father reminded him of Henry Fonda. He never "got into arguments with anyone," and he was a "peacemaker." At times, he would be at sea for a two-year stretch. When he returned, "he would be very generous with people he hardly knew but were down and owed rent." He closed by writing, "He did like to drink but aside from that he was an outstanding Christian gentleman." Even in this hint that my father might have, on occasions, drank too much, his drinking seems too normal, too harmless, too controlled.

After Donna read the letter, she asked, "Do you think that he even knew your father? She too was having trouble making James's view of my father mesh with the father of my simple story. How could this man who James described be the man who went on horrific binges, who left his family and disappeared, who only sent money once, who even lost contact with his own mother?

"I think he did," I answered. I can't say that I can make logical sense of how the binge drinker became the social drinker if that's what really happened, but I saw some ties between the man I believed my father was (or could have been) and the man I found in New Orleans. I had always thought that my father was a quiet and sensitive man, intelligent and articulate. This is the man I thought he could have been. While I was skeptical that he really was a social drinker at 519½ St. Philips Street, I was pleased that James seemed to like the "Commander" and that he had fond memories of him. I was pleased that my father had friends. It seems like I should—or maybe could—have been angry that he was giving money to people he hardly knew without sending anything to his family, but I wasn't. It would be easy to say that he didn't care about us or that he was trying to buy friendship. But I choose to believe that he felt too much guilt to contact us. I choose to believe that, as he was helping others, he was making amends to his family. His mother. His wife. His sons. All of us.

Even though my father seemed to have a better life than I expected, I still think he lived with depression and probably fought hard against a pervading sense of guilt. The despair, loneliness, maybe even self-loathing, that I saw in his eyes when I looked at the photograph on his Merchant Seaman's license was probably there. Not all the time. The camera caught a moment of what he tried to avoid feeling, what he fought to put behind him. In the eyes of that photograph, he seems

GEORGE H. JENSEN, JR.

to be seeing the eyes of those he left behind. In our eyes, our gaze, he probably believed that he was unforgiven, unforgivable. As for me, until recently, he would have been right.

When he died, I was only twenty-four and I couldn't conceive of any reason to contact him. Now, I have read his letters. I am stronger. I have let go of a great deal of pain. If he were still alive, I would write him. It would be a short letter. I would say that I had turned out okay, that I had a family and that he was a grandfather. I would tell him that I don't think much matters but love. I would tell him that I love him and hope he has found a place that feels like home, a place with friends. I would give him my address and say that he could write me, if he wished. I would end by saying that I would understand if he doesn't want to write.

It would be hard to write because it is so hard to predict how letters will be read. I would like to say that I hope he can let go of his self-blaming or guilt and find peace with himself, that I am not asking for anything from him, that I only want to say that I care and I have tried to understand, as much as I can, from a distance. But all this could sound so condescending. Maybe I could say that, when I think now of the family split by his drinking, what I feel is sadness and loss, that I miss them all, including him.

If he were alive, if I did write this letter and mail it, I would have to realize that it might never reach him or it might only reach him after years. I might never know if it were lost in the mail or if he read it and then threw it away. It would be an act of faith, like Whitman's poem about the soul being a spider, suspended in space, shooting out filament after filament.

I will never put this letter into words because it is too late, but I know what I would say.

On August 4th, the governor of New Orleans declared a state of emergency to cope with an outbreak of West Nile Virus. We decided to leave New Orleans early and drive to the Florida coast for a few days. It was J.C.'s (or John's) birthday. We played "Birthday" from *The White Album* for him.

Donna said, "If J.C. were alive, I bet you two would have fun researching your father's life together. I could just see the two of you on a trip to New Orleans."

When we returned home, the search continued. In early September, I wrote the Pearl Harbor Survivors Association to ask for the names and addresses of members who had been on the USS *Dewey*, my father's ship. The secretary sent me a list of twenty-two names, but I was apprehensive about contacting them. I had heard that many Pearl Harbor survivors never talked about the December 7th attack or the war, and I didn't want to intrude on their silence or privacy. I sent them a cautious letter, apologizing in advance for bothering them, asking them only if they knew my father's battle station so that I could imagine what he might have seen as the Japanese bombers dove toward his ship.

As I drafted the letter, I realized that I would need to sign it "George H. Jensen, Jr." I hadn't used the "Jr." since I was in the third or fourth grade. My decision to drop the "Jr." was conscious and symbolic. It was my way of telling myself that my father was not coming back. When I registered for the draft in 1968, I insisted that the "Jr." remain off my draft card. In fact, I argued with the secretary at the Draft Board. She kept saying, "But your father might come back." I kept saying, "He won't come back." Now, I had to include it, because my father's shipmates would need to know that it was "George H. Jensen, Jr.," the son, writing them, not "George H. Jensen" their shipmate. It also felt right. As I was coming back to my father by learning about his military years, I was warming to the notion of being a "Jr."

I sent out the letters, and the answers trickled in for over a month. A few letters were returned with "deceased" written on the unopened envelope, but most of my father's shipmates were alive and healthy and wrote back on Pearl Harbor Survivors Association letterhead. Many began, "Welcome aboard!" Almost all of them remembered my father and shared that, during the attack, he manned the phones on the bridge that connected all parts of the ship, an extremely important and difficult job. Some sent me histories of the *Dewey* and photographs of the ship. Stephen Yorden sent a photograph of all the chiefs of the

Dewey, as they knelt together on the fantail of the destroyer. He also sent me a copy of *Typhoon*, Raymond Calhoun's book about a typhoon that almost sank the *Dewey* in December 1944, shortly after my father was transferred off the ship. He inscribed the book: "For Dr. George Jensen, Son of Chief Yeoman Jensen of the USS Dewey DD 349 with warmest regards, Stephen P. Yorden, Chief Warrant Officer, U.S. Navy Retired." Maria Dawson wrote to say that Joseph, her husband, had passed away. She later sent me a videotape of an interview with Joseph about his experiences at Pearl Harbor. Robert Reece wrote to tell me that he did not remember one person from the *Dewey*. A few weeks later, he wrote me again, this time to send me an application form for the "Sons and Daughters of Pearl Harbor Survivors, Inc." In his letter, he added, "If you need a sponsor, you can use my name." I wrote him back to thank him for the form and for being willing to stand in for my father, his shipmate, a man he could not remember.

I was struck by the generosity of these men, and I felt welcomed among them.

Many of the men wrote a paragraph or two about how their lives had turned out, what happened after Pearl Harbor, after the war. They had children and grandchildren. They had worked as a teacher or a milkman. They had long and happy marriages. After they had survived Pearl Harbor, attacks by submarines, and dive bombers, they wanted to tell me they had a simple and good life.

I spent most of my life looking for a surrogate father and had only experienced frustration. Once I began to look for my real father, I found men who stood in for him. As I continued to read and reread the letters from my father's shipmates, none of whom I had ever met, I began to miss my father, maybe for the first time, certainly for the first time since I was seven or eight.

On December 7, 2002, I went to the Pearl Harbor memorial service at the national cemetery in Springfield. Four survivors of the attack laid a wreath at the memorial for those who lost their lives on December 7, 1941, while about six or seven people watched. Then on December 13th, my father's birthday, I laid a rose at the Pearl Harbor memorial at the national cemetery. Donna bought a birthday cake. These became new family traditions.

CARS

SHORTLY AFTER WE RETURNED FROM VACATION, DONNA BECAME SICK. FROM the time she was nineteen to twenty-two, she had six or seven operations for Crohn's. The adhesions that naturally develop from any abdominal surgery were now causing an obstruction. In September, she underwent an operation. Then, she developed an infection. Antibiotics had no effect, and her doctors thought, for a while, she might even have "the flesh eating bacteria." She underwent three more operations to deal with the infection, three trips to the ICU. She was eventually transferred to Barnes Jewish Hospital in St. Louis, where she underwent another surgery. She was in the hospital for over seven weeks, and, a few times, I didn't think she would make it. I began to worry how I would raise our two sons, who were then fourteen and fifteen, on my own. Then, I thought of my mother, who raised two sons from the ages of seven and ten, and I was embarrassed for being so weak. Slowly, Donna recovered.

On December 19, 2002, Jay turned sixteen and took his driver's test. Even though Donna was still recovering from her surgeries, she took Jay on a few short trips to look for a car. They found a 1992 Legend for $4,500, which seemed to be in good shape. Jay really liked it, but Donna insisted that we take it to the Acura dealer and have their mechanics look it over. The mechanic said the car needed about $2,500 in repairs and that it would probably continue to need repairs. Obviously, we backed out of the deal.

Since Donna didn't have much stamina, I had to take over helping Jay buy his first car, which was a situation that no one expected and no one wanted. My family had banned me from car lots. I had simply never learned how to buy a car. Most boys turn sixteen and their father takes them to car lots to look for their first car. In the process, these fathers teach their sons *how* to buy a car. One of my favorite episodes of *Leave It To Beaver* is about Wally, Beaver's older brother, buying his first car. He saves some money and goes car shopping on his own, without his father. He thinks he has a good deal, but Ward insists on looking at the car before the deal is finalized. The father looks at the tires (bald) and under the car (oil leak); then he pushes down on the bumper (bad shocks). The father saves the teenage son from making a boyish mistake.

I never had this kind of experience. My father was gone long before I was sixteen, and my mother tended to buy used cars from close friends. When I was commuting to Old Dominion in undergraduate school, I drove my mother's VW Bug. When I was in graduate school, I rode my bicycle or walked. When I worked in Chicago, I rode public transportation. It was only once I moved to Atlanta in 1983, at the age of thirty-three, that I needed to buy my first car—on my own.

One Saturday morning, I was riding my bike down Roswell Road and stopped at a car lot. I saw a metallic blue 1975 Fiat Spider, and I was a goner. When I started to work a deal (if you could call it that) with the car salesman, he realized I was naive, and he actually tried to help me out. They were asking $7,600 for the car. He told me that they would probably take a good bit less. After he talked to the used car manager, he came back and said, "They'll go $7,450." I said, "Okay." I'm sure the salesman thought, "What an idiot. I was trying to help him out. I told him they would go much lower, and he takes their first offer." I loved that car—for about six months. Then reality hit. The monthly payments of $270 strapped me, especially once I discovered that my dream car needed $300 in repairs every couple of months.

If I had waited a few months until I met Donna, I would have had some help, because Donna and Lenny, her father, were masters at buying cars. When Donna was as young as nine or ten, she and her father would look at cars on the weekends, talk to the salesman for hours, and try to work a deal. Once Lenny worked the salesman down as far as he would go, he would act mad and say something like, "This is bullshit!" Then he would storm out of the showroom, his daughter trailing behind, and go to another car dealer, find another car they didn't actually want to buy, and start all over.

On a Saturday morning shortly after we met, Donna and Lenny took me out to look at cars, almost as an initiation into the family. Lenny started to talk to the salesman like he was helping me to buy a new car, and I broke into a cold sweat. After about twenty minutes of haggling back and forth, Donna and Lenny noticed that I had turned pale. They broke off negotiations and took me home, gave me a few drinks, and applied a cold compress to my forehead. After that day, I let Donna buy all our cars. She enjoyed haggling with the salesmen (they were always men), and I think they actually enjoyed the challenge of arguing with a woman who knew the ins and outs of deal making. While I never went to car lots, except to sign contracts, I did listen to Donna and Lenny and I started to become less naive. So, while Donna was justifiably worried when she passed me the task of helping Jay find a car, she had some hope that I had benefited from contact with her family.

After about a week of looking in the papers and visiting car lots, Jay and I found a Honda Civic that he liked. When we returned from the test drive, it was 5:25 pm on a Saturday. The showroom was about to close at 6:00. The car salesman, Bill, someone Donna had bought cars from in the past, quoted us $7,999. Relying on one of the strategies I had learned from Donna and her father, I told him that we wanted to look around some more on Sunday, that we liked the car, so, if we didn't find anything else, we'll be back on Monday. Then the price came down to $7,700, then $7,500. Repeating a strategy that was producing good results, I told Bill we wanted to look some more. I stood up and started to leave. Bill said, "There are a lot of people in town right now looking for cars like this. It might not be here on Monday. Not an automatic like this." I started to move toward the door. Bill said, "What would it take for you to make a deal, right now?

271

Would you close if I could get it for you for $7,300?" "Why don't you see," I said. When Bill went to talk to the used car manager for his approval on the deal, I told Jay that the manager might not approve that figure, that Bill was trying to keep us in the showroom. I also told him to watch how Bill and the manager worked off of each other. Soon, the manager came over to us with a sheet of paper. They always have a sheet of paper, I later told Jay. That's their way of telling you that this price is the bottom line. In reality, I told Jay, there is no bottom line. He said, "Look, I know Bill said $7,300, but this is what I have in the car right now." He pushed the paper toward us. On the paper, the figure is $7,475. He continued, "I know your family has bought some cars from us, so we will let you have it for that price."

I said, "We're going to look around some more."

As we were leaving, the manager said, "It might not be here Monday."

"Have a good evening," I said.

I thought I had handled the stress pretty well, but I was just barely holding myself together. When we arrived home, Jeff had some friends over, so I decided to call Pizza Hut. The operator asked, "Do you want to know our specials." Then, she started to reel off the specials: The Manager's Special, The Three Medium Special, The Meatlovers' Special . . .

I panicked. I said, "I'll have to get back to you." When Donna walked into the kitchen, I was banging my fists into my forehead, repeating, "I panicked about buying pizzas, I panicked about buying pizzas." I just couldn't take anymore wheeling and dealing. Not about cars. Or pizzas. Or anything. Donna took over and called Pizza Hut.

Sunday, after I had regained my composure, I talked to Jay about the Civic. I told him that it seemed to be a good buy, even at $7,475, but I also mentioned that we shouldn't be swayed by the manager saying that he had "that much in it." It's all accounting, I tried to explain. When the previous owner traded in the car, the dealership might have paid more than the trade-in price for the car instead of discounting the sticker price of the new car. Bill had said that they put $1,400 into repairs, which could be viewed as good or bad. Some of the repairs were new parts on the engine that simply made it look better but may have nothing to do with how the engine performed. Also, if the car needed $1,400 in repairs, then maybe it was a lemon.

Monday, we went back to see Bill. We said that we would probably buy the Civic for $7,475, providing it checked out. Unfortunately, it didn't. So we started over again. A few days later, we saw a Honda Accord for sale by owner. The owner wanted $8,600. She was ready to trade it in a few days and had been offered $6,800 by the dealer. We offered $7,300, and she said yes. The car even checked out with a mechanic. We both felt pretty good. We had avoided buying two bad cars and finally found one that was a good buy and in excellent condition. We had both learned a great deal in the process. I wasn't exactly Ward Cleaver, but I did okay. Donna even said, "I'm proud of you." I think she was pleasantly surprised.

Soon, both of my sons will be driving their own cars to their own destinations. My life will be easier, in some ways. I will not have to rush all over town, picking up kids and dropping them off, but I will miss our conversations. It seems like we have our best talks in cars. Just last fall, I picked up Jeff from his high school football practice. He was, at the time, playing on the freshman team.

He asked, "Can we go for ice cream?"

"Sure." On the way to Andy's Frozen Custard, Jeff said he wished that he didn't go out for football. The coach yelled at him every time he made a mistake. Other kids made bigger mistakes, more mistakes, but the coach kept yelling at him, saying, "Get me someone in here for Jensen." Or, "Jensen, are you ever going to learn?"

Neither of us spoke for a while, then I said, "Some coaches yell more at the better players. The coaches feel like these players have more potential. They might not yell at some players because they know those guys won't even be on the team next year. The coaches don't yell at them because they have already given up on them."

Jeff said, "That might be what's happening."

We bought ice cream and ate it in my car. Then, it was dinner time. Without saying much more, we went home.

SOME OF THE WORDS ARE THEIRS

The relationship between a father and his sons is more fragile than any man wants to admit. We want to believe blood is its own bond, but it is not. All relationships need attention, and we have to accept that the dynamics change moment to moment. We need to recognize our bungled attempts to express love, and we need to make amends when we let fear overshadow love. We need to worry less about being men and find ways to be more human.

It took attention and acceptance to find my father, and now I want my sons to know him. I sat down on my father's birthday and wrote my sons a letter so they could know the grandfather who died before they were born. I knew they might not even want to read the letter until they were older. Someday, when the moment is right, they will read it. Someday, in a difficult time, it will lend comfort.

A Letter to My Sons

December 13, 2002

Dear Jay and Jeff,

I NEED TO APOLOGIZE TO BOTH OF YOU. I NEVER TOLD YOU MUCH ABOUT YOUR grandfather, and I am certain that you tired of me saying, "He was an alcoholic. He drank himself to death." That wasn't fair to you or to him. At some point, I began to feel a need to have a different—a fuller—story to tell you. Over the last year or so, I've been researching his career in the navy. Now, I can tell you a little more.

As you know, I was only seven when I last saw him, so I never heard him speak about the war. I don't even think that he spoke of the war to my mother, except in generalities. When they met, he was still in the navy, so it was obvious that he had been in the war, and I'm sure he told her that he was at Pearl Harbor when it was bombed and that he served in the South Pacific campaign. I doubt he told her, or anyone else, much more.

Some veterans just don't talk about the war. In *Goodbye, Darkness*, William Manchester remarked, "For years, I had been trying to write about the war, always in vain. It lay too deep; I couldn't reach it." Before he could write his memoir about being a Marine during World War II, he had to travel back to Guadalcanal "to search for meaning in the unconsummated past." I had friends who served in Vietnam. When they returned, I always asked them what it was like over there. They might say, "It was bad," but not much more. I imagine that they thought, "There is no way I can make him understand." They couldn't find a place for their stories, even their unspoken memories, with people who never experienced war. I would guess that my father also felt that he couldn't bring war stories home with him. He might have even felt that he had to act like the sailors in war movies, because that is what his family, neighbors and old friends expected. Even if he wanted to tell stories about the war, he might have felt that he could have only told these stories to his shipmates. I think this happens to a lot of veterans. They cannot find a way to tell their stories, so their experiences, in Manchester's words, "lie deep in one's subconscious, squirreled away, biding their time."

278

Before the war, my father saved photographs of his adventures in the navy, personal pictures of him and his shipmates in exotic locations, which he neatly arranged in photo albums. He wanted to preserve these memories. If he ever had any personal photographs of his wartime experiences, none survive. The photographs that were passed on to me, as part of my mother's documents and memorabilia, depict scenes of Pearl Harbor, a task force in the Pacific, and a destroyer with DD 349 on its bow. On the back of these photographs is stamped: "OFFICIAL U.S. NAVY PHOTOGRAPH: PACIFIC FLEET." Toward the end of my father's career in the navy, he was a journalist. He must have had access to archival photographs, and, as he was ready to retire, I imagine he went through some file drawers and made his own collection of photographs that would remind him of his connection to historical events, but not so much his actual experiences. It was like he wanted to say, "I was a part of history," but not so much preserve a personal account. I don't think that he was ready to say, "This is what I witnessed." Or, "This is what I experienced." It was too early for him to tell his story, to his friends or even to his wife, and so I thought it was lost to all of us.

Of course, I wanted to know more. For years, whenever *Tora! Tora! Tora!*, *In Harm's Way*, or *The Battle of Midway* was on television, I watched the films, even though I had seen them all at least a dozen times. Repeatedly, I spent the better part of Memorial Day watching Hollywood versions of the attack on Pearl Harbor or the Battle of Midway, or other films about World War II, never consciously connecting any of it to my father, your grandfather. Then, about two years ago, I started to realize that watching these films was a way of connecting with my father, learning a little more about his war years. I would never hear his stories of the war, but I could see the events that he and thousands of sailors and soldiers experienced, the men played by extras in the Hollywood films, the men who did their duty and won the war.

In the last few years, I have found myself wanting to know something more specific, more than I could glean from official Department of Navy photographs, more than I could learn from the frames of actual battle footage spliced between the scenes of John Wayne or Glenn Ford, shot on a Hollywood sound stage, for it was during the war that the man can most clearly be seen. Now, once I have passed fifty years of age, I feel a need to find a story that I can tell you about your grandfather, a story that you might later pass on to your children.

I began to research my father's war years by obtaining his military records, reading histories and first-hand accounts of the Pacific campaign, and watching documentaries. I eventually wrote to his shipmates, who told me that he was well liked and that he was "all navy." This seemingly simple phrase means that he did his job, as expected, even in the most difficult experiences, even when Japanese fighter planes were strafing his ship, even when torpedoes were in the water, closing in, even when bombs hit so close that salt spray washed across the deck near his battle station. Because he was "all navy," his shipmates could count on him.

When I reviewed his military records, I learned that he served on the USS *Dewey*, DD 349, but his military records only provide a sketchy outline of when he was transferred or promoted. As far as I know, he didn't keep a diary, which was against policy. The letters that he must have written home to his parents have not survived. Even if I had his war letters, they probably would have been written to his mother and father back home. He wouldn't have wanted to worry them, so his letters wouldn't have told the whole story.

It might seem like the man he was from December 7, 1941 to August 15, 1945 is lost to us. But maybe we can find something of him in the events of history. From his military records, from the history of

SOME OF THE WORDS ARE THEIRS

the USS *Dewey*, I know when he was in battle. From Harry A. Gailey's *The War in the Pacific* and other histories, I know something about these battles. I can also find accounts of the kinds of experiences he must have had in memoirs, like Richard C. Epps's *Life on a Tin Can*, collections of letters, like George B. Lucas's *Every Other Day* or James Orvill Raines's *Good Night Officially*, and diaries, like James J. Fahey's *Pacific War Diary*, first-hand accounts, such as recollections of Pearl Harbor survivors, C. Raymond Calhoun's *Typhoon*, and studies of the psychology of war, like Paul Fussell's *Wartime*. All this would say little

if we knew nothing of the man and his character. To know the man, we will listen to his shipmates. They will help us to tell his story. They will give me my father and you your grandfather.

Some of what I am going to tell you will give a sense of what he experienced by sharing some of the experiences of other sailors on his ship or on other ships around him. These will be events that he could have experienced or emotions that he might have felt. So I will tell you about possibilities, about what your grandfather could have seen. These possibilities might not be history in the truest sense, but we are actually looking for what history usually ignores. Not the turning point of battles, but the experience of battle. Not the legend of heroes, but the bravery of real men. Not the actions of generals or admirals, but the place of regular men facing the unthinkable.

Your grandfather was born in Ranier, Oregon, on December 13, 1912. He and his three brothers were raised in a small house in rural Vaughn, Washington. I don't know much about his childhood, but I assume that he spent a lot of time playing in the woods and fishing with his brothers. From one of my cousins, I heard that he had a good friend named Bob Africa. From some old photographs of the two, it seems like they liked to clown around and act silly, even long after they were teenagers. Your grandfather was a good student (I know this from one of his report cards), but, at the time, most people from his community did not go to college. After he graduated from high school in 1931, he worked for a brief time as a mail boy and a clerk in a department store in Seattle. It was the depth of the Great Depression, and he was lucky to have any job.

On September 20, 1933, he enlisted in the navy to learn a trade. Because he was a good writer and speller, the navy decided to send him to Stenographers' School. During the early years of his career, he served with the Pacific fleet, on the USS *Antares,* a cargo ship, and on several battleships, the *Utah, Arizona, Maryland,* and *Tennessee.* He was a good sailor, but, as with many young sailors, he was in trouble from time to time. On February 28, 1933, he was cited for "Inefficient performance of duty as a Ship's Library Yeoman." He received one week's restriction. I would like to think that he was spending too much time reading and not enough time re-shelving books.

On August 6, 1941, your grandfather transferred to the USS *Dewey,* which was then in San Diego. By this time, he was a Yeoman, First Class, which means that he was trained as a stenographer and spent most of his time doing clerical and administrative duties. My mother told me that many of his shipmates called him "Jens" (short for "Jensen"), so that's what I'll call him for the rest of this letter.

By the time that Jens transferred to the *Dewey,* World War II had already started in Europe, and many Americans feared that the United States would soon be drawn into the conflict. War also loomed in the Pacific. Throughout the fall, President Roosevelt was becoming more concerned about Japan invading China and other countries. As a message to the Japanese, he decided to send a large task force to Hawaii, which included the USS *Dewey.* The task force left for Pearl Harbor on October 29ᵗʰ, 1941. By this time, Admiral Kimmel, the Pacific Fleet's Commander in Chief, was aware that the Japanese might attack territories of the United States, but he and his advisors thought the attack would come far from Hawaii, perhaps in the Philippines. At Pearl Harbor, they were more worried about sabotage.

Because Admiral Kimmel felt war was eminent, all of the ships stationed at Pearl Harbor spent a great deal of time drilling. The sailors drilled until they were sick of drills. You have experienced something like this when your coaches make you shoot free throws until you can hardly lift you arms, or push a blocking sled across the football practice field, again and again. The sailors on the *Dewey*, all of them, hated the drills, and they didn't like the captain much better. He was C. F. Chillingsworth, a demanding officer, who drilled his sailors even harder than most skippers. Some of the drills prepared the crew for battle, but many of them were what sailors call "chickenshit." As Paul Fussell, who has written much about the experience of battle, says, "Chickenshit refers to behavior that makes military life worse than it need be. . . . Chickenshit is so called—instead of horse- or bull- or elephant shit—because it is small-minded and ignoble and takes the trivial seriously." Stephen P. Yorden told me that Captain Chillingsworth drove Jens "up the bulkheads." However, Dorwin Hill told me that Captain Chillingsworth got them out of some difficult situations.

After the war, Jens loved the play *Mister Roberts*. When he was stationed at Charleston, South Carolina, about the time I was born, Jens even played a supporting role in a local production. The play is about Lt. Roberts who serves on a supply ship in the Pacific; he has to deal with the chickenshit of a crazy captain who demands that his crew deliver more and more cargo. After Lt. Roberts is transferred off the ship, he writes back to his former shipmates: "The unseen enemy of this war is boredom." The play was later made into two movies that will, like *Tora! Tora! Tora!* and *The Battle of Midway*, give you some idea about what Jens experienced.

In early December, the *Dewey* was tethered in a nest with four sister destroyers, the USS *Hull*, USS *Worden*, USS *MacDonough*, and USS *Phelps*, all of the Farragut class, alongside the USS *Dobbin*, a destroyer tender, on the northeast corner of Ford Island. Most of the destroyers in the Farragut class, built in the 1930s, were considered to be the first class of modern destroyers. They were called "gold platers," because they were outfitted better than earlier destroyers. After they were built, however, naval warfare began to shift away from the kind of sea battles where ships closed on each other at top speed and launched broadsides from their gun turrets. Carriers, air power, and submarines were emerging as the dominant offensive weapons, and battles would soon be fought between fleets that might remain a hundred miles apart. To prepare for the changes in tactics, the *Farragut* class was refitted with more depth charges and anti-aircraft guns in the late 1930s. Such refittings would continue throughout the war. At this time, however, the *Dewey* and her sister ships were undergoing routine maintenance. Their engines were in pieces, and they relied on cables from the *Dobbin* for power. Most of their ammunition had been removed. The nest of destroyers could not have been more vulnerable.

On the morning of December 7, 1941, reveille was sounded at 0650. Most sailors across Pearl Harbor rose, showered, had breakfast and then settled into a lazy Sunday morning. Arthur L. Critchett was sitting with some other crew members on the fantail of the *Dewey*, smoking cigarettes and shooting the breeze. Dorwin Hill was studying for upcoming exam for first class machinist mate. Jens, your grandfather, was probably reading the newspaper in the Yeoman's office just below the bridge or maybe in the radio shack across the hall, where he often drank coffee with Lloyd Gwinner, one of the radiomen. Jens's duties included decoding messages from the fleet, so he spent a lot of time in the radio shack.

By 0745, he would have heard the buzz of a large squadron of planes approaching from the north. He might have thought, "Why the hell did they order drills for a Sunday morning?" Then, the low, dull buzz shifted to the high-pitched whine of planes in a dive. Then explosions. Then a sailor ran across the deck yelling, "The Japs are here! The Japs are bombing us!"

Most survivors of the Pearl Harbor attack speak of how difficult it was to shift from relaxing on a Sunday morning during peacetime to accepting that the Japanese really were attacking, that they had been at peace one second and war the next, that they needed to be at battle stations, that they needed to fire on the enemy planes. You have to remember that these men had not yet been in battle. They were well trained, but training can never teach as well as experience. For seconds that seemed like hours, they were in shock. Dock Campbell later recalled: "I got to the bridge and there wasn't a soul there. Everyone was over on the port side hanging over the rail watching this torpedo wake go on by the ship. It had been sent for a battlewagon and it went right under us." From the fantail, Arthur Critchett saw the USS *Utah* explode when it was hit by a torpedo. The battlewagon began to list almost immediately. The seconds that seemed like hours were over.

At 0757, the *Dewey* sounded General Quarters, which meant that every member of the crew, whether he was sleeping or in the shower, ran to his battle station. Some of them still thought, "This must be a drill." Or, "Why are we drilling on a Sunday morning?" Or, "Damn that Captain Chillingsworth!" I am sure that Jens, who was probably in the Yeoman's office, also had trouble accepting what he was hearing and seeing. Once he was at his station on the bridge, only then would he have seen explosions on Ford Island, diving gray planes with red balls on the wings, and bombs exploding along battleship alley. Only then would he have to believe that this was real.

He probably muttered a few cuss words under his breath and then manned the phones that connected all parts of the ship. He probably thought, "All hell is breaking loose." It is important that you understand he was in the middle of it all. Standing on the bridge, at his battle station, he would have seen everything happening around the *Dewey*. Manning the ship phones, he would have relayed every order from the officer in charge to the crew in the 5-inch gun turrets or standing at the .50 caliber machine guns.

Of course, even before the crew received orders, they began to act. Dorwin Hill threw the power switches so the *Dewey*'s guns could open fire, but the demand in power from the *Dewey* and her sister ships tripped the generators on the *Dobbin*. Without power, they could not use the elevators to get ammo from below or operate the guns. Sailors even had to use bolt cutters to open the ammo stores. Then Joe Dawson and others began to run ammo to the guns, and sailors topside began to operate the guns manually. They were, as Joe Dawson later said, "shooting at planes like crazy." They didn't think. They had drilled so much that they didn't have to think. They just reacted, even though they were all confused, in shock, even though they had not yet heard orders.

The entire crew scurried to shift the *Dewey* from being a destroyer in pieces to a destroyer in battle, but every time they began to get something working, something else fell apart. Without power, the water pumps that cooled the .50 caliber machine guns could not work. These guns soon melted, but the crew continued to fire the 5" dual purpose guns at Japanese planes that flew so low they could see the enemy pilots smirking. From the bridge, Jens also might have seen the faces of the Japanese pilots. He certainly would have seen the *Oklahoma* hit by three torpedoes and the *Arizona* explode, sending a wall of fire in all directions. He might have even felt the heat of the blast.

The second wave of Japanese planes hit the harbor at 0900. Concentrated fire from the *Dewey* and her sister ships disrupted this wave enough to prevent it from doing extensive damage. Then, at 0945, a third wave hit. These planes began to attack smaller targets, including the *Dewey* and her sister ships. Several bombs hit close to the *Dewey*, but luckily she sustained no damage. During the brief lulls in the battle, Jens would have seen the burning battleships from the bridge. He would have seen sailors jumping from the decks of sinking battleships into the water, covered with burning oil, and he would have relayed the order to launch the ship's rescue crew.

Barbara Kelly, who was thirteen years old and living on Ford Island, remembered watching sailors jump from burning ships into oily water. She watched as some sailors swam through flames to reach the shore. Her mother and other women handed out rags and towels so that the sailors could wipe away the thick oil and then gave them their husbands' uniforms, pulled from the clothes lines. All of this was close enough for Jens to see and hear. He would have smelled the burning oil.

As soon as the attack was over, the crew of the *Dewey* prepared to be underway. Dorwin Hill and other machinists had to retrieve the engine's valves from the *Dobbin*, reassemble the engine and fire it up. Hill later said, in his calm understated manner, "It was a hectic day." When the steam was up, they tried the condenser pumps and discovered that a powder case from a 5" gun was caught in the impeller. It took an additional hour to extract it. At about midnight, the *Dewey* was underway.

The *Dewey* was the last of the ships in her cluster to head for sea. She rounded Ford Island and headed south toward the channel, through Battleship Row. From his station on the bridge, Jens would have seen the superstructure of sunk battleships still burning, including the *Arizona*, on which he once served. He would have seen only the hull of the *Oklahoma*, which rolled after it was hit, trapping some of her crew. As they passed through the channel, which led to the Pacific Ocean, he would have seen the *Nevada* beached off his port side. During the attack, the *Nevada* had attempted to break for the sea. After the battlewagon was hit repeatedly by dive bombers, the harbor command ordered the ship to beach herself so that the channel might be kept open for other ships.

I try to imagine what your grandfather must have felt as the *Dewey* passed the sunken and burning *Arizona*. He probably knew sailors who still served on the ship, but I doubt that he would have heard that some of the crew were trapped below deck. I am certain that he was horrified by the scale of damage, and he must have worried about whether his country would survive an attack of this scale. He probably feared that the Japanese were, at that moment, staging an invasion of the Hawaiian Islands. He would not have known that the Japanese fleet was already heading home.

As soon as she was underway, the *Dewey* received orders to find the USS *Enterprise* and escort her back to Pearl Harbor. The *Enterprise* had just delivered a squadron of fighters to Guam, and the *Lexington* had just delivered a squadron of fighters to Midway. The aircraft carriers were supposed to enter Pearl Harbor by December 6th but were delayed by bad weather. If the carriers had been in port, the attack would have been far more devastating. The outcome of the entire war might have been different.

Carriers like the *Enterprise* and *Lexington* were becoming so important that it was the role of destroyers like the USS *Dewey* to defend them. At the beginning of the war, the US Navy had 8 carriers, 17 battleships, 18 cruisers, 20 light cruisers, 113 submarines, and 171 destroyers. Throughout the course of the war in the Pacific, carriers became the dominant offensive weapons, but they could not easily defend themselves. Because destroyers were cheaper to build, the navy could order more of them. So, destroyers were viewed as being more expendable. They were used to "screen" larger ships, especially carriers. In a typical task force, the carrier would be surrounded by cruisers and light cruisers. At the outer perimeter, destroyers "screened" the carrier by being the first line of defense. When enemy planes, or bogies, attacked, the destroyers screened by firing their anti-aircraft weapons. Their job was to shoot the bogies down or, barring that, become the target. If a submarine fired torpedoes, the destroyers "screened" by taking the hit. If a periscope were spotted, the destroyers "screened" by breaking from the Task Force to seek and destroy the submarine with depth charges. The crew of destroyers knew that they were expendable, and they knew that it was their job to be a target.

After the *Dewey* found the *Enterprise* and escorted her back to Pearl, she returned to sea to patrol for submarines. The USS *Ward*, another destroyer, had sunk a two-man submarine shortly before the attack on December 7th, so the admiralty suspected that Japanese submarines were in the area. The crew of the *Dewey* was still new to battle. Stephen Yorden said, "That night everybody was trigger happy. Geez, if there was a seagull flying, they'd shoot at it." The *Dewey*'s sonar kept pinging, and the crew launched all her depth charges in five days. As Dorwin Hill later said, "Many whales and schools of fish received a headache that week."

On February 20, 1942, the ship was in Task Force 11 when several waves of Japanese planes attacked. They watched as Lt. Edward "Butch" O'Hare shot down six Japanese planes in about four minutes and became the first navy ace of World War II. During the Battle of Coral Sea, the *Dewey* was among the ships that defended the aircraft carrier *Lexington*. The *Dewey* was strafed by Japanese fighters, and five of her crew were wounded. When the *Lexington* was hit and abandoned, the *Dewey* rescued 112 of her crew. During the Battle of Midway, the decisive battle of the Pacific campaign, the *Dewey* screened for the oiler *Platte*, which was a prime target. Then, the *Dewey* participated in the invasion of Guadalcanal.

The sea around Guadalcanal was hot and humid. As you can imagine, sleeping quarters could be steamy, and this was before ships were air conditioned. Even though large fans moved air through the ship, the sailors' bunks, which were one on top of another, with barely enough room between them to turn over, were often too hot for sleeping. Even the chiefs' quarters, which had hatches smaller than the diameter of a basketball, were suffocating. So, many of the crew slept outside on the steel deck, but, even outside at night, they never stopped sweating. Many of the men developed rashes and sores.

Unlike the modern navy, the food was not particularly good, partly because the best supplies went to the war in Europe. In May 1943, James J. Fahey, a sailor on the USS *Montpelier*, wrote in his diary: "We got dehydrated potatoes and no one eats them, they are like soft cement, they stick to the trays like glue." On August 11, he wrote: "We have been eating bread that is full of little hard bugs for quite some time and this will not change because of the heat."

But they had good moments, too. When Jens was on watch at night, he could have looked to the sky and seen the Southern Cross. When he was off duty and didn't need sleep, he might read an Armed Services Edition of a novel or listen to Tokyo Rose on the radio. Some nights, he could have watched a boxing match or a movie on the fantail. On occasions, his ship anchored near a small island and allowed the men to go ashore. They could swim, pick fruit, have a warm coke or beer, and eat a few hot dogs. During these picnics, some sailors let off steam by starting fist fights. When at sea, during moments of calm, they could dive off the ship for a short swim, as long as a few sailors with rifles kept watch for sharks. They needed breaks like this from battle, for even the strongest and bravest man will break down after 200 to 240 days of continuous combat. I am sure that Jens thought the good moments were short and infrequent. Mostly, he was bored or dog tired or wondering what the next battle would bring.

On August 6, 1942, the *Dewey* steamed with Task Force 62 for Guadalcanal. The ship came alongside a tanker to top-off the fuel tanks and highline two new seamen. Highlining is a way of transferring sailors from one ship to another where the sailor rides in a small chair and is pulled across the gap between two ships while they try to keep the line tight. If the line becomes too slack, the sailor drops into the sea. If it becomes too tight, it snaps, and the sailor drops into the sea. The new guys must have thought being highlined was exciting, but the crew of the *Dewey* probably looked at them and thought, "They have no idea what they're in for." Most veterans will tell you that it is impossible to envision the experience of war or understand it from books or movies. As Walt Whitman said, "The real war will never get in the books."

On the morning of August 7, the *Dewey* was coming around the island behind four World War I vintage destroyers, "four stackers," that had been refitted as minesweepers. Jens would have been at his battle station on the bridge when Captain Chillingsworth received a message that a Japanese barge was headed for Henderson Field bearing 050 speed, 6 knots. The captain issued a series of orders: the number one and two 5" guns, those at the bow, should standby to fire, sound a long whistle blast to let the minesweepers know the *Dewey* was overtaking them, and increase speed to 20 knots. The captain, the entire crew, knew that the area was heavily mined, so the ship was already in danger. As the *Dewey* approached the Japanese barge, the number 1 and 2 guns began to fire. After two rounds, the captain turned the *Dewey* so all of her 5" guns could open fire. Of course, this also meant that the *Dewey* presented a larger target. The Japanese barge was soon hit and in flames, so the *Dewey* began to fire on other enemy ships in the area.

After firing and being fired upon for four hours, the lookout on the main direction, one of the new sailors who had just been highlined aboard, shouted, "Dive bombers overhead!" The Captain yelled, "All ahead flank speed, hard right rudder." The ship heeled over about twenty-five degrees and the first bomb missed the ship by about fifty feet, close enough to send spray to the deck. As soon as the bomb hit, the Captain yelled, "Hard right rudder!" Another bomb barely missed the ship.

The immediate danger was over, but the crew remained at battle stations. Sometimes, the crew might remain at their stations for days, with only short breaks. One sailor at each station would go to the galley and bring back sandwiches, which they would then eat as they watched for more Japanese planes. After about four hours of tedious quiet, an entire squadron of Japanese torpedo planes attacked. The Captain called for flank speed and ordered the ship to zig-zag. One torpedo plane headed directly for the *Dewey*, and the anti-aircraft guns hit the plane just as the pilot released its torpedo. Luckily, the plane was too close to the ship. Torpedoes released from planes dive deep, due to the angle of the attacking plane, and then rise and level off just below the surface. The crew of the *Dewey* watched as the torpedo ran deep under the ship, rose to its pre-set depth on the other side and hit the USS *Jarvis*. During the same attack, a torpedo also hit the USS *George F. Elliot* and set her afire.

I want you to try to understand what your grandfather and his shipmates did in the moments between the Japanese plane releasing its torpedo to the torpedo hitting the *Jarvis*. If Jens didn't see the plane launch the torpedo, he would have heard someone at one of the .50 caliber machine guns send the message that a torpedo was heading straight toward the ship. He would have relayed this message to the captain, and the captain would have ordered hard rudder right. Jens would have relayed this message to the engine room and then waited. He wouldn't have moved. He might have wanted to run to the starboard side to see if the torpedo was going to hit his ship and then run to the port side to see it level off, and know that his ship was safe, as some of the crew had when a torpedo ran under the *Dewey* during the attack on Pearl Harbor. But he didn't move for thirty or forty seconds. He and his shipmates were now seasoned in battle. I am sure he stayed at his post and did his job. And I am sure that the entire crew of the *Dewey* stayed at their battle stations.

It is also important to understand that destroyers are called "Tin Cans" because they have no armor on their sides. Larger ships, such as battleships, had thick steel on their sides, so they could stand a hit from a torpedo with less damage. Destroyers, smaller and without armor, usually didn't survive torpedo hits. As Jens and his crew mates were waiting for that thirty or forty seconds, hardly breathing, they

---

would have known that the torpedo, if it met its mark, would kill most of the crew. And they all stood at their battle stations and waited.

After the torpedo attack, the *Dewey* was ordered to pick up the Japanese pilots who were swimming toward the beach. The crew lowered a Jacob ladder. As the ship approached the pilots, the *Dewey*'s crew threw a heavy line so that they could pull them aboard. The Japanese pilots refused to take the line three times. Japanese soldiers and pilots were indoctrinated into the Bushido code, the same code that Samurai followed for centuries. They were taught that, if they surrendered, they would offend their family and their ancestors, so the pilots continued to swim. The captain of the *Dewey* could not allow the pilots to escape to the island and he did not want to tarry in the area, which would have left the ship an easy target for Japanese submarines. He ordered the pilots to be shot. He had no choice.

291

During operations in the Pacific, Jens and his shipmates would have only seen a small part of the battles around them. They would have heard rumors that helped them to imagine what sailors on the other side of an island or marines on the island were experiencing. When on the *Montpelier* off the Solomons, James J. Fahey wrote in his journal that Marines said the Japanese "have some Imperial Marines who are 6 ft. 4" tall." The Japanese were fierce, clever fighters, and their defense of islands was, as Paul Fussell said, "suicide stubbornly protracted," but they didn't have giant Marines. In battle, rumors fly in all directions. Neil Callum, a soldier on a troop transport, deliberately started a rumor to see how long it would take to get back to him: "I told someone we were to be sent ashore for a route march and the story went round the ship and came back to me in twenty minutes." It was said, in one rumor, that "Henry Ford was going to give each prisoner of war a free car when the war was over."

In the days that followed, the *Dewey* was involved in more battles. Japanese submarines in the area sunk four cruisers and damaged six destroyers, so the crew was often on battle stations for long stretches, and fatigue set in. On July 11, 1943, Fahey wrote in his diary: "Your mind goes blank and you find yourself walking around some part of the ship, some distance from where you want to go, and then it dawns on you that you are not supposed to be there. You forget what day it is, what you had for breakfast, what you did in the morning. You find yourself in the washroom with no soap or towel. When you turn the water on, then it dawns on you." During these times, Jens probably longed for his peacetime life, the simple events he once took for granted. Getting a cream soda at the drugstore, going fishing with his brothers, seeing a movie on Saturday afternoon.

After some action in the Solomon Islands, the *Dewey* headed north to the Aleutian Islands, southwest of Alaska. The ship participated in the occupation of Amchitka Island on January 11, 1943, and the occupation of Attu Island on May 11. When the USS *Worden* sank, they rescued her crew, which was a dangerous operation in frigid, rough seas. It was so cold in these northern seas that the crew, when on watch, had to wear flannel masks, heavy gloves and pea coats. Even simple maintenance tasks became difficult and dangerous, and many of the crew were seasick. The small size of destroyers and the shape of their hulls, designed for speed, meant that they were rough rides, even in moderate seas. In heavy seas, the bow often cut through swells, and the deck would dip underwater; hatches and doors leaked, which meant that the crew's quarters were also wet and cold. As William H. McBride wrote: "Destroyers moved less predictably than larger ships. Vertical motion was perhaps the most debilitating, the up-and-down pitch of the bow, or the vertical heave of the entire ship, made simple matters such as eating a meal or staying seated on the commode a difficult task even for a seasoned sailor. Rolls were usually more predictable but could easily cause the loss of balance, and destroyer sailors heeded the old saying, 'One hand for the man; one hand for the ship.' Several days in moderately bad weather induced deep fatigue. Trying to sleep while wedged into a corner between a piece of machinery and a bulkhead or with legs and arms wrapped around a mattress while grasping a bunk frame was exhausting."

The *Dewey*, as Lloyd Gwinner said, went through some "hair raising" times in the South Pacific. When the ship was still in the Aleutians, the captain received orders to transfer a second class seaman off the ship. Gwinner said, "Since I was senior, I had first

crack at it. I figured our luck was about to run out so I took my leave."
He made a good decision. Gwinner spent the remainder of the war
on a submarine chaser in the Caribbean, but the *Dewey* had more
"hair raising" times ahead. For the rest of the war, they island hopped,
seeing action in the Gilbert Islands on August 16, 1943; the Marshall
Islands on January 17 and 31, 1944; Milli Island on March 8, 1944;
and Woleai Island on March 30, 1944. Jens transferred off the *Dewey*
to the USS *Arctic* on April 8, 1944.

For the rest of the war, Jens had smooth sailing. The *Dewey* did
not. In December 1944, the *Dewey* was part of a task force that was hit
by a typhoon. In the rough seas, the *Dewey*, which was top heavy with
its many refittings, rolled so far that the depth charges on the deck
were underwater. Three destroyers were lost. Dorwin Hill and Steve
Yorden, both friends of your grandfather, received medals for helping
to save the *Dewey*.

I believe that Jens would have heard about the *Dewey*'s close
call in the typhoon, and, if he were still alive, he would have told you
stories about Dorwin Hill and Steve Yorden and his other friends
on the *Dewey*. He would have said that the crew of the *Dewey* were
seasoned sailors. Even though they knew the ship could go down at any
moment, that being rescued in rough seas would be nearly impossible,
they never hesitated. They were "all navy," and he was proud to call
them his shipmates. As he was telling this story, you would know that
he was one of them.

After the war, Jens edited newspapers at Fort Slocum, New York, and
Little Creek, Virginia, where he retired from the navy in 1956, with
twenty-three years of service. His performance ratings were always
stellar. He was a talented man who seemed to succeed at almost any
assignment, as can be seen in this quote from an article that appeared
in his hometown newspaper:

> Jensen was assigned to the navy complement at the Armed
> Forces Information School at Fort Slocum in October, 1951,
> to save the school's newspaper, The Islander, from folding.

The paper, with Jensen as advisory editor, was designated the outstanding army paper of its kind twice last year. Jensen is an instructor at the school.

In the last years of his life, he lived in New Orleans and worked as a Merchant Seaman. He was a member of the Seafarers' Union, which had a reputation for being "radical." I assume that he was well respected as a seaman, for he could always find a berth. When he was in port, at his home in New Orleans, he liked to sit at a bar in St. Philip Street and discuss politics. During these times, he had money, and he often helped his friends when they were behind in their rent. A man who knew him during this time described him as a quiet man who was gentle and kind, a Christian.

As I read through the letters from my father's crewmates, which trickled in over weeks, I kept thinking about a memory, a short episode, seemingly hardly worth remembering or writing down or passing on. I was six, probably in the first months of the first grade. Like most of the elementary school kids in the overcrowded schools of Virginia Beach, I was on a split shift. I went to school early in the morning and was dismissed about noon so another group of kids and a different teacher could use the classroom in the afternoon. On the day of this memory, my father picked me up at school and took me out to lunch. At a diner, we sat on stools with red leather seats; the lunch counter was covered with turquoise Formica, speckled with brown, black and white dots. We had both ordered hamburgers and Cokes. The short order cook, wearing a tee shirt and a white apron, both covered with stains, asked us what we wanted on our hamburgers, mustard or ketchup. I didn't know how to answer. My father said, "Why don't you try both?" It seemed like such a big decision, but I think I eventually said, "Okay."

This is such a vivid memory. For a long time, I wondered why I remembered this simple episode when I certainly forgot so many others, so many that might have suggested more of the man. It was only when the letters from his friends came in that I remembered the look on my father's face when he said, "Why don't you try both?" He

GEORGE H. JENSEN, JR.

was looking down at me, smiling, in the presence of this other man, a stranger, a short order cook in a 1950s diner. Even before this stranger, he was proud of his son, as I am proud of both of you.

When I wrote back to my father's crewmates, thanking them for sharing a part of their lives with me, for telling me bits about who my father was then, which told me something of who he was even through all the turmoil in our family, I found myself missing my father in a way that I don't think I ever had before. Through this letter, I hope that you will come to know him as well. On Memorial Day, December 7th, and December 13th, your grandfather's birthday, I hope you will remember the crew of the *Dewey* and your Grandfather.

Love,
Your Dad

A Brief Sermon on Love

WHEN MY SONS WERE TODDLERS, DONNA AND I ENROLLED THEM IN A DAYCARE center operated by the College of Education at Georgia State, where I was teaching. The center had observation rooms so that education majors could study childhood behavior, and parents were also allowed to visit. So, when I had free time between classes, I occasionally walked over and watched my boys for a few minutes, just long enough to reassure myself that they were okay. I did worry about the ethics of the situation. Was I violating my sons' privacy? Was I being an intrusive parent? I can see how some might interpret my secreted observations as a violation of boundaries, but I came to think of it differently. I came to view my short observations of their lives apart from my life and our family as an early step toward allowing them independence. Even when they were still toddlers, even when they depended on me for so much, they had found a place in the world apart from our family. They made friends, and they established relationships with adults who would nurture them. It gave me immense pleasure to see that they were learning, if only in rudimentary ways, to find a place in the world and be persons who could find friendship and love among those who were once strangers.

299

As I have sorted through the memories of my first family, my family of origins, I have learned about the power and limits of family. *Alcoholics Anonymous*, the Big Book, says that alcoholism is a family disease, that every alcoholic harms at least seven other people. Even after my father left, the presence of his drinking remained in his wake. Even after we lost contact with my father, the alcoholic structure of my family survived and split us into roles that kept us together even as it kept us apart. We fit the pattern of an alcoholic family is some ways, we broke it in others.

My mother asked the alcoholic to leave, the alcoholic left. If my mother had not grown up in a normal, supportive family, she would not, I believe, have found the strength to ask my father to leave and save us from the worst of his drinking. If she had not attended Al-Anon for a while, as I believe she did, she would not have known how to move our family closer to the kind of family she knew as a child and a young woman. In the early years after my father's departure, my family remained alcoholic. As the years passed, we slowly found our balance and became a little more like a normal family, if there is such a thing. In writing this memoir, I have learned to see my family as changing in time rather than fixed in a moment of crisis.

I have also learned that members of fractured families can become people apart from their families. My brother, who was most harmed by my father's drinking, moved past being only J.C. to being John, a person who had more devoted friends than anyone I know. While I believe that my brother carried a great deal of pain from his childhood until the day he died, I also believe that his life was full of victories. When he felt safe, when he could overcome his fear of abandonment, he found love. I also believe that, had he lived longer, we would have investigated the history of our father together. He might then have come to feel, as I do now, sadness that our father's drinking caused so much pain and loss that he could not become the kind of husband and father that he wanted to be. Now, when I think of my father, I miss him and I am proud of who he was apart from his drinking. Not everyone will be able to find a way to look beyond the drinking of an alcoholic who has done harm, and not all relationships can be salvaged. I was lucky. I had the help of many people, especially my father's shipmates. Others will need to find a different path.

At this point of my own journey, I like where I am, and I have hope. I have written myself through many drafts. But even before the writing of this book, from observing AA meetings and reading the Big Book, I learned that the two most important emotions are love and fear and that we cannot experience both these emotions at same time. On page 65 of *Alcoholics Anonymous*, my favorite page, a chart, which has three columns, shows alcoholics how to begin working the fourth step, the "searching and fearless moral inventory." The fourth step is a way of starting to dig out from years of drinking, years of being a hopeless alcoholic to becoming an alcoholic with hope. In the first column, alcoholics write the names of persons they resent. In the second, they write the cause of the resentment. In the third, they return to the self by writing about the source of their resentment. This is the example that the Big Book supplies:

I'M RESENTFUL AT:	THE CAUSE:	AFFECTS MY:
Mr. Brown	His attention to my wife.	Sex relations. Self-esteem (fear).
	Told my wife of my mistress.	Sex relations. Self-esteem (fear).
	Brown may get my job at the office.	Security. Self-esteem (fear).
Mrs. Jones	She's a nut—she snubbed me. She committed her husband for drinking. He's my friend. She's a gossip.	Personal relationship. Self-esteem (fear).
My employer	Unreasonable—Unjust —Overbearing— Threatens to fire me for drinking and padding my expense account.	Self-esteem (fear). Security.
My wife	Misunderstands and nags. Likes Brown. Wants house put in her name.	Pride. Personal sex relations. Security (fear).

301

The simple chart, a plotting of the core of a person's life, shows alcoholics how their resentment toward others ultimately harms *them* more than the person they resent. So they need to move past their resentment, stop harming others, so they can stop harming themselves. But the chart also shows the hidden cause behind resentments and character defects. It is fear, which pops up parenthetically in the far right hand column, as if it were peaking out of the subconscious.

The chart is a homily on the dangers of fear. As alcoholics work on the fourth step, as they learn about fear during their "searching and fearless moral inventory," they begin to open themselves to the possibility of loving and being loved. After they complete the fourth step, they will tell it to another person and their Higher Power (Step Five), become ready to remove their defects of character (Step Six), ask their Higher Power to remove the defects (Step Seven), make a list of those they have harmed (Step Eight), and, if possible, make amends to them (Step Nine). This is how they dig out; this is how they move past fear to love.

Making amends may be the most important part of this process, for this is how they begin to reconnect with the world and build a new way of living, sometimes even salvage relationships. My first encounter with the Ninth Step was from the other side of it, as the recipient of an amend. During the summer after my first year in graduate school, I worked for my friend Skip, who was then a subcontractor. That was the summer that Skip was in the process of bottoming out. He starting drinking early in the morning and also did his share of drugs. As the summer progressed, he was around less and less. I kept things going and even volunteered to forego my salary for a few weeks when Skip was short of cash. A few years later, after Skip had found his way into the program, he handed me some money and explained that he was making amends. I am certain that the act and, maybe much more importantly, the story that came with it, helped him. It certainly helped me. Skip now has over thirty years in the program. Members of Alcoholics Anonymous call this a miracle, a God thing.

As I have seen Skip and others stay sober in the program, become stronger, hold their families together, I have come to believe that my

GEORGE H. JENSEN, JR.

father could have had a different life. I have come to find possibilities intriguing and reassuring. In alcoholics who have come to AA and stayed in AA, I have seen persons my father could have been, and, in these persons, I have found the good in my father that was too often hidden by alcohol. It is easy to stop caring for the alcoholic, but we do so at the risk of harming ourselves. As I have learned to love my father, something has changed in me. I have learned—through days and meetings, years of searching, working through the photographs and letters in my mother's papers—to love more completely each member of the alcoholic family of my childhood, my father, my mother, and my brother. Documents, letters, and photographs have changed my simple story and given me new memories. Especially the photographs. In some shots, I see tension or a point of crisis, but in many I see joy. Even in the worst of times, my family had moments of real joy. Sometimes, the moments were minutes; sometimes, hours; sometimes, days. Too often, these are the moments I have trouble remembering.

303

Something of my ongoing journey is on these pages, and it suggests that I worked to understand the members of my family separately. I still have not come to terms with the structure of my first family, but I have attempted to move past it. I have come to believe it was the very structure of our nuclear family that kept us apart, and so what I have come to love are the individuals that alcoholism and that structure kept from me. This means learning to live with contradictions and multiple versions of reality. When my father wrote to my mother after he left, when he wrote of suicide, I need to understand that his pain was real even as I understand that my mother might have thought he was trying to manipulate her into taking him back. When I read my brother's letter to me, when he wrote that he never felt loved unconditionally, I need to accept that his memories—other memories—of our mother can exist besides mine, even though they seem to describe a different mother. I have not tried to reconcile their stories, to make my brother's reality of our family mesh with mine, or make my view of my father stand beside my mother's. I cannot reconcile these stories without doing violence to them. I have decided, as much as I can, to let them stand alone on these pages. It was their words that helped me to move beyond my childish memories and so come to understand my own story better, at least, to see it more complexly, even if full of gaps, questions, and contradictions.

As much as the lives of my father, mother, and brother are beyond my understanding, I feel that I have learned something of their *essence*. A word not in fashion these days. Postmodernists and social constructionists say that we are the people shaped by our ideology, culture, history and circumstance. They are not wrong. Certainly, alcohol (or, a way of consuming alcohol in a particular moment in history) shaped my father and deeply affected every member of my family. But postmodernists and social constructionists are not entirely correct. We are something beyond the foods we eat, the clothes we wear, or the technology we embrace. Postmodernists and social constructionists cannot explain everything; they are particularly inept at explaining love. To love someone, we must find that person's essence. I best understood my mother's essence when I thought about how her resolve to raise her sons apart from my father's drinking never faltered and when I read what she wrote about being a high school counselor. I best understood my brother's essence when I read his journal and when, at his funeral, I understood his impact on the lives around him. I best understood my father's essence when I read his letters, when I saw him through the eyes of his shipmates, and when I thought about possibilities, the kind of husband and father he would have been, had he been able to stop drinking. Possibilities have helped me see his essence.

I am glad that I have come to know more of the lives of my father, mother, and brother. I now know more of how they were away from me or the structure of our family, and I have thought about what could have been. This is all good, but I also have regrets. I wish that I had come to this place earlier. I wish that I had let my father know I was okay. I wish I had raged harder and longer against the walls between my brother and me. I wish I could have imagined the extent of my brother's pain. I wish that we would have celebrated our accomplishments, the ways that we moved beyond the kernel of our family. These regrets do not lead to guilt. I think we all did the best we could. The regrets are about loss. They lead to sadness. Sadness leads to love. And hope.

When I attended open AA and Al-Anon meetings, I often left feeling sad. Not depressed, but sad. Connected to others. When I am in a place of sadness, I am a better teacher, friend, husband, and father. I hope that my sons will have more good memories than bad, more joy than sadness, but I also hope that they know that sadness is about connecting to the pain of others. It is not like depression, when we are trapped in our own discontent and feel alone. Most of all, I hope my sons know they are loved. I hope they know my father, mother and brother, if only from the memories recounted on these pages, and that they will connect with their past but not live the past of others. I hope they know the importance of possibilities.

I have given up my simple story for the complex stories of my father, mother, and brother, for stories that reflect their lives as lived apart from our family. These are not stories that can be shaped into a single narrative. Yet, even though their stories must be told separately, the process of coming to these stories is part of a larger movement. This book has been about questioning assumptions, listening to the words of others, and trying to understand what is always beyond our grasp. It is about learning to care, and caring exists somewhere beyond certainty, in sharing our stories, even if all we can tell are bits and pieces.

In an age of mass media, it is hard to tell stories, but my current family tries. When we gather for a big meal, we tell stories about the time we drove our mini-van to the river on Christmas day and got stuck in gravel for three hours, how the boys and Cole, their best friend, used to dress up as Ninja Turtles and terrorize the neighborhood, the names that I call Betsie, our crazy dog (Ratface, Big-Butt-Little-Brain, Yippy, Shit-For-Brains, Psycho-Pup, Barf Bag and Gansta-Bitch Betsie), our vacations at the beach, or our paddle trip on Yellowstone Lake. We talk loud and laugh hard.

Love, fear, and laughter all appear to be part of our evolution, remnants of our collective survival. Psychologists are starting to realize that it is laughter that moves us from fear to love, and all this is part of the structure of the brain, essential to what it means to be a human being. Laughter reduces stress and elevates our immune system; it also brings us together. This I learned from listening to oldtimers at AA meetings; reading psychology only confirmed it.

Indeed, I find most of my truths in stories, and one of the stories I come to again and again is *A River Runs Through It*. While I was writing much of this book, I ran the film on a small television as I searched for the story of my family on paper, reworked my words to try to get it right, and sometimes I found a member of the Maclean family had already captured what I was trying to say. Toward the end of the film, we see Norman's father at the pulpit, giving one of his last sermons, searching for a way to understand Paul's death, and the Reverend Maclean says,

306

> Each of us, here today, will at one time in our lives look upon a loved one who is in need and ask the same question: "We are willing to help, Lord, but what, if anything, is needed?" For it is true that we can seldom help those closest to us. Either we don't know what part of ourselves to give, or, more often than not, the part we have to give is not wanted. And so it is those we live with and should know who elude us, but we can still love them. We can love completely without complete understanding.

Norman once said that all he knew of Paul, his brother, is that he was a good fisherman. After all I have written, all I know of my brother is that he wanted, once known in all of his complexity, to feel accepted and loved, even if only by one person, yet he feared that showing himself completely would lead to complete rejection. We all, I believe, share his desire to be known and accepted and loved. We all share this fear— his fear.

After a friend read a portion of the manuscript of this book, he said to me, "With a book like this, it is important who will have the last word." The last word will be my brother's, an entry from the journal

---

that he started and never finished, and they are words of how he felt at one moment in time, as he was looking back at the effects of our father's drinking. Maybe these words will find completion on the pages of this book, in the chorus of my family's voices, the words of those who have passed on, and even in the history that is emerging in another family, the family that my wife and I have created, a history that is largely unwritten. My brother ends with a question. You will need to find your own answer:

I don't care if people dislike me or don't want to be around me. What I can't accept is someone loving me with all its ensuing pain. My most successful relationships are, and have been, with people who are incapable of love, or incapable of loving me or who are so consumed with their own problems that they have nothing to give, at least to me. Loneliness is still painful, but less so than the pain of love, which would destroy me if I gave it a chance. Why should it be this way?

307

Moon City Press is a joint venture of the Missouri State University
Departments of English and Art and Design.
With series lists in "Arts and Letters" and
"Ozarks History and Culture,"
Moon City Press
features collaborations
between students and faculty
over the various aspects of publication:
research, writing, editing, layout and design.

LaVergne, TN USA
03 March 2010
174864LV00002B/4/P